BODY,

VESSEL AND SEA OF SELF

BODY,
VESSEL AND SEA OF SELF

JOSEPH A. AMATO

Body, Vessel and Sea of Self
Joseph A. Amato

Cover illustration by Abigail Rorer, The Lone Oak Press.
Cover design inspired by Rosalia Amato Bauer.

Editing, book coordination, and book design by Wendy J. Johnson of Elder Eye Press – a design and concierge publishing house dedicated to designing with the best design practices for legibility and clarity, to benefit all eyes, of all ages.

First Edition, 2023

Amato, Joseph A.
Body, Vessel and Sea of Self / by Joseph A. Amato
ISBN: 9798857043394 (alk. paper)
Library of Congress Control Number: 2023915301

Crossings Press, 12800 Marion Lane West, #705W
Minnetonka, MN 55305, USA
www.josephaamato.com

Manufactured in the United States of America by the KDP Independent Publishing Platform.

CONTENTS

PREFACE

The body makes us the one and the many we are. It is the sole and mortal vessel in which we cross the deep seas of self and life.

  – Joseph A. Amato, Author

We carry our evolutionary history in our biological makeup, while every day, we go about our lives using hard-won ancestral skills that now seem second nature. When it comes to deciding what it is to be human and even more when we ask what constitutes humanity, our bodies are as important as our cultures, our minds as significant as our biology.

  – Clive Gamble, *Origins and Revolutions: Human Identity in Earliest Prehistory*

We may be sexists. We may be racists. But surely, we all are "bodyists" who know one another by our noses, faces, postures, manners, gestures, and quirks.

  – Joseph A. Amato, Author

We may never slip the bonds of our physical nature, nor perhaps should we wish to, since our embodiment gives us our humanity and brings us, weak and mortal though we are, the immeasurable riches of conscious experience. But when we reach towards the transcendent, then the soul "soars enchanted," and, so far as our finite imperfect nature allows, we rise "with silent lifting mind . . . and touch the face of God."

  – John Cottingham, *In Search of the Soul*

The self is one, the self is many. Yes, the self is one, yet many—a complex multitude to be known and shown in different and even contradictory ways, which I do here under the broad and loose proposition that the self is the body and the body is the self.

I set aside the self as mind and brain, soul and spirit only to suggest the fertility of this proposition that the self is the body. I do not struggle to define the singularity of individual consciousness and autobiography or explore the self as a creation of others as persons or groups. I set aside considerations of how much the self is the sum of distinctions, associations, identities, and metaphors we, as individuals and creations of culture, make across a lifetime.

Furthermore, I do not seek here to examine how the body locates us in place and time, be it a moment or a lifetime in society or on the earth itself. Language itself is rooted in bodily experience, for the body is the source of the first metaphors of our experience and existence.

Finally, I do not avoid affirming the body as an elemental source of feeling and emotions or pre-rational and pre-conscious senses—sixth, seventh, and a multiplicity of the senses—of the self as a body in the world and in relation to its own needs and functions. Finally, by choice, I weigh in as a critic of materialism and those who make the body a mere agency, a type of machine, in a causally and even determined knowable world. As will be apparent, I side with pre-historical and traditional classical and religious systems that do not separate the body from belief, symbols, and interaction with a transcendental world and God, as creator and restorer of the living and dead.

However, this work is not a thesis-driven monograph. On the contrary, the equation of the self and body produced for me a most fertile union, birthing asymmetrical chapters composed of insights, assertions, anecdotes, and poetry—or simply a collection of open reflections on how the body shows that the self truly is a profound and inseparable one and many.

The body places us in being. It is the source fact and metaphor of our being and identity. It is the vessel and arguably the first captain of our lives. The body is a true amphibian in space. In our very soul, it gives us something in common with rocks that hold space, plants that grow, and animals that move and reproduce nature. Our body defines the places, circumstances, conditions, and means of comprehending life. More simply, it is buoyancy in the sea of being and time.

We experience, remember, imagine, and project ourselves in the body. We tell the stories of our lives in our bodies, for skin, so to speak, needs skin. Our bodies interact, give and receive, nurture, love, are intimate, and fight in flesh. They are the first boundaries in public and private lives. They accompany us in action and understanding.

The body also makes us a singular being that knows loneliness and solitude. It is a *prophetic* voice dictating needs and wants, which are multiple, compounded, as well as divided, and contradictory. For the body has a chorus of separate parts, functions, and events. The body can deny consciousness rest and make for restless sleep. It gives rise to impulses and is quick to adopt and slow, even tenaciously against, relinquishing habits, however quickly learned.

From a different perspective, the body not only perceives different worlds, persons, and peoples but excites us with senses, feelings, suspicions, wanting, and having.

The body defines life, sex, conditions, stages, and eccentric conditions from birth to death. Ever present to being, it constantly signals itself, its conditions, and its surroundings. Indeed, to a chorus of multiple voices, the body sings and hums us through our days. It establishes our presence and proclaims our being at every turn and moment while murmuring our mortality and declaring our coming deaths.

The body accounts for mood and temperament, our sense of the inner and outer worlds. It beams us with a sense of fullness and depletes our spirit with a sense of emptiness. It gives rise to our emotions, spurs our wishes and hopes, and underpins our conditions and plans, even informs us when death is near and inevitable.

The body, which accounts for the pleasures of eating, drinking, and sex, accepts the discipline of everyday life and even the drilling of boot camp. The body puts us on a mixed ground of our being and meaning. While it can be

beautiful in form, the body can also be bent and twisted—
with the comic backside of unexpected farting and the ordeal
of lives of constipation or diarrhea. The body's contrasts,
juxtapositions, and open contradictions furnish the tap root
of our cultures, traditions, and folklore.

As the source of such primary metaphors as those of
want and desire, resistance, conflict, completion, place,
movement, and direction, the body plays into the highest
aspirations for unity, peace, and plentitude. The Old and New
Testaments testify to this with such body-rooted metaphors
as blood, sacrifice, bread, eucharist, crucifixion, and rebirth.

After exploring the body and self in the early chapters, I
conclude with three chapters on things, tools, and machines
as extensions of our bodies and makers of our modern
selves. With things, tools, machines, and engines, we change
the world and enact and make the self of groups, world, and
mind. In this sense, as deep history shows, from our known
beginnings, we are creatures of our advancing handiwork
and artifacts. While beginning with cities and civilizations
and dramatically accelerating in modern times, we radically
extend the powers and energy of the body, causing us to re-
imagine and invent ourselves and the world anew.

I hope this book will excite its readers to think about
themselves as the story of their own bodies. In turn, I hope
that this will increase an appreciation of themselves as
a wonderful plenitude of body and mind, place and time,
cultures, words and metaphors, and inheritance of family, the
dead, myths, the church, and God.

Acknowledgments

M y thanks here are of two kinds. As revealed throughout the text and especially in its personal anecdotes, poems, and reflections, I owe much not only to parents, family, friends, wife of fifty-five years, and four children but also to culture, inheritance, institutions, ideas, and beliefs that made my body "a vessel and sea of self."

In truth, the body creates life and self. It can be treated as the axis of an autobiography and a multifaceted thematic hub of a hundred different types of memoirs. An older person of my age can paradoxically concede that the most ancient local and rural cultures formed their life and understanding of their body and may know that, in all likelihood, they survived as long as they did thanks to modern science and technology. They might even be aware that a full diet and public health not only defeated sickness and disease but made possible the pursuit of passions and pleasures, travel and recreation, and even imaginative journeys to the depths of the sea and space.

I was born healthy and have remained so for the last eighty-five years, thanks to good health, diet, and condition, along with a heart bypass at fifty-five, a pacemaker at eighty-three, medical doctors, "continuing access to a drugstore worth of medicine," and the social and financial support from governmental programs. I, an only child, had the gift of good, healthy, industrious, and loving parents. They accepted and taught me to accept myself as both a body and a person. At the same time, they taught me that I had a potential place and duty in society.

My multi-ethnic working-class family and three grandparents gave me a traditional world in a microcosm. Their lives and stories belonged to the rural world of a village. At the same time, they were generous with food, talk, and meals on Sundays and holidays. They joked and teased, danced, and cared for children. They suffered a few early deaths and tragedies and knew second marriages; meanwhile, all worked hard, did their military service, and unabashedly after the Second World War, took to refrigerators, televisions, new houses, and goods. In a lot of ways, they were friends of the body—the peasants of old on the loose in new times.

As good Catholics, they celebrated and taught me that God was of body and spirit, and his son, Jesus Christ, was God incarnate, who knew, cured, suffered, died, and was resurrected, and would do the same for man. While one could sin in their body, communion, Mary, and the saints lived and graced us to the earthly and heavenly depths of our bodies.

In my childhood, there were spaces, places, and things of play everywhere. At home and in schools, things were set up and organized for my full development. Boy Scout days, when I was eleven to thirteen years old, mixed discipline and play. Scouts meant proper saluting and standing, days at the cabin, in the woods, hanging at a campfire, playing night games, walking river banks, being on guard for poison ivy, learning to row and canoe, collecting nests, tying knots and bandages, and learning to sleep out in self-made sumac shelters.

Then too, there were sports. I could swim well, and I skated with a sense of turn, speed, and freedom. Hockey allowed me to participate with clashing sticks and boys and clever glides of self and passes of the puck. As a teenager, I traded baseball for carrying clubs and the golf course. Managing the driving range, I took to golf, a discipline (in fact, a dozen disciplines depending on the shot to be made, the lie, and the club). There were true mysteries to the swing, the ball's flight, and the bounce of the ball. I failed to become a champion despite wishes, thoughts, and practice, even though I practiced until my hands bled and achieved high school awards.

In other things, I found limits to the command and grace of my body. Distances were marked between my body that was given, dreamed, and willed. I had to give up writing left-handed, admit I had no talent for singing, was clumsy in many things, not quite as strong as others, and without patience for practicing the trombone. I also couldn't run quite as fast as I wished. It didn't help to blame my large, slowing thighs.

More significant distances, experienced as high fences topped by barbwire, existed between my body and me and my body and a girl's. Intimacy and sexuality, singularly and together, escaped me until marriage at twenty-seven. As much as I liked their soft feel and luscious mouths, and how much I liked to kiss them and dance very close with them, I didn't know their anatomy or my own, by experience or even study or vicarious browsing. Only in marriage to Catherine, my wife of fifty-five years, and through life with four good but physically and spiritually different children, did I begin to understand the fullness and richness of the body, what a wife, mother, and woman's body could become, and sense all that the body meant to her, meant to me, and to each other through days and nights, in love, unity, and the long-coming and separating of age and death.

How, then, do I give thanks to what made my body, that made me, and makes my world real and interpreted? I am too old and without time to write a detailed autobiography or a dozen memoirs. I can only say thanks to God, nature, family, society, wife, friends, and children for being, living, and becoming what I am.

In sum, I can't say thanks to all that gave and taught me my body—its reality, potential, and fulfillment. I couldn't write enough memoirs (though I wrote *Golf, Beats Us All, So We Love It*, and *Bypass*) to thank the persons and institutions, society, and culture that gave me life, opportunity, and imagination to be a self—a body that is a vessel that carries me through life and across a sea of meaning.

I hope this work follows from book one, an intellectual and cultural history of self as a *One* and *Many*, and I hope it anticipates book three on self, which is an exploratory and thematic autobiography. Titled *The Spring of Springs*, the work is a memoir of this eighty-five-year-old man who both mourns the recent loss of his wife of fifty-five years and yet grows in gratitude for all the gifts he has been and still is given. Despite my diminishment by age and loss, I am filled with thanks for the life I was given by my parents, family, and wife; thanks for what I continue to find in religion—its

doctrines and sacraments, inspiration and hopes; and thanks
for an education and a chance to study and teach intellectual
and cultural history. These have given me the ideas,
traditions, times, places, things, and events that went into my
self-making.

Finally, I wish to express my gratitude to my deceased
wife, Cathy, who lived out her life and body in my presence,
teaching me, an only child, about grace, generosity, fairness,
beauty, and love. As a founder of a La Leche chapter, a food
co-op, and as a public health nurse, ardent biker, and reader,
Cathy ministered to the bodies and spirits of others. In our
own home, she worked, sang, and produced four children
and taught me how to love five grandchildren and use and
celebrate the gifts of the body. She turned our everyday life
into a liturgy of our ways and days.

In many ways, our four children—Felice, Tony, Adam, and
Beth— have been a blessing. They furnish their widowed
father with occasional good meals and conversations,
medical aid, and financial help while supplying me with
needed household goods and cooking supplies. Beth's
husband Brent and son Adam purchase "my gadgets" and
make them run. Beyond all this, my children, in their half-
century, have been good, honest, and a matter of pride in
sports, education, work, and family.

Specifically, for *Body, Vessel and Sea of Self*, Felice's
oldest daughter, Rosalia Amato Bauer, inspired a second
cover's design. And again, I trusted two "old hands" along the
long road of writing. Craft person Wendy Johnson of Elder
Eye lent her many talents to afford me the text and book I
wanted, while Dana Yost, writer and poet, proved himself a
friend and critical and imaginative copy editor. A very recent
note by the archaeologist and anthropologist Clive Gamble
reminded me of my indebtedness to multiple students of
pre-history, European and French historian Eugen Weber
of UCLA, and so many other French and Italian writers of
rural, local, traditional, and popular cultures who accent life
and experience, culture, and language inseparably tied to the
body.

INTRODUCTION
SING AND THINK BODY
THE ONE AND MANY IT IS

I am the poet of the Body and I am the poet of the Soul,

The pleasures of heaven are with me and the pains of hell are with me,

The first I graft and increase upon myself, the latter I translate into a new tongue.

I am the poet of the woman the same as the man,

And I say it is as great to be a woman as to be a man,

And I say there is nothing greater than the mother of men.

  – First verse of Walt Whitman's "Song of Myself"

Why not praise the body as Whitman did? The body makes us flesh, bone, blood, and much more. The body is our closest companion, ever with us in and through our days. Yet, the body can rage and war against us, stealing our days and mind, and painfully and abruptly end our lives.

The body is our inner and outer door to being. It is the platform and motor of our being. It acts upon the world and is acted upon by the world. It goes into the world, and the world enters us through it. It is our birth, life, and death. With and by the body, we pledge, consecrate, sacrifice, and dedicate our lives.

Arguably it makes us conscious or surely comes continuously of our consciousness across a lifetime. It fills us with feelings, moods, symptoms, warnings, images, rhythms, memories, hallucinations, and core senses of right and wrong, touchable and untouchable, pure and sacred, and filthy and contaminating; at least, this is how I read Mary Douglas' 1966 *Purity and Danger*. She suggests that cultures, thanks to the body, are a mix of feelings, senses, and thoughts. They tell us quietly and by shouting what is *in place and out of place*, what is sacred and pure, and what pollutes, contaminates, and must be set apart and treated as taboo.

My friend James Rogers, in the wake of the death of his beloved wife, reports that keeping, moving, and getting rid of things filled him with a sense of them having right and wrong places. It led him to argue, whether admitted or not, that ghosts and presences haunt things; they ooze in and out of places and are incorporated with memories and senses that go to the bones and heart.

We, creatures of the body, live in a corporeal world, or in the words of A. Richard Turner, "Body is our corporal, visceral self. We can feel a clear head on awakening, the pain of arthritis in the joints, the exhilaration of exercise, the sting of a scrape."[1]

The body enters us in space and time. It is the agency of our contacts, interactions, comparisons, and projections. It is the skin, flesh, and spirit of our communities, even the practice of our memories. We take things into ourselves, and we name and put ourselves into them. They come with feelings and emotions registered in the senses, consciousness, and mind.

Our bodies make and hold our memories. They are our first cabinets of curiosity. Memories recall prior experiences—the things that tell of once-encountered places, times, works, peoples, and societies. When I walk, I look for stones that hold in microcosm the materials, surfaces, colors, and history of the ground my feet travel, and my eyes scan.

Bodily memories—along with the senses, feelings, and emotions—recall, foretell, and gesture things that happened and things we did. They evoke fear and confusion, pride and shame. In this way, the body pervades the mind and mood and what we think, feel, do, and imagine.

The body puts us among others, placing us in a world of energy and forms and plants and animals. Bodies come with what we hear, touch, and love; what we see, hear, tell, and imagine. Bodies can mean situations, possibilities, and

2

crowds. Bodies are a primary source of stories, cultures, myths, and selves.

We assume everything we meet has a body with an outer shell and an inner substance. So, hands, mouths, tongues, and minds must break into the world to know and have the world's fruits and secrets. This assumption of the nut and gem within underlies our conception of the good, special, beautiful, and sacred. We experience and know our own and the world's bodies in many ways through a glance, sight, touch, exploration and investigation, and myths.

Bodies form early mythology and folklore as godly and invisible, grotesque, gigantic, and mutating. Greek literature and myths mingle man, animals, and the gods in multiple ways. The Centaur has a man for his front and a horse for his rear. The Sirens sing, pulling Odysseus both toward the sucking whirlpool of the Charybdis and rock shoals of the Scylla. Zeus chases and impregnates earthly maidens with generations of lesser gods and spirits. Achilles' vulnerable heel, held by his mother, who dipped him in the pool of the immortalizing waters of the river Styx, proves the fatal spot found by the wavering arrow shot by the young Trojan, Paris. The stare of the Medusa turns all it catches into stone.

On an intellectual track, the twentieth-century historian Ernst Kantorowicz found the genesis of medieval political theology in, to cite the title of his seminal work, *The King's Two Bodies*. He showed how the monarch's sovereign power derived from the religious duality of the moral and fallible corporeal person and the elected and infallible head, which first belonged to the Fathers of the Church and is resonant in the 1870 doctrine of papal infallibility.

Ever protean and elastic to our imagination, the body defines our place, movement, and goal in the world. The woman's body, in contrast to the man's, remains a symphony of beauty and holds the mystery of new life. As we shoot rockets and astronauts into the sky, fascinated by the power and reach of our modern science and technology, similarly, we, with new and deep-penetrating instruments, examine the hidden bodies of cells and viruses. In the evening at home, we watch the radiant, strong, admirable, and alluring bodies of athletic heroes who are contemporary cousins of Greek Olympic athletes.

Our earthly and secular body seems to increasingly anchor the self in being. According to reviewer Julian Baggini (*The Wall Street Journal*, May 4, 2022), Noga Arikha contends in her very recent book, *The Ceiling Outside* (2022), "the sense of self is profoundly anchored in the body," and accounting for our inseverable tie with others, "the mind is inherently relational, not isolated." Drawing on the pioneering work of Antonio Damasio, Arikha, according to Baggini, goes so far as to say that "the brain serves the body, not the other way around."

According to contemporary neurologist Oliver Sacks, who wrote *The Man Who Mistook His Wife for a Hat* (1985), self and the world can be disassociated and even turned upside down in the cases of people who have mistaken or broken contact with their bodies. This is illustrated by cases of individuals who can't read faces, understand sounds, or keep in order their sights, memory, and language as inseparable from the body. Often these conditions result from suffering hallucinations, experiencing epilepsy, undergoing strokes, or other trauma.

Disorders of the mind can be understood to arise from our singular, finite, and mortal body, which unpredictably throws us into a world of experience beyond our control and surprises us with delight and terror. The body moves in and out of worlds of things and people, alternately attracting, repelling, and compelling, awakening streams of associated emotions, feelings, and thoughts. Thus, bodies make and enrich experiences and can form the inner lining as well as axes and turning points of biographies.

Bodies, which distinguish male and female, young and old, family and friends, and others and groups, make the stages of our lives. When young, at least for the healthy, the body is our trusted companion, the moveable and adaptable platform of our days. When young, the body, not without surprises and even traumas, accompanies, grows, and develops, which, in retrospect, we judge to be natural and normal. It joins us in learning to play and compete, be at the table, in bed, and love.

A woman's body tells, suggests, all. As sacred and profane, alluring, reproductive and mothering, and then aged, fallen, and in decline, her body reports her life: her attracting, giving, loving, caring, remembering, and imagining. More than the body of a husband and father, whose scars might reveal his work and prowess, the mother—at least the traditional wife and mother—carries in flesh and spirit her life of dedication, children, and family.

With great variation by individual and sex, our bodies deliver us to old age and death. Their routes have been set by choices and habits. They have been improvised, compelled, and even biologically determined. An old body, taking my own as an example, increasingly commands. It can become a frail and fickle friend, a nasty and arbitrary dictator who rules with the frequency and urgency of the kidneys, the reluctance and even hardened resistance of the bowels, and the weakening of lungs and heart. Infections, itches, and scratches turn us all into nurses and doctors or drive us old with midnight trips to the emergency room.

As we age, of course, with immense individual variation, the body overtakes and can even dominate our minds and daily conversations. It locks us more and more to ourselves as it limits our movement, diminishes our minds, weakens our limbs, steals our breath, and leaves us afraid and atremble.

With our revealing and disguising mask of face and gestures, the body inwardly constructs and outwardly enacts our life in tropes, figures of speech, such as clichés, oxymorons, and paradoxes, or with the four classics used to classify types of plays and motifs of histories, comedy, tragedy, irony, and satire. The body undergoes a thousand tests and makes millions of gestures as it conducts a life's story, even coaching us when it is right to die, to let go.

The body, as stated above, denies our autonomy. It does not allow us to make ourselves one thing, have a single defining secret, or be forever truly alone. The body puts us in a common life amidst the changing elements, light, earth, water, and air, alongside the chosen and rejected, the brilliant and stupid, the wise and mad, and the common and unusual. The body forever puts us and our world in a discourse of contrasts, comparisons, and differences. At the same time, it draws on reigning clichés (like *the girl next door*) while sparking metaphors that join things, places, times, societies, and gods. By proximity and association, gratitude, reciprocity, jealousy, wish, and dream, we live the lives of others.

Philosophers and religious thinkers incorporate us whole—incarnate, body, spirit, and soul—into transcendent beings. Speaking in Athens, St. Paul, telling of his faith in Christ, declares that "in Him, we live, and move, and have our being" (Acts 17:28–29). He goes on to say, being of Him, the Son of God, "we ought not to think of the divinity is like an image fashioned from gold, silver, and stone by human act and imagination." In Romans 6:4, Paul seals the earthly body and the divine, "We are buried with him by baptism into death: that like as Christ was raised up from the dead by the glory of the Father, even so, we also should walk in newness of life."

Traditional early cultures spiritually and mythically knit our bodies into other living and dead bodies and spirits. Many of these cultures made the earth the sacred repository of bodies and sprinkled ashes as seeds of transcendence. The dead made the ground and place holy. The ancients of Greece transported their selected dead from the mother city to plant and consecrate the walls of their new colony. Early Christians located their churches on the burial grounds of their saints. The best-known saints set the foundations for the churches which drew the most distant and, thus, tested pilgrimages in hopes of attaining the greatest miracles.

Bodies, alive and dead, still call us in this deaf, secularized world. Traditional believers and poets still are haunted by spirits. Spirits still inhabit places and things. Memories still vivify the present and link us to the dead through words, fidelities, and duties beyond place and time.

As a young man who protested the draft for the war in Vietnam, I understand that young men are called to sacrifice their bodies and their mortal lives for a temporary war. As a father and grandfather, I understand how young women hear, from childhood on, the dutiful call of love to give their lives to a man, the start of a household, and the bearing of children. They must let a man and child into their body, lives, and spirit.

With the question of what do I owe my body goes the question of what do I owe the bodies of others. Is the body a living temple? Is the body the seat of freedom and humanity? The body claims axial deliberations in matters of possession, residence, law, constitutions, and rights. Debates over the rights and responsibility of the body and its actions and fate go with questions and judgments of slavery, racism, banishment, imprisonment, capital punishment, and abortion, along with prostitution and pornography. "When we go to the center of the hoop," do we, in the words of Black Elk's *Sacred Pipe*, cry out knowing that "anything born into this world . . . must suffer and bear difficulties."

Contrarily, as I discuss in the closing chapters, there are contemporaries who aspire, believe, and propagandize that progress can, should, and will eliminate suffering. Some even direct their sympathies to campaigns against the cruel and unnecessary pain of humans and domestic animals. Some extend their empathy to all of nature—the entire ecological system.

Certainly, new markets, technologies, and international communication have extended sympathies and have made fellow feelings global. The body of the others becomes present to me; they pass the front porch of my feelings and mind. Their most basic bodily needs are heard within me. Democracy, social work, foreign aid, education, medical therapy and research, and philanthropy plant the seeds and feed the roots of a universal sensibility that suggests we are all one in being and body on an advancing but ever-fragile earth.

CHAPTER 1
PERPLEXING BODY

M any have chosen to make the self a mind or the work
of the mind. They have chosen to define us by our
thoughts, memory, conscience, habits, and duties. Yet,
for certain religious thinkers through the ages, we are a
spirit or soul that connects us to God and His creation. To
define the self by one's thoughts and doubts sounds as early
modern as it is romantic to identify oneself with controlling
feelings and dominating passions. Some contemporary
writers make us inseparable from the flow of consciousness,
while existentialists define the self by circumstances,
choices, and freedom. All these ways of thinking—in addition
to individuals who know themselves by their choices and
their right to choose—overlook, ignore, and even deny the
body's role in making self.

To be is to be in the body. The body puts us in the flesh; it
locates us in time and place and in the world. We arise from
and die in the body. Nevertheless, the body is not one and
does not make us a singular one. The body is a multivalent
plurality. It makes and expresses, reacts and remembers,
reveals and masks, and voices and projects us across our
entire lives. We forever live and talk as if we are inside and
outside of ourselves and as if we are of one body and mind
and many bodies and minds.

To use the dichotomy articulated across a long career by
the British archeologist and anthropologist of human origins,
Clive Gamble, the body is a *container and instrument*. He
writes in "Thinking inside the mask," our bodies, the source
"of our experience of living in the world," are made of heads
and torsos, "which contain brains, bellies, and orifices,"
that take in and store, nurture and propagate ourselves.
In contrast, we have limbs, which "have no openings, even
though they are part of a whole, the body. Our legs, toes,
arms, and hands grasp, kick, hit, gouge, pound, and with the
right implement, do almost anything else we want."[2]

As Gamble explains, the body as a container and user of containers and an instrument and user of instruments interact and define the poles of our actions and lives. They define our relations to things, tools, and the language of our understanding and metaphors.

For Gamble, masks stand out as "containers without walls."[3] They enfold us within and express what we symbolically make and project. They connect our inner selves to others, nature, gods, and the world. In this way, I take the body to join our inward and outward being with action and word, making the body both "a vessel and sea of self."

The body both throws us up against picket fences and floats us on mysterious waters. In "Pascal's Wager," the most well-known section of his classic *Pensées*, seventeenth-century mathematician, philosopher, and religious thinker Pascal wrote of our inescapable dependency on the body. "Our soul has been cast into the body, where it finds number, time, and dimension. It reasons thereupon, and calls it nature, necessity, and can believe nothing else."

Of our genesis born out of the relation of body and mind, Antonio Damasio wrote, "A mind is closely shaped by the body and destined to serve it. . . . For any body, never more than one mind."[4] However, in the same stroke on the same page, Damasio acknowledged our ignorance of the exact relation between the body and mind with a quotation from Nietzsche, who described that in the mysterious mix of body and mind, we are "hybrids of plants and ghosts."

Poet, philosopher, and religious thinker T. S. Eliot offers a conclusion to the question of what, who, and where we are with "Dry Salvages," gathered in his 1943 book, *Four Quartets*:

> Or the waterfall, or music, heard so deeply
> That it is not heard at all, but you are the music.
> While the music lasts. These are only hints and guesses,
> Hints followed by guesses; and the rest
> Is prayer, observance, discipline, thought and action.
> The hint half guessed, the gift half understood, is
> Incarnation.

We struggle in poetry, prose, and life to locate the self, ever-changing, metamorphosing, disappearing, hogging the stage of our consciousness until it sneaks off with a few words and something to do. In *The Unseen Body*, published in 2021, Jonathan Reisman plunged the body into changing times.

> We are clockwork creatures. . . . In adults, the heart beats about once per second, . . . and lungs inhale and exhale with the same cadence as ocean waves pounding the shore and retreating. . . . But there are many more beats in the body, each an actual biological clock keeping its own idiosyncratic times. Eyes blink every few seconds, and blood cells circle through vasculature every five minutes or so. Regular meals lead to (hopefully) regular excretions, bladders and intestines filling and emptying in dependable quotidian replay. . . . The human body depends on the rhythms of habit and gets used to, and becomes dependent on, almost anything—even the drumbeat of inebriation.
>
> Though our lives seem to proceed in linear fashion with one day following another and days progressing forward, human biology is best understood as not a single consecutive progression but a complex circular weaving of overlapping and interlaced musical meters. Homeostasis is an intricate blending together of beats, with melodies, varying in tempo as we go round [Sic.] and round.[5]

In the Introduction to *The Hand*, Raymond Tallis confessed his ignorance about our place as a body and mind in life. "We will never get entirely straight about ourselves in the way that we may get straight about things that lie outside ourselves. We must always live our lives opaquely, acting out body, desires, and thoughts that we find ourselves possessing and being possessed by."[6]

In my poem on the body, I made the whole body as Tallis treats the hand, as a great and non-reducible one and

many, whose embrace we cannot compass, fathom, or stand
beyond.

Body,
Marvel of being,
Flesh incarnate,
Arrives in womb.
Becomes the infant,
That becomes the child
Who moves out towards and into being
With sucking mouth
Absorbing eyes,
Fingering, touching, and prying hands.
Walking,
Wanting,
Riding
He is on the lookout
As he finds balance and direction.

His body, a dozen organs,
Five major systems,
Cells, nerves, organs,
Brain, bones, teeth,
Marvelous machine,
Of growth, learning, and reproduction,
Lasting across ages,
Exists ever
Temporal, mortal, vulnerable.

Body harbors hidden cancers,
Develops an irregular heartbeat,
A nervous tick,
A life-long twitch
A hundred maladies,
Orifices,
Broken ducts,
Sealed, and herniated tubes,
The old man pisses too much
And shits too little.

Symptoms become manifest—
A tremor, a shake,
Vertigo, and a backache,
Ever felt but never pinpointed.
Death hides below skin,
Within tunnels and organs unexplored.

Like the earth,
The truth belongs at times to guess,
To diagnosis:
The skill of a dozen crafts and feeling and poking hands,
Ten probes,
And five shadowy frames,
Twenty blood and lab tests.
And two hundred treatments
Lie ahead
For another restless night
In my crumpled bed.

The body puts us in life and being. It is inseparably of our soul and somehow indescribably apart from it and the spirit. At the same time, the body is in and out of us, with, and even, as the old know well, against us. It is never to be completely and permanently emptied short of death, no matter our therapeutic cleansing and lofty intentions.

The body locks us in different, ambivalent, and contradicting realms. As much as it is our companion and trusted friend, it can, especially with age, turn into an enemy. Few of us long-lived healthy moderns and contemporaries are quick to join St. Francis in thanking God for all-taking Sister Death.

The body, however, is with and in union with our consciousness, birth, and death. The body can be bold and joyously buoyant; it can also be leaden, awkward, timid, and a hundred other negative things. While right there with us, to be seen and touched, it also is sly, covert, and clandestine. While it can be beautifully disguised by the cosmetic, clothing, dietary, and surgical industries or penetrated by the beams and waves of atomic scanning machines, it can hatch malign plots never suspected by either doctor or patient.

The body puts us impenetrably deep in life as the mind arguably can carry us high in truthful vision. The body fits and even slots us in and blends us into places, occasions, and communities. It is the threshold, home, and grounds on which we meet, learn and interact with others. (This makes me think of the soft plea in the song "Take my hand, I am a stranger in paradise" that played in my slow-dancing youthful days.)

The body animates us. It enters us in motion and movement. It moves in sync and out of sync. It also presents fears and attractions, makes for pleasures and pains, and offers assumptions and projections. The body grows, reproduces, acts out, and ages us. It distinguishes us by age, sex, and conditions. It marks us out and individualizes us for a lifetime.

The body harnesses us to the reins of pleasure and pain. It recognizes simple and complex things and situations and acknowledges superior and inferior powers. The body fills us with certainties and hunches and sheer suspicions.

The body takes us into the world. It does this through our traditional five senses—or a sixth *mystical* sense, which operates in terms of presences beyond matter, space, and time. Or the body does this, as contemporary neurologists theorize, through somatic senses, which number from seven to nine or many more. Their counting goes from *proprioception* to senses of heat, pressure, and pain, to all-important recognition of people, things, and situations, the loss of which produces the *wildest aberrations*—the sort that led Oliver Sacks to write the now classic, *The Man Who Mistook His Wife for a Hat.* Cases of paranoia, schizophrenia, and depression, or the symptoms of alcoholism and drug addiction, multiply how much the hidden body and its ties and missing ties to the mind determine lives. Simply, we are a nest of sensations, impulses, reflexes, feelings, compulsions, hunches, feelings, and emotions.

At the same time, the body has amazing positive powers to ever so quickly learn and localize learning in its senses, fingers, hands, eyes, nose, tongue, and other parts of the body. Intuitively, instinctively, without hesitation, the body grasps that a thing or a whole situation is safe and solid or tentative and precarious. At the same time, the eye, ear, nose, hand, and foot need no coaxing to recognize what approaches as dangerous and hostile or useful, welcoming, and benevolent.

Our body, at least until recent times, constantly works the earth. It hunts, plants, culls, harvests, builds, and takes apart. Our body is a box of tools that, over time, learns to make a greater box of tools, which we call technology. It reconfigures and places us, starting with fireplaces and campgrounds, and advances to make our houses, villages, and societies. The self and body go hand-in-hand through life as they make our world.

Our body behaves in accord with spaces being intimate and private or communal and public. It senses itself in touch with spirits, the very powers of ancestors, and gods. As the sight of our beloved lifts our souls, the mere glance of an alien eye fixes us in shame and guilt. Our body can be taken up by the movements, feelings, and passions of the crowd, and it can be literally crushed and stifled by a crowd.

Our body joins, links, and makes us dependent on others from infancy on. Others, with their bodies, form and make our being. Their bodies nurture, punish, and teach us. They enable, invite, block, discipline, and control us. Bodies make us distinct individuals and even solitary individuals and also make us collective and gregarious beings.

A particular body of another captures our attention. It alerts our senses and activates our interests and thoughts. We name individuals and assign them traits by their bodies. This person is a drag, that one a snake, weasel, owl, a cow. Indeed, we imaginatively make ourselves animals and put ourselves in them. What child in play does not purr like a cat or roar and hiss like a lion—not embody self in the skin and movements of a hundred animals? Indeed, whole armies march in goosestep in our imaginations.

At times, especially when healthy and young, prior to questions of our sexual identity and bodily prowess, we presume we and our bodies are one and in harmony. With the onset of adolescence, the body becomes a new sun and moon in our lives. Our conversations with it become as varied as the body's parts, changes, needs, elevations, and vilifications. My adolescence body became a cross of shame—a shaky bridge to others, especially unknown girls.

At all stages of maturity and old age, the body forms a cacophony of voices and noises. With speaking and meaning-making tongues and ever-touching, constructive, and expressive hands, we explore, make, and tell both the world and the self what and whom they are while identifying and establishing relations between them. As feet travel, shape, and interact with the earth, so eyes, ears, and noses take infinite sensations, while the unresolved throat, grumbling stomach, and noise-making rectum signal the presence of a human self. The body not only experiences but interacts with the world and constantly gestures, shouts, whispers, and mumbles as it goes. The same body sitting in old Hollywood musicals finds itself imaginatively dancing with Fred Astaire and Ginger Rogers or dancing in "Singing in the Rain" with Gene Kelly.

We are both a puppet of our body and its puppeteer. We move our bodies to fit the mind's script, scene, and music. At moments, we even become the body we know we are not. Males blow up their chests on the back page of a cartoon ad for bodybuilding from the 1950s so as not to have sand kicked in our faces by the *beach bully*.

Admittedly, we use appearance to beguile and lure. Girdles, bras, braces, shoe lifts, wigs, dentures, and false eyelashes are our tools of artifice and disguise. By choice and habit, we become the look of the world we idealize. With dress, posture, and language, we fit our bodies into the world we seek.

There are even good reasons to know our body as a many that make us a many. Our body is never a solid, certain, and definite thing or a single object for investigation and reflection. Nor does it fit an identity or a cast of words or an image, however crafted. Who, at least at moments, does not think of him or herself to be but a mere single frog egg in the flush of a gathering spring river? When old, who does not see his skin as the cracked clay of a dried marsh? From youth on, we know a snooty nose, however loftily pointed, can hold a big *booger*—and does not, from time to time, even the shapeliest rear sneak out a rude and smelly fart. Even the feet of our stars and heroes stink. Children take pleasure in noticing, identifying, and making bodily sounds and smells.

In old age—my stage and preoccupation—the body rudely defies commands that aging imposes. In senior apartments, the daintiest women and the largest men wear diapers of one brand or another. Accidents multiply as the "call of nature" becomes more frequent and welcoming bathrooms are farther away.

No news increasingly becomes welcome news. Our very conversations account for the body's changes. I hear, "I am going gray; getting old." Out of the blue, we are told, as I was recently, "You have skin cancer, carcinoma below your right eye."

We cannot hide the fact that we have passed our heyday. Our body stiffens and weakens, and our balance falters as our energy slackens. Our digestion flags, our arthritic limbs stiffen, and our breathing falters. We suffer our own bowels and feel we are the bowels of the earth. We are afraid of falling—to fall once and for all or again and again until we rise to the fall of death. With old age, the body enters a dialogue with us about pain and hurt. This dialogue is not just within us but is spoken all around us. At times we wish we could be dust and fly away into starry heavens or disintegrate in the compost pile to fertilize new life.

Age leads us to ask how we will end. We are constantly reminded that our strength wanes, intelligence dims, and of what we fear if suffering becomes manifest—not only in us but also in those of our age. My shorthand for this condition: *Constant constipation/frequent urination! Take another pill* and *buy a new pillow.*

The body is an interruption. Its signals can be sharp, intense, and yet tediously repetitive. For those with a nervous and reflective nature, it announces advancing mortality. The body's complaints are not easily turned aside, for according to Cicero's account, old age's misery battles us on four main fronts. It withdraws us from an active life, weakens our bodies, deprives us of most enjoyments, and stands us not far from death.

Creeping senescence can become the self's preoccupation. It can drive us to mount a counteroffensive. To take up Stoicism's harness: remember and do one's duty to the end. It may cultivate an Epicurean dismissal of death and indulge oneself in what moderate pleasures one can. From it, one may learn detachment and the emptying of oneself of all illusions and images. One can be grateful for what was once had and hopeful God will return us, fresh, reborn of Heaven's spring rain, to flourish in the world again.

Aging can also even assault our important rooting in gratitude and hope. It literally kills off mates, parents, family, friends, dates, customs, and causes in which we invested our hearts. It chokes off our recollection of blessings received and things achieved. Even mental activity, once generated by teachers, friends, and books, can be diminished by the "loss of synapses" and pity for the self. The mind seems incapable of consoling our pain with purpose and putting memory against what has been lost. In age, the captain has lost his grip on the wheel, he cannot read his compass, he has retreated to his cabin, depressed, and he cannot rally us to port ahead.

In so many ways, the more we are conscious of our bodies, the less they seem, at least at times, our own. As I learn what I am medically or surgically to have done from books or studies, my body becomes ever more alien and distant. It becomes more an object and less me, I, and self.

The body I assumed to be my own now increasingly seems like a third party. It demands that I surrender my life to medical advice and treatments. It becomes ever more dependent on authority and under the care of others. It is contagious to the misfortunes of others. It takes in the accidents, illnesses, and deaths of others as they are germs against which I have no immunities of presumption and optimism.

Many of us, who once gushingly sang out in joy about the gifts of our body, end up disliking, even hating, our body for what it is making us. Counseling and medicine, at best, abate the inevitable slowing inertia of our multiplying years. There is no end to the types of self-hate stemming from aging. Some of the old are obsessed with their failing public appearance, while others suffer at home alone with their real and imagined ailments.

I mull how body hate and self-hate are joined. I find that thought in-depth in literature with its exploration of types of irrationality. I hear it in the classical philosophers' prescription of moderation, duty, and discipline, and the theologians' concern with vice and sin, speculating on sin as a source and state of self-corruption. And when I think of ravenous eating, compulsive and killing fasting, or suicidal bulimia, the type that thirty years ago killed a young student of mine, I even speculate on the question of whether we are an animal that hates itself because its body and mind can become a broken and even evil alliance.

Of course, we must always bear in mind that our body belongs to others as much as it does to ourselves. We forever live, think, and feel inside ourselves as we think we are seen and talked about on the outside. Unquestionably, we all live by our interior and exterior bodies, and as we try to take hold of ourselves, others take hold of us. Near the beginning of his *Body in Question*, Jonathan Miller wrote:

> Of all objects in the world, the human body has a peculiar status: it is not only possessed by the person who has it, it also possesses and constitutes him.

> Our body is quite different from all other things we
> claim as our own. We can lose money, books, even
> houses and still remain recognizably ourselves, but it
> is hard to give any intellectual sense to the idea of a
> disembodied person.[7]

The body leads, follows, prompts, and gnaws at the mind. It
alerts, suspects, and receives through senses: sights, sounds,
smells, and touches, in addition to unifying impressions and
images. It gathers and passes on such signals even when
the person sleeps. The body, as a student, learns what the
mind cannot at first imagine, and it can be taught a wealth
of things by instruction and repetition. It can be harnessed
to routines by discipline and refined by new experiences
that alert, caution, surprise, satisfy, and hurt. It takes in and
makes part of itself as perceiving, acting, and behaving with
good habits. Good habits, ideally, refine temperaments into
character.

From another perspective, the body can be said to know
no master. It is wild. It is the voice of unconsciousness, an
entity Nietzsche attributed to an uninhibited metaphysical
will. It is expressed by Freud in terms of the Id's incestuous
and irrational impulses. Or found in wild and untamed
unconscious polymorphous impulses in Norman Brown's
Love's Body, a voice of the liberating 1960s counter-culture.

Under certain conditions, including illness, disease,
and extreme solitude, the body becomes disobedient, turns
savage, and belongs to orders defiant of self and anything
resembling common humanity. The body saves, protects,
remembers, and reproduces all the signals it stores up. It
repeats instantaneously and spontaneously while not denying
great individual variation of the body's failing, wasting,
injuring, and destroying selves, unbeknownst to the mind and
its cautions. Who could not write his or her autobiography
or fill a long ledger inventory of self-violations, reoccurring
temptations, and unintentional slips and falls? Plus, I do not
list suspected paths to suicide. Without an education and a

river of experience, I cannot even sketch the tributaries of self-hate, which end in self-mutilation and suicide.

Nevertheless, I contradict myself in measure. Though vulnerable, fragile, complex, and mortal, with a jumble of hundreds of millions, even billions, of years of mixed and jumbled evolution, the body is unimaginably rich and undeniably triumphant over extinction. With all of its evolved parts and organs, it is a changing and surviving vessel that carries us out, into, and through the world of things and life. A mixture of repetitions, constancy, and surprise, and a choir of faces, hands, feet, fingers, toes, chests, bellies, and buttocks, our body has produced remarkable harmonies and even symphonies of being.

The body forms our house and home. It puts us on the front porch, in the kitchen, living room, bedroom, basement, and attic. At the same time, it forms our villages and joins us to society.

As our embodiment and incarnation, the body is our glory and shame—our earthly infinity and finitude. It marches us through life. Surely, the body makes us the great multitude that God created and of which the mortal Whitman sang.

As much as we would like to define, judge, and treat the body as one, it escapes us. It goes beyond our words, wisdom, and philosophy. It tests our most reaching metaphors and myths. It multiplies beyond theorists and actuaries.

A poem about the body could never be complete. It is great in fact and detail and beyond our metaphoric reach. The body can be told as tragedy, comedy, irony, satire, and their mix. It can be understood as a matter of causes and orders, a result of events and surprises.

In his films, Charlie Chaplin joined the hilarious and melancholic. He stood forth with frantic, repeated, single, and slow movements. We, his audience, cannot separate him from his body—his bowler cap, big shoes, baggy pants, twirling cane, tear-plucking hands, and a face full of gestures. As a melancholic comic, he entered wonderfully out of sync with the newborn mechanical world of the factory.

Death can come to us through the suicide of others. It did so to me when I was a young college teacher. I recorded this in two early poems—found in my *Death Book: Terrors, Consolations, Contradictions, and Paradoxes* (1985)—that conclude this chapter in verse, as I began it.

Deaths by suicide can turn into stories that painfully speak to us across decades. I think of the suicide of our university swimming coach.

PALM'S DEEP WATER

Palm, our swimming coach, had been drowning for years.
Something had cut him adrift
From his career,
His self,
This shore.

He kept casting off from his job
And they kept hauling him back,
Until the last time
When he said (it is reported)
That he would never be saved
If they kept bringing him back on board.
And so he disappeared
In the wake of this school
And those churning days.

Only when people spoke of
How once we had a championship team
And now we have no team at all
Was Palm mentioned.
Then his name echoed
In our great pool,
It lapped from side to side,
Up over the rails.
From swimming tank
To diving well,
From the top of the three-meter board
At one end

To unused Olympic clocks
At the other.

Palm, Palm,
His name echoed there
Like the softest wind
On this prairie.

Now, years later,
From across this prairie
Comes
Word
That
Palm, seeing no light,
Let his body descend into great darkness
For the peace of deep water.

I also have not forgotten the suicide of a former young university student of mine. He, a promising poet and writer, married himself to a terrible blizzard's wind and cold one winter night:

A WINTER PEACE DANCE

God is cold,
And I am lost along the road again.
For the last twelve years I kept getting lost.
My blue eyes grow paler all the time,
Losing hold of what they see.

I am in front of this farmhouse.
I am walking around it, swirling like the snow,
Seeing the house and not seeing it.
Its light, this snow, my loss.

They guide me in as if I am a blind man.
They talk nicely, they offer tea,
And as they phone the highway patrol,
I slip out.

I know too much,
I have thought too long,
I have felt too strongly,
And been lost too often
To be found again.

I'll sleep out,
And when I awake on that hard, frozen earth
I'll dance my last dance,
I'll embrace the prairie winds,
I'll dance the winter I have been,
I'll finish the winter I suffer.

No voices, no bands, no houses.
Cold and moonlight in a crystal silence
Too cold for any howling dog,
My dance,
And winter peace.

CHAPTER 2
I SING OF THE AGES
OF THE BODY

I sing the body I am. Embodied and incarnate, I incorporate
the world, its touches, liquids, food, faces, voices, and
movements. I never stop taking in things and the world.

I come and go and carry out my ways and days with
my body. It embodies and makes me mobile. It puts me in
nature and with others. It joins me to things (like homes,
rooms, beds, and blankets), and I appear in and with it on
all stages, public and private. It goes with underpinning and
consecrating my life by deeds and sacrifices to individuals
and groups of others.

I also treat my body as my vault. In it, I store my inner
senses, intentions, and energy. However, as much as the
body can be wild and out of control, I claim it as mine. When
young and well, it was my faithful horse. Now, at eighty-four,
my body has declared its full independence. It is rebellious,
headstrong, and even subversive. As an invisible clock, it sets
the length of my days but knows not of exterior happenings
and fatalities. Ambiguously, it is the agent and victim of my
fate and fortune.

My body, elementally and in the presence and relation to
things and other bodies, affords and denies energy, action,
and movement. It creates symmetrical and asymmetrical,
harmonious and cacophonous worlds of one and many things
and situations. It does this with its own ones and twos—two
eyes, ears, nostrils, arms, hands, legs, feet, breasts, nipples,
testicles, cheeks of the face and buttock, but has one mouth,
which takes in food and drink and holds a wagging tongue
that spins out all sorts of words. Also, there is, Heaven, Help
Us!, a single head filled with many teeth and a brain beyond
plummeting. It is mounted on a turret-like neck and a torso
that stands straight, turns, and slouches, with a solitary
and protruding navel. And, as males count their fallen and

risen penis as a metronome of both the moment and years, females, with protruding breasts and wombs, softness and protuberances, host more alluring and mystifying systems of ones and twos, expanding with pregnancy and births and collapsing with age. The bodies of men and women, different by face, hair, skin, musculature of back, legs, feet, arms, hands, neck, walk, and movement, make the great human contrast, which made and still makes dualities of metaphors, cultures, societies, and traditions.

The body plunges us into the world and consciousness, situations, and feelings. Through body and face, we first meet, name, and come to learn of inner things and persons. Alerted and cognizant by diverse senses, the body beacons the world in which we have been placed. It tells us about our insides and glimpses, acknowledges, and accepts the revelations of worlds outside—about, around, and even upon us. The body finds, defines, and makes paths to things, landscapes, others, places, and communities.

The body is our given and life-long companion. Like an accordion, it opens and shuts, playing to what is around. It accepts, learns, and makes habits and regimes to meet the world's necessities and take its pleasures. It keeps memories immediate to the mind and puts first and unusual experiences in its cabinet of curiosities.

HERE I AM

My body encapsulated me in life and the world, creating so many reflexes, experiences, feelings, and memories which were decisive and unforgettable, ever puzzling and yet given sense. My body goes to the very heart and forms of my being, exceeding the touch of my hands, the rub of my body, the count of my fingers, and my most adroit words and reaching metaphors.

By its own automatic commands, my body sets me in movement and action. Through pains, it instructs me about the order and nature of things and even the limits of self-indulgent pleasures. As a compliant and even dutiful servant, it instructs me gently and brutally about limits and control.

It brings me to realize that, over time, discipline and good habits, virtues if you wish, help one along the road to good days and good ways.

My body afforded me my first identity in the world. I remember myself as an ambidextrous boy, as quick to use one hand, side, and eye as the other. I also remember myself in the first or second grade as a boy who had a stutter and was effectively cured in a few minutes by a speech therapist who said, "Quit trying to say too much at the same time." Later in life, I came to identify myself as the son of a quick-talking and wise-cracking mother, whose first cousin said of her, "The tongue will be the last organ to go on that woman." He had the same quick tongue as my mother.

When very young, again, I would guess six or seven, on the threshold of falling asleep with relatives talking and playing cards in the nearby dining room, I clearly thought, if only for a few moments, I fear I might not wake again. I might not be anymore. Now old, this childhood reoccurs: soon there will be lasting dark, in which I and all may *be* no more. I counter this thought with prayer and sleep.

I came into being in a body. It was a body, incarnate as the world recognized with my mother suffering my long-coming arrival. Upon my birth, a nurse weighed me and described my sex. My parents named me not by appearance but by ancestry. They blanketed, fed, and cared for me. They had my first shoes preserved in bronze.

I discovered my body long before I began to live by my mind and for myself. My hand touched my hand, fingers opened, clutched, ran, and touched my skin. I relished my fat, my mother, and the nipple of a bottle. I sucked my thumbs. To no one's delight, once, I was told, I plastered the wall brown with my fresh feces. By the time I was five or so, I was in basic command of my body and its movements, and on a soft evening, I loved to play outside and wrestle on the grass; and once, I remember, with one arm extended, I went around and around a street pole until I fell down dizzy and laughing. I set myself and the world awhirl. (I never did like roller coasters, although I liked to climb trees and ride bumper Dodgem cars.)

27

My body recorded my entrance into life and play. I was spared long and crippling diseases, like the polio epidemic of my youth, that could result in life-long paralysis and distort or even build character as it did in the case of President Franklin Roosevelt. A childhood scar on my right wrist reminds me of playing in a field behind my house and being cut by a sharp piece of broken glass. I got bee stings on my bare feet while crossing over a clover-filled lawn on the way to play with Herbie next door. Terrible bouts of poison ivy, which I found everywhere, even blowing in the wind, attacked me often and required shots. When quite young, I got a case of ringworm, suspected from a theater seat, and as a punishment, I had to wear my mother's nylons to school and experience the mockery of classmates. A nail in the knee, playing "tanks" in a field with an empty bicycle box, earned me a tetanus shot, while an early appendectomy was followed a year or two later by a doctor's office tonsillectomy, which introduced me to inescapable spinning ether-made dreams. So, disease, accidents, and therapy punctuated and marked different chapters in my life.

In elementary school at Stellwagen, on the east side of Detroit, I explored and fit in another space, and there, if I press my memory, its front was defined by a road with a median strip that held a few crabapple trees whose large thorns could be harvested to prick another student. On the building side where we entered, there was a stand of poplars in whose shade we stood and talked while our terrain of free horseplay was out back with large yards of gravel, fields of grass, one outdoor skating pond that I loved, and a baseball field on which, in the early grades, I didn't excel at either batting or fielding.

At Stellwagen, I learned to accustom my body to new spaces, regimes, and other children. They lined us up and marched us to classes. I remember sitting at a desk with a slanted top that opened for storage. At its top, the desk had a groove for a pencil and a small metal ink holder, both of which made games for rolling pencils and sinking index-finger shots with small balls. At the same desk, I learned the stroke of the alphabet, drawing the capital and lower-case letters with the tip of a steel pen that was easily bent. I also learned to judge myself at a lowly score of 40 out of 120—sloppy and slipshod by the Palmer Method of penmanship rules.

Mrs. Thomas, the short, second-grade music teacher who branded me a "listener," once took my attempts to sing as acts of purposeful disobedience and tried to slap me in the face. To her great anger, she failed as I blocked each of her blows. She told me to march to my locker, which I gladly did, free of her for the day.

In kindergarten, they taught us to skip. In second grade, they tried, without succeeding at all, to teach "slap-dash" me to draw and paint. In the second or third grade, they even taught us to dance. I swung my square dance partner, Judy Lintz, the lightest girl in the class, too hard and high, and she came down in tears, and I felt myself a monster of my own doing.

Out behind the school, where more boy fun was to be had during recess, I learned to pitch pennies and baseball cards, play catch, arm wrestle, and find out just what kind of boy I was, which meant what my body could comparatively do. As a competitive boy, I put my body to the test in almost all things at most times, whether in our ongoing neighborhood fighting of the Second World War in the fields out back, wrestling under the street light, or biking and running fast and far, counted by city blocks, twelve of which equaled a mile.

My elementary days belonged in large part to my growing body. While growth, skills, and pride were often out-of-joint, my body, nevertheless and without choice, underpinned who and what I took myself to be as a boy and to become as a man. Both sensitive but not easily cowed, while growing up, I had memorable experiences around confrontations and fighting. It seemed a necessary and honorable path for a boy to follow.

While already by First Confession and Communion at seven, I believed and, to a degree, understood myself as capable of committing mortal sins. Also, at around seven years old, I knew how to insult by the body by calling someone a *sissy*, another a *pee pants*, someone else a *shit-ass*, a non-athletic kid a *cream puff*, and the flat-rear-ended office guy who sits and diddles with books all day, a *satchel ass*.

As much as I enjoyed names, I knew my reality was when push came to shove, "sticks and stones may break my bones, but names will never hurt me." In the second grade, we often initiated a boy with a solid punch to the back. When I initiated the large but clumsy Arthur Rubin with a hard punch to his back, he profoundly cried, and I profusely apologized, giving wailing Arthur my two new pencils in hopes he wouldn't tell our teacher. Arthur and I did make amends, and he and his mother invited me to his house to play.

Another confrontation and its fall-out occurred when, in third or fourth grade, I threw smaller and younger Herbert Sudeman down on the ground. I confessed to doing this to the summoned principal in the presence of my *victim* and his father, "Yes, I threw Herbert down on top of his violin case. He refused to put it down and fight after he spit on me. Yes, I taunted him, but he insulted me." The principal took my side, and Herbert and his father took the broken violin and left. I liked Principal Donolan thereafter.

Of course, the dutiful and affectionate attention I received from my black and white-breasted furry Border Collie, Spikes, counted greatly. It somehow compensated in some way for the respect I didn't get from my neighborhood and schoolyard friends. Having my dog made me special, loved. With Spikes, I had a true buddy until his *girl-chasing* earned him permanent exile on my grandfather's farm 240 miles north in Vanderbilt, Michigan. There, Spikes had new adventures, including once sniffing the tail end of a porcupine. His adventures ended when he took to chasing cars and got run over. On hearing this, I wept bitterly for an evening. Spikes was gone, and a part of me was missing.

In Boy Scouts, I found another open terrain larger than the fields and alleys of my neighborhood and freer than the school and schoolyard. Hiking and exploring, swimming, canoeing, rowing, and fishing, handling a large knife and axe, tying knots, making tourniquets, splits, and bandages, learning to smoke and, once, trying to chew tobacco, were in play at camp on the north branch of the Clinton River. The troop tested bodily skills, intelligence, and knowledge with merit badges and ranks and broad allegiance with salutes and marches to the Scout's oath and nation.

I remember one solitary hike along the river when I entered a marsh thick with stinging nettles. They made me itch so painfully that I fought my way directly to the river's bank to escape. I entered the water, tucked my hips boots under my arm, and sided stroked to the other shore, losing only one boot in my crossing.

Even after I became an ardent canoeist and rower, I never lost respect for water's grace and powers. In 2014, at seventy-six years old, I, a passionate reader of *Moby Dick*, Melville's great embodied spirit of the sea, metaphorically turned my body into a ship that stays afloat by the mind in *Buoyancies: A Ballast Master's Log*, keeping ballast in balance as we sail through the shifting seas of life's experiences.

My thirty or so merit badges with ranks that reached Eagle Scout and beyond, and my special awards like the Order of the Arrow, all taught me about and tested my body. When I was eleven, I embarrassingly recall an event at our Boy Scout Christmas party. In front of our whole troop of scouts and their parents, I, first to choose, greedily chose the biggest box under the tree, only to discover it held nothing. I cried bitterly. I had been tricked and then terribly embarrassed by revealing my oversized desire and my tearful disappointment. I could do nothing other than remember to, in the future, choose a moderately sized box and smile.

CLOCKS OF AGE

Clocks and rhythms punctuated my childhood. At school,
I got in step and found synchronicity with my peers. Aside
from a camp gong that called us to lunch and supper, clocks
punctuated my youth. In school, big, *seriously authoritative*
wall clocks taught me that institutional time outweighed the
ordinary tick-and-tock of my days (the small clocks set by
my mom for rising and sleeping, school and work, weekdays
and weekends). Likewise, we learned to keep time when we
ran, speed-skated, took a long hike, took a pulse, or tied a
bandage in First Aid classes. Our Boy Scout troop ran its
meeting like the military organization it feigned to be.

Wristwatches, work days, and vacations timed my
habits, play, and expectations. My father's clock-like life,
defined by missing only two days of work in forty-three years,
established the rhythm and calendar of our home. Each day
he got up at six, dressed and ate, and prepared for his forty-
minute bus trip downtown to work at Western Union. He
returned every day on the same bus, making me believe that
downtown and all its happenings were synchronized with
my father's schedule. When home, just after five, he changed
out of his suit and into his work clothes. He then did an hour
or so of chores, sat, and hastily ate as if at a peasant's table
for which quick taking was required to get one's share. Then
after another job or two, indoors or out, he took up his post
on his easy chair in the long living room, and finished the
day's crossword puzzle which occupied his bus ride to and
from work, turned on the radio to listen to his beloved Detroit
Tigers or a special major boxing match featuring Detroit's
Joe Louis or a nationally-known Italian fighter. Sunday
usually meant Mass and trips to two sets of grandparents, a
get-together with relatives, or, occasionally, friends. Shopping
also punctuated the calendar. Aside from an incidental
shopping trip or my mom taking me on an annual Christmas
shopping expedition downtown to Hudson's department
store. When I was three or four, my father took me to buy
a used white, four-door 1940 Plymouth, and again two or
three times more when he bought brand-new Chevys. These

cars subsequently often drove us out into the countryside to buy fruit, visit a park, and took us on our memorable long-distance two-week vacations out east and even once all the way to Florida for Dad's national union meeting. He and my uncles loved to brag about *the good time they made* across hundreds of miles to and from Detroit.

My body marked off my days. Meals made the mornings and evenings predictable in the same way that snacks and treats add an occasional surprise of pleasure. Whereas head colds meant days at home in bed listening to the best radio shows, and constipation brought dull and listless periods followed by castor oil and painful enemas. Aside from physical accomplishments, such as being the self-declared fastest skater at Stellwagen, accidents such as being hit in the eye with a baseball in Kelayres, Pennsylvania, and wearing a patch from there to New York City, falling out of a tree with no serious injury other than damage to my pride as a tree climber. An appendectomy and tonsillectomy before I was ten marked points of my advance in life. I remember my first ejaculation and my confused and mixed reaction to my shooting fluid.

ANOTHER AGE AND STAGE

As only a full-length biography could suggest, each new stage of life brought new experiences and ideas about encountering, feeling, reflecting on, and identifying with my body. My body, call it a "multiplicitous many," nourished my experience and, in large part, made my fortune.

My childhood and early youth turned on witnessing and identifying with my surprising body, which made and remade me at home, in school, outdoors in play, and at camp among family and familiar and unfamiliar others. As adolescence dawned on me, I was sent to Jackson Intermediate for eighth grade. This school was located three miles to the south and east, in an alien and rougher part of town. Jackson meant not just new teachers and a new building but required an inventory of who were the tough and mean guys, those who might punch you in the face without you saying a word, or with whom it was dangerous to be caught alone in the bathroom. The bus ride to Jackson put me in the company of unknown boys and girls from the surrounding neighborhood. It was about choosing seating partners and fighting my way toward the back of the bus where the *lords* sat. The mightiest princes sat in the back row, and the king sat in the center seat of the back row. Over a period of three months and several tussles, I advanced toward the back and took a place on one of the back-facing seats. There I tested myself against a big blond-haired guy who put an unforgettable vice-like headlock on me. As a consequence, I moved up a few rows, found a steady seating companion, and amicably rode to school for the rest of the year, letting the strongest rule.

I entered nearby Denby High School, a mile and a half north and east of my home, with pimples on my forehead, amidst the throes of puberty. I most often rode a public bus to school. My mother counseled me in several ways to "look good and don't baby yourself," consoling me that the pimples would rough up my skin so I would look like a man and not be a smooth-skinned sissy. My father taught me by his daily example and life-long regime: don't complain and quietly, steadily go about your business, restraining feelings and never forsaking duties for pleasures. So, I entered Denby neatly dressed—at one point really stylish with my white bucks and my black and white varsity coat—and ready, so I thought, to go to work on the pre-college curriculum of algebra, science, Spanish, world and American history, and physical education.

Denby, located in a relatively young and thriving middle-class neighborhood, was built in 1920 for two thousand or so students and was bursting with over four thousand students split into four grades, divided between *A* – fall entries and spring graduates and *B* – spring entries and graduates. Indeed, there were too many to know, and too many clubs to join and sports to play. I felt like a stranger at Denby for my whole four years, even though I was elected to be the sergeant-at-arms of my six-hundred-student senior class.

I learned to kiss a bit (but no more!) and dance slowly and close, but I never entered any desired and forbidden lands. I had no idea of how a girl was made or how to treat one. I, an only child without sisters or brothers to share experiences and ideas, simply did not know girls, who they were, how they worked, and what made them go. I only knew, somehow, that I should match up with one of them (a pretty and friendly one!) and eventually date and hug myself into love and marriage. With an array of messages—familial, bodily, and culturally, though not delivered to me by music or movies of which I was no fan—I was told that joining my body to a girl's would somehow make me a full-blooded male, an adult, *a happy and responsible somebody.* In a word, I lived through my high school years, and for that matter, my university and post-university years, unable to solve the quadratic equation of my body, sex, love, marriage, and happiness. I satisfied my mother even less as she pleaded ever strongly for grandchildren as my bachelordom loomed greater and more certain.

I found no niche at Denby—not with its girls and certainly not with math. I had no car, and learning to drive didn't mean much to me. The only opening for my body, energy, dedication, and success came from golf. Therein was a test, competition, and hope through which tenacity and skill would deliver me to adulthood.

I dreamt of becoming a winning tournament pro. From the ages of twelve to seventeen, as a caddy and, later, manager of the driving range at the exclusive Country Club of Detroit in Grosse Pointe Farms, I took account of myself by working my first full-time job and playing a game that made me a caddy champion and a freshman starter on the Denby golf team, which I captained my senior year.

While caddying and running the ranges on weekends and after school, especially during my half-day junior and senior years, I learned manners and etiquette and developed my body and strength. Already by fourteen, I could carry "doubles" (two bags which might weigh as much as sixty pounds) for eighteen holes, then carry another bag in the afternoon for nine more holes, and, additionally, walk and hitchhike home. The game itself confronted me with the test of creating a good swing, which required learning the fundamentals of stance, complexities of grip, subtleties of alignment, and mastery of take back, swing, and follow-through. Then, too, I had to learn to see and think a shot, hole, and entire round—play different clubs in diverse lies, in different grasses, fairways, roughs, bunkers, and greens. As I wrote in my *Golf Beats Us All, So We Love It*, there was no end to what was to be learned and mastered, and though, at times, my hands bled and my heart ached, I concluded I would not be good enough to really shine as a champion. Or put more simply, by the spring of my junior year, I painfully discovered the loss of a first-sought dream that clubs don't have erasures, pencils do, and tournaments don't ever grant degrees, while colleges commonly do. I decided that I would think, not play, my way forward in life.

My body continued to make and tell me who I was and what I might become. As it once made me an energetic child who was good on his blades and at the swinging of a golf club, it led me to *dancing and marrying* my good wife and made me the father of four energetic children. Her body, its changes with pregnancy, and her ability to reproduce, nurture, and serve us all, made "home" with its feel, rhythms, and seasons. Home grew within and out of her. Her energy, moods, and exhaustions fashioned a clock of biology, ritual, and love, which joined spirit and body.

My body was my personal yardstick of the world. It afforded home protection, security, loyalty, and continuity over the years. It allowed me to compare myself to everything and everyone else by health, strength, performance, work, and income. My body underwrote and went with my experience. Its actions, adventure, and projects created a rudimentary narrative of where I have been and what I did. It made me, at times, proud and embarrassed.

My body wrote, writes, and will write my life. I could not write an autobiography without my body at the center and narrating my life. Surely, my childhood lived in the flesh with loving parents, grandparents, aunts, and uncles, at holiday gatherings, an aunt's cottage, a great aunt's cabin, and as a Scout as I forged an unbreakable bond with water, earth, bark, leaf, rock, stone, gravel, asphalt, concrete, and a hundred other surfaces. The stories of learning to smoke and quitting smoking after twenty years merit telling.

In my autobiography, which forms book three of this exploration of self, I detail how my growing body and awakening mind led me into, accompanied me, and emerged me out of each age. In the last thirty years, I have written poems about my body as a sailing vessel, skating across black and cracking ice, and my growing identification with old and large trees. Death now surrounds me inside and out, recently taking my wife of fifty-five years and several dear friends. My body seeks a new tyranny over consciousness as my heart stalks me again after a quadruple bypass I had thirty years ago.

Multiple autobiographical stories spill out of my body in interior actions and outward associations. My body underpins experiences and actions. It not only made my senses, formed habits, and afforded me words and metaphors, but also primed the source of my interests, my shame and pride, and formed my reciprocity and gratitude. My body's truths, real, willed, imagined, and ambiguous, make me a multitude. As I age, my body wells up in me with symptoms and signs of my mortality.

Key to so many experiences and relations, my body's metronomes now set me to moving at an erratic pace, marching seemingly as fast as I can towards an approaching but undefined end. The ground I walk on is filled with those I love, with whom I hope to be reunited. Somehow, young again, we will take hands and circle right, left, up, and around and around in fullness and joy.

Conversely, my body clocks my entropy. As I grow old, I slow down and hoard. I am harnessed to stiff muscles and move with rheumatic joints. My stride shortens. I have quit skating and am riding a bike and swinging a club with less freedom. The fluidity of my movement is gone. My appetite is less. Constipation clogs my bowels and mind. My catalog of maladies grows as my pill caddy swells. I am haunted by tales of fallen others and fear of my own loss of balance.

Then, too, across my whole life from childhood to today, the bodies of friends and others not only attracted and repulsed me but also established senses of familiarity and surprise with the strange, puzzling, and threatening. They left me comparing and wondering and expanded my ideas of what others and I were and could become. In my own family, I saw and grew used to the exterior differences of young and old, male and female, short and tall, thin and heavy, blue and brown eyes, and heavy and really heavy eaters. I loved a grandfather with a glass eye, and I liked a "deaf and dumb" great uncle and aunt who spoke with gestures and sounds and one of their boys who purposely urinated his way out of military service. I also remember an infant next door who couldn't speak and rhythmically rocked back and forth from foot to foot. Once, on our neighborhood block, I remember a begging blind man slowly poking along the street until it began to rain; then, he surprisingly ran straight and without hesitation to the bus. On the city bus, there would occasionally be amputees and someone with a cleft palette. At the city camp, I encountered a six-toed boy. Of course, I saw children hurt and wondered what was under a girl's skirt and how things worked and grew under and in there. In a word, for me, bodies created experiences, questions, and wonders, and made a self of greater variety and possibility.

POEMS FOR CATHY AND GETTING OLD

My elder eyes increasingly absorb and internalize the bodily condition of my fellow elders. Their size and conditions, trembling hands, failing sight and hearing, limps and hobbles, and canes, walkers, and motorized chairs converse with me, often saying, but for the grace of God, there go I.

In my middle sixties, I wrote the following poem in empathy with a group of women exercising in the pool of the town's new YMCA.

SHALLOW-WATER AEROBICS

A chorus line
Of ten women
Baptized in play,
Smiling, buoyant,
Up on their toes,
Gently prancing,
Traipse and glide in circles
By a grace
Stored deep within.

These gentle nymphs
Grown large with age
Circle in the shallows,
Gingerly bobbing up and down,
Their wombs grow cool,
Forgetting yesterday's wear,
The hard heat of zealous men,
Awkward births,
And perhaps a few recall
Even an abortion or two.

Like full-suited astronauts
Taking their first rising steps
On the round moon—
Gently springing off the mosaic tile floor,
Grinning, celebrating
Buoyant womanly flesh!

With tummies, thighs, and breasts,
Bodies afloat,
They enjoy this Y's waters,
Having lived a life
Of deep-water aerobics.

Given how forty-five years of marriage and raising four
children had grafted me in body and mind to my wife Cathy,
her sudden, totally out-of-the-blue diagnosis of a serious case

of double cancer—myeloma and lymphoma—altered the next
ten years of our lives until her death at the age of eighty. To
miss a person, as I miss her, is to miss a body and spirit—a
person—her presence, willing hands, quick movement, and
quick tongue brought a home's comfort as now her absence
spells vacancy and loneliness.

I entered a void without a woman and her body, work,
and habits. My days lack a rhythm. I am a ship without
ballast. I am like a marsh without grasses and the surprise
of a duck taking flight. I have been rushed towards my own
death and thrown back to my graduate days when I lived by
sandwiches and books alone.

In a personal booklet for my wife of fifty-five years, I
gathered the following four poems suggesting how lifetime
braided us together in body and soul.

CATHY

The wind moves on the lake,
Poplar leaves spin,
Martins test their darting flight,
Our children rush in and out
Of the water,
And we walk
With easy steps
Across welcoming years.

OUR ZEN MASTERS

Children plant strange flowers
In forgotten spaces.
Tony, our oldest son, sends us a valentine;
On it, two pea-green tanks
With yellow hearts on their sides.
Felice, our oldest daughter, says,
"Night ends where morning begins."
Adam mistakes my athletic cup for a catcher's mask
And insists that he wear it downtown
On his head
In case of a hailstorm.

Ethel asks a hundred times a day,
"Do birdies bite?"
She says, "March comes in like a lion
And goes out like a monkey."
One blizzard day my children bring a dozen frozen
*   sparrows*
Into the house,
And when the birds revive
They fill this Buddhist monastery
With flight
And the sound
Of gleeful Zen masters.

CATHY, ON YOUR EIGHTIETH

We raft and sail together,
Body and spirit
Husband and wife
Mother and Father
Cousins of these places and times.

We sing in each other's hearts and bones.
As blessings and offerings
We go
Celebrating and consecrating each other
Through days and years.

ANNIVERSARY

Cathy,
Nurse,
Mother,
Woman and wife,
No wife better for this life,
For me.

On your closing picnic days
We spread out the blanket of our final years
With biweekly cancer treatments extending years,
Maladies of diverse sorts punctuating our calendar.

41

And longer trips postponed
Until new wings are fashioned.
We settle for meals and walks,
Grandchildren's games
And attendance at Sunday Mass.

We carry on with such ordinary fare.
On uncertain ways.
We cross these days
Without celestial augury,
Only adjusting therapy.

These days so ordinary,
This life so extraordinary.
Only this flesh
This love,
These prayers.

Our bodies, attracting magnets, carried us on life's journey; to passageways and bridges, we crossed to each other and into life. With touch, feel, affection, food, church, and ways, our bodies wrote the narrative of our lives. Affording proportionality and energy and wrapping us in flesh and senses, our bodies shaped our home and life. With her death and the absence of her body came this empty world.

MOURNING AND REFLECTING ON BODIES

While mourning my wife, I dwell on how women's bodies make home, place, and the center. Throughout all stages of their lives, most women make and care and join us by habit and familiarity with things.

I struggle to grasp what the aging and loss of the body mean to a woman. It occurs over the years—loss of fertility, fallen flesh, and lost curves, shape, proportions, beauty, and attractiveness. Diet, exercise, jewelry, clothing, and hair-dressing barely fight off the loss and do not undo her mortality.

I find the loss of Cathy has readjusted the calipers of my own aging, loss, and pending death. I, of a male body, have long known the body's signs of mortality, with bulging stomach, weakening muscles, reflexes, and speed. This decline took a sharp and accelerating turn with my heart diagnosis in 1988, and with my quadruple bypass in 1993, the year my father died. I began to bid my own body adieu. I felt so many things. I stood on the windswept platform of an old and lonely station waiting for that dark train only a couple of stops away.

Feelings and thinking about my body brought to mind St. Augustine's question: *What is so much yours as yourself, and what is so little yours as yourself?* And I was led to try a poem on my relations to my body and myself.

FAREWELL OLD BODY

Goodbye body, my old and true friend,
We have shared the cocoon of the womb, and lived years
in this earthly home.

The world rubs up against my body and me,
And we press back and grind against it.
Together body and I discern
By senses and thoughts,
We make meanings out
Of big and small,
Hard and soft,
Still and moving,
Slow and fast,
Smooth and jerky,
Thick and thin,
Straight and round,
Singular and common.

Around the horn we go,
Knocking down the Walls of Jericho.

Body and I are a couple,
Awake and in dreams.
We are married in twos,
The axis of our compass,
Up and down, left and right,
So we travel hand and hand,
Across this land,
From first breathe and light
To suffocating death's irrevocable night.

As one and two,
In violent opposition and graceful harmony
Body and I know,
The give and take of the world.
It speaks with a Pentecost of tongues,
Body and I reply
In our ten thousand tongues.

After all,
We have learned to eat and drink light,
Sail strange seas,
To strange shores,
Buoyant with words
Metaphors are my sky-scooping sails.

Body and I,
We bed down
And we die together
As one,
My body and I.

So now eighty-four years old and for almost ten years since
the early onset of my wife's treatment, having lived in a senior
residence on the western edge of Minneapolis with three
hundred and more people whose average age is the mid- or
high-eighties, I receive daily evidence that the old spend
a good portion of their lives caring for and talking about
their changing bodies. Somehow, we all mourn the loss of

the body and self, and, like prisoners, we live by medical
worries, visits to doctors, and pains ranging, to speak in polar
opposites, from hangnails to pacemakers and constipation to
undefined consternation. Here is a bit of a poem I started but
never completed:

> *We talk to our body*
> *And it talks to us,*
> *When we itch, twitch, and scratch*
> *Groan and moan.*
> *We pray*
> *Only certain*
> *We are on a short-term loan.*

I think of a neighbor who steadily, then suddenly, lost his
mind. When no longer capable of recognizing his own wife,
he was placed in a total care residence. There he treated
everyone he met as if they were a customer who had just
entered his clothing shop. He patted them and sized them up
for a sale. He comes to mind now and then, and I, too, fear, if
only momentarily, I will lose my mind. I truly will be without
a memory. I will end a nobody, a nothing, a void. I won't even
know how to pray. I wrote the following stanza:

> *My body,*
> *My life raft,*
> *Steals me from Trinity and eternity.*
> *It floats me to nowhere, oblivion*
> *Ever far from resurrection*
> *And loving communion.*

To rely on ideas from Cicero's classic *Cato the Elder on
Old Age*, old age attacks me in four ways. It withdraws me
from active life, weakens my body, deprives me of most
enjoyments, and stands me, knowingly, not far from death.
I would add to Cicero's list that age steals my sleep and
waking.

My aging body imprisons me in self-preoccupation. It peppers my attention with irritations and pains and taxes my saving disciplines of work and prayer. Age cloaks light, form, and spontaneity with a worsening condition and puts me in that ragged medical game of *diagnosis and prognosis*. Yet, I have not become a medical *agnostic* as my father did during the last decades of his life, leaving each appointment with the departing phrase, "They don't know what they are talking about."

Aging, some suggest, can assault one's gratitude. It can even strangle the memory of gifts and exchanges. Severe cases of Alzheimer's can steal one's recognition of one's spouse. My body and life become a ship without a captain, and even prayers for a gracious and peaceful end are forgotten.

So, we are driven to euphemize our *senior* years. Even Shakespeare described what he called the sixth age in the first act of *As You Like It*, a stage when we are entered "into the lean and slipper'd pantaloons." Yet in Act II, Scene Seven, he declares it a time of "second childishness and mere oblivion. Sans teeth, sans eyes, sans taste, sans everything."

In a collection of quotations, the bard tells us that the last years do not hold the best. They may well deliver us to a state when we are lame in body and dead in the brain. Shakespeare wrote in *King Lear*, "I fear I am not in perfect mind," and pointedly in *Much Ado About Nothing*, "As they say, when the age is in, the wit is out."

"Age," he declares in *Hamlet*, "with his stealing steps/ Hath clawed me in his clutch." It brings us to "that time of year thou mayst in me behold/When yellow leaves, or none, of do few do hang/Upon those boughs which shake against the cold/Bare ruined choirs, where late the sweet birds sang."

And this condition, as Shakespeare tells us in *Richard II*, lacks remedy even by any royal touch.

> But not a minute, king, that thou canst give / Shorten my days thou canst with sullen sorrow/And pluck nights from me, but not lend a morrow/ Thou canst help time to furrow me with age/But stop no wrinkle

in his pilgrimage / The word is current with him for my death / But dead, thy kingdom cannot buy my breath.

With no consolation from Shakespeare, I approach death, which I do not know, cannot truly name. It escapes me in essence and ending. And I cannot cease the fear it sparks that I will be no more. In this way, the body perishes, and takes me on a journey of disintegration, one of no return. It will carry me to a nowhere, of nothing, or Heaven, a rebirth, a reunion, a *Spring of Springs*, alive with light and grace.

CHAPTER 3
ON THE SURFACE OF THINGS

What tells us more than a face? It speaks so many languages with words and gestures. Emily Dickinson depicted a hard and hateful face.

> *A face devoid of love or grace,*
> *A hateful, hard, successful face,*
> *A face with which a stone*
> *Would feel thoroughly at ease.*[8]

My body speaks to me in so many ways! Its conversations with and in itself over such elemental matters as light and heat, stimulation and imitation, immediate reaction and reflexive habit, and memory, multiply with science's growing explorations and understanding of the nervous system. It can murmur and go about its business with the brain merely eavesdropping. It even whispers its feelings and moods as quietly as a penitent in a crowded church confessional. But also, at times, it can shout out with urgency, implacably, "Something must be done!" So, my body speaks to me with a cacophony of voices.

My body carries on daily and continuous conversations with my conscious and thinking self and responds to the appearance, acts, and words of others and the size, shape, movement, and condition of things. My body, like yours, makes and mirrors moods and intentions. It offers testimony, makes vows, and proves that appearances can be deceiving. From an early age, people incorporate their bodies into hiding the impulses, thoughts, and designs of their inner selves.

Across youth and into adolescence, the polyglot body learns many languages of deceptions, all of which say, one way or another, things are never quite what they appear to be, and the self is not revealed exteriorly, *prima facie*. However, disguises do not completely harness the revelations of face, eyes, and hands.

A person is made up of their appearance and twitches. I had a friend who rubbed his index finger against the side of his nose whenever he lied or exaggerated, which was quite often. Much later, I knew a college president who, when talking under pressure, rubbed his neck with his thumb and forefinger alongside his Adam's apple. When I pointed this out to him, he was quite taken aback by his confession that *what he said wasn't necessarily so by testimony of his gesturing*!

Cultures, passing styles, and fashions put the body in the service of communications of all sorts. They dress and enact who, where, and when they are and what they want. Tattoos often profess identities and memberships had or wished. Of course, people use their bodies, their comportment and gesture along with dress and jewelry, to confess, pretend, lie, flatter, show disdain, and fit the occasion.

Sometimes, our approach to others seems like putting one's self down on the runway of a carrier ship caught in roiling waters amid shifting winds. There is simply no end to what bodies say to us. No wonder when confronting complex social intercourse, my grandfather concluded he would hew his own course, and those who didn't like it, to use his favorite phrase, "can kiss my ass!"

Popular and mass cultures use the body as a bulletin board. The body's shape, pose, and actions are the wrapping and, in part, the substance of the fashion, love, beauty, sports, and film industries. Bodies sell everything from health products and toothpaste to bathroom cleaners and new cars. Wars convert societies into body counts. In the case of the American Civil War, society allocated prosthetics for limbs, while in the wake of the First World War, the world counted bodies to be repaired and even the number of surgeries required for a single prosthetic mask to repair a disfigured face.

Movies and video games shoot and kill abstract bodies for commercial entertainment. Serial killers reduce life itself

50

to bodies that can be shot. As I write, in Uvalde, Texas, an eighteen-year-old loner, ironically named Salvador, translated as savior, committed mass murder with an automatic rifle and pistol. After shooting his grandmother in the face, Salvador drove to an elementary school and, in a murderous copycat action, locked himself in a second- and third-grade classroom, where he proceeded to massacre 19 children and two teachers.

Indeed, in the vernacular, we classify groups around us by their bodies and functions. Until the 1960s, society classified people with the vernacular as *lame, club-footed, crippled, blind, mute,* and *deaf. Midgets, dwarfs,* and *giants* were the spine of the Midway, to which barkers called crowds to see the *freaks* of nature. The common classifications of the past eras are the enemies of contemporary science, therapy, sensitivity, and politically correct language. Body talk, direct and cruel, is on the outs. A cultural war is at hand.

Society commonly took the person to be an extension or the essence of his or her body. Traditional and classical cultures continued to find identity, meaning, and value in bodies as seen and depicted. Gravettian fertility figures (Venus figurines) of the Upper Paleolithic Period, roughly from 22,000 to 33,000 years ago, featured the breasts and hips of a pregnant woman as the source of fertility and, as argued, many other ends. To jump ahead in history, Greek sculpture married men and women to the gods, while early modern literature, as voiced by Erasmus, Rabelais, Montaigne, Cervantes, and Shakespeare, used bodies to treat their characters, both low and high, with irony, satire, humor, and caricature, while there can be no full and agreed upon index to describe all the purposes and ends contemporary art makes of the changing and polyvalent body

The body spoke to us before we had words. The body brings feelings and emotions before we know and express them. At the most rudimentary level, the homeostatic body tells us when it is out of balance, hungry, or off-kilter. The body tells us to get up or down and so much more about the size and shape of the world and self before we learn to speak, skip, and learn good posture. In fact, the body instructs us in making such elemental distinctions as fertile and sterile, pure and impure, hard and soft, edible and poisonous, young and old, living and dead, and so much more, long before we have discussions and read literature on such elemental colors, forms, and shapes of being.

Our bodies primordially encountered earth, life, and other humans before language and culture named and valued them. Before we can describe and count, we have feelings about good and bad things and people who deserve and don't deserve trust and affection. Prior to understanding any ethics, we sense what is giving, fair, and generous and what is denying, miserly, refusing, and hurting.

Surely, traditional, folk, peasant, and village cultures had their foundation in the presence and interactions of bodies with things and other bodies. Proof of this abounds in stories and jokes of bodies that are dead, invisible, and transformed by good and evil. When trying to get at the essence of the body, multiple meanings of size, age, condition, senses, potency, and magic powers are ever at play. The very speed of the eye and the quickness of wit and tongue define the presence of the body and the self.

Neighborhoods and villages skated on nicknames for the body, its parts, and functions. Nicknames made slang and filled the schoolyard language that I heard. To mind come words like: "four-eyed," "cock-eyed," "lame-brained," "duck-footed," "pigeon-toed," "drag ass," "even-handed," and "dirty mouth."

BODIES ARE SURFACES AND SELVES

The elemental proposition that the body is a set of surfaces in a world of changing surfaces might offer a key to unlocking the first and most elemental stages of the relationship between the body and self. I already approached this thesis in my work *On Surfaces: A History* (2013) and as summarized in the introduction to my *Everyday Life: How the Ordinary Became Extraordinary* (2013).

In accordance with a phenomenological approach, I suggest in *Surfaces* that, in the beginning, surfaces present themselves as sensations and perceptions. They are taken into mind as conceptions and shaped into images, symbols, and language as conceptions. Surfaces furnish primary encounters with the outer and inner layer of things—their cover, epidermis, membrane, bark, rind, hide, and skin. They also give humans their first experiences, defining the body's primary disposition toward objects and the surrounding world.

Human bodies meet and interact with a world dressed in surfaces. Surfaces are the wardrobe of being. They present the world as animate and inanimate, parts and wholes, singularities and particularities, and yet, faces and gestalts of self, others, animals, objects, places, situations, and whole horizons. According to the British archaeologist Clive Gamble, we experience, act in, and know the world as sets of scapes—bodyscapes, soundscapes, mindscapes, task-scapes, landscapes, and sense-scapes.[9]

For humans, skin—as feathers, scales, or bark for other species—is our face in the world. It identifies us to the eye and touch, defines us as one, and identifies us as human.

To pursue this phenomenological course, skin is the first proof of our incarnation—the fleshy dress of our being. While buffering and resistant to sun, heat, and cold, skin is also plastic and self-replacing. It reveals our age and condition.

Skin tells of our life and labors. It shows burns, wounds, scars, blemishes, tumors, warts, and infections. As the partially transparent boundary and mediator between the interior and exterior worlds, skin is one of our culture's much-read books. It tells of the fair who enjoyed the privilege of staying out of the sun and those who toiled long and hard in the sun. Tattoos and scarification assert many things—an individual sentiment or tribal identity, allegiance to a way of life, membership in a gang, or imprisonment.

Skin is revelatory. As the whole history of cosmetics confirms, skin can be decorated to suggest, even profess, the type of person we would be. We incorporate skin in the image and act out what we project to the world. At the same time, confirming appearance can only be skin deep; a blush can confess the truth we disguise.

Our face, of different skin, shapes, and functions, is our front door to the body and the mind's porch on the world. The face is a personal link between the self, the world, and others. By saying words and casting glances, it throws baited hooks into passing rivers. It is one of the body's biological wrappers and tools.

THE WORLD ENGAGES US IN CONVERSATION

The world of surfaces, with its wide and diverse variety of bodies and faces, form a Pentecost of tongues. Surfaces evoke basic responses, feelings, and emotions. They even foster myths, ideals, and aesthetics. While they evoke reflections, they exteriorly and interiorly impose themselves on us. They deliver hugs and slaps. They lure, repulse, terrify, and injure us.

Surfaces awaken so many conversations in our body, calling up reflexes, reactions, sympathies, and simulations. They direct our energy, generate motives, and become ends in themselves. Surfaces shape space; they measure change and reveal movements and motions. Surfaces signal what is, what is leaving and vanishing, and what might be coming. They stretch before us as open and inviting fields and confront us with imposing thickets that bar entrance.

Surfaces speak to us on the most concrete, elemental, symbolic, and metaphorical levels. Bodies distinguish the inner and outer worlds and make pairings and oppositions, establishing contrasts and similarities. In the world, the body experiences and teaches us with senses, feelings, and the rudiments of up and down, front and back, around and across, without and within, hot and cold, tight and loose, smooth and rough, transparent and opaque, heavy and sinking, or light and afloat, and make so many other polarities. Infinities reside in the body's experiences and notions of contrasts, differences, similarities, and unities. In the recent therapeutic work, *Awe* (2023), Dacher

Keltner suggests we listen to music with our bodies, which experience and express awe.

There is truly a "poetics to our bodies," to borrow the title of a long-time favorite book, the 1958 French classic *The Poetics of Space*. In it, twentieth-century French philosopher Gaston Bachelard suggests that, within space resides an ontological perspective on the cosmos. There are mysteries in such homey things as the inside of a drawer, chest, cabinet, or other containers.

Humans read the world and one another by reading surfaces, hands, and faces. With the tip of a pencil, a sheet of paper, and a keen and leading line, artists design, decorate, and express interior and exterior worlds—even suggest what Leonardo da Vinci proved with pen and charcoal, that *Drawing is Thinking*—to use the 2008 title of a book by the popular New York designer, Milton Glaser.

In nineteenth- and twentieth-century societies, despite societal revolutions, national competitions, and wars, Western society progressively transformed the surfaces of the world. By transforming nature and environments, it engineered landscapes, farmed fields, and organized cities and bodies. Its hands and minds were regulating government and democratic national society; its tools were technology, business, transportation, communications, science, medicine, and public health. This was seen where increasing majorities shopped, played, and acted on their lives.

In this world, born of the Industrial and Commercial Revolutions, we become the things we make, have, desire, dream, and design. We enact and know ourselves in constant transformation. With medicine and chemistry, dress and appearance, we take our place in the world, which is comprised of the fields we farm, the forests we harvest, the rivers we dam, and the cities and buildings we live and work in. There is truth in saying we are the tunnels, bridges, sewers, and plants we make, the roads and vehicles we drive, the ships we build and captain, and the planes we fly. New machines, things, and their surfaces lead us to new experiences, meanings, minds, and selves.

We become self-inventing. Created surfaces and the routes, roads, bridges, and railways we travel are proven pathways to our new selves. In store windows and parading on public streets, at play in public parks, and on stages and athletic fields, we see the new selves we dream ourselves to be.

Starting at the end of the nineteenth century and at the beginning of the twentieth century, physics and chemistry began to both explore and engineer the atomic world. We artificed new molecular materials; plastics and nylons were among the first. Plastic, the protean material, found its way into all things. The polymer, nylon (developed in the 1930s and introduced at the World's Fair in 1939), drew attention to a woman's shapely and clean-shaven legs in a more cost-effective way than silk. In the form of parachutes, nylon also guided the descent of airmen and paratroopers back to earth during the Second World War.

In a different form and for a different end, nylon's younger cousin, Velcro, patented in Switzerland in 1954, put people and things under tighter wraps with a fresh array of hooks and loops. Teflon took on a different assignment. It lined pots and pans so that food didn't stick to them. Polymers produce superglues and adhesives and make many of the light and strong materials that characterize contemporary industries.

As I wrote in *Surfaces*, current research in biomacromolecules is developing a new polymer in the genes of spider silk proteins, which, as a fiber for thread, is stronger than nylon or Kevlar and antimicrobial, hypoallergenic, and completely biodegradable, making it medically beneficial for surgeries and bandages. Biomacromolecules are also potential materials for engineering membranes of slow-release capsules, lightweight waterproof fabrics, biologically friendly plastics for surgery, and for strong, flexible components for aircraft manufacture and space capsules—industries ever in search of strong, light, malleable, and smooth wrappers for hulls and wings.[10]

We find ourselves repeatedly marveling at ordinary things and machines shaped to our body's pleasures and needs. There are machines as light and extra-strong as snowblowers, car tires that grip wet surfaces, Velcro bands that hold shoes tight, glued heads of golf clubs that don't fly off, and skate blades that don't come loose after decades of use. Then, too, there are paints that don't chip and woods as strong and smooth as stone. From across the globe to our freshly created screens come images, pictures, and words of exploding people and soothing presidents. We find ourselves in a cocoon of made surfaces.

In our *superficially constructed world*, we have grown accustomed to soft surfaces, travel on fast and smooth surfaces, and live in a selective, colorful, and near-odorless world. We banish nuisances and the rough as best we can. We expect to be smooth, fast, painless, and pleasingly made—a designed and chosen "natural."

Made surfaces serve and enwrap us. They house our bodies, our senses, and our consciousness in a pleasing order. We accept and buy into a world of design and invention. Despite our calls to be natural and simple, we accept the made, synthetic, and innovative world of exterior and interior surfaces. We take to the wilderness in our Kevlar canoes (that is, our plastic boats made of a chemical compound called poly-para-phenylene terephthalamide).

We have become a society made fresh by ever-new means of living, speeding, moving things, and interacting across ever-greater distances. Unwittingly, we embrace our creations and the altered perceptions and sensations, conditions, situations, lives, and meanings that go with them. Truth verges on becoming the sum of things made, invented, lived with, and displayed.

Surfaces become fresh windows for seeing and wanting; new doors open to possibilities, wants, and dreams. In this world, keen eyes turn restless and relentless hands seek transformations. Surfaces become new doors to the body, self, and world.

CHAPTER 4

IN THE BEGINNING, WAS THE FOOT

From our animal beginnings, we entered and participated in the world by walking, seeing, sensing, touching, picking, and gathering. We explored, learned, and developed as we went on our ways.

When we quit our trees in Africa, we fully entered the world as bipedal creatures. So, on immediate and local grounds and through generations of continental migration, we developed paths and made ourselves at home in the world.

Walking on two feet shaped our bilateral bodies and mobile minds. By shaping our posture and orientation, bipedalism lifted up our eyes to see near and far, from side to side, and freed our arms to reach and our hands to touch and examine. It formed our inner and outer compasses and carried us into the world we encountered and experienced.

WALKING, OUR NARRATOR

As quoted in my *On Foot: A History of Walking* (which is the source of much of this chapter), "In the beginning was the foot," wrote anthropologist Marvin Harris.[11] The earliest hominid species walked on two feet from two to four million years before a subsequent hominid species made tools and from four to six million years before *Homo sapiens,* our kind, appeared about a hundred thousand years ago.[12] "Anthropologists and evolutionary biologists are now agreed," science writer John Noble Wilford recently wrote, "that upright posture and two-legged walking—bipedality—was the crucial, and probably, the first major adaptation associated with the divergence of human lineage from a common ancestor with the African apes."

However, biologists and anthropologists dispute where and when a bipedal species abandoned its arboreal habitat and got up and off its knuckles.[13] Using only patchy material evidence and conjectures based on the molecular clock of genetic change, anthropologists writing the narrative of bipedal man struggle to determine when our African ancestors abandoned the forest for the prairie. Scientists have yet to explain when our earliest ancestors emigrated from the African plains and what connects tool-making, meat-eating, and increased brain size. Earlier hope of finding a single, featured actor in this multimillion-year narrative has steadily faded with the growing consensus emerging that, until the unexplained disappearance of Neanderthal man thirty thousand years ago, the earth was home not just to a single species but to multiple bipedal hominid species.

Bipedalism produced and depended on a body that differentiated man from ape.[14] Being anatomically vertical and walking on two feet altered the human pelvis and limbs. The thickness of the pelvis set limits on the size of infants at birth, which resulted in longer postnatal nurturing and the development of family life. The freeing of hands opened the way for human tool-making. Upright walking required hominids to dedicate a considerable portion of their muscle and torso to balance rather than to forward thrust. Integral parts of the balancing act of walking, human shoulders and arms, formed a marvelous system of extension in the service of ever-grasping hands. Bipedal locomotion also facilitated humans' capacity to walk and talk simultaneously.

Psychologist Robert Provine speculates that bipedalism permitted hominids to make fuller use of their breath and vocal cords, enabling them to issue more complex and diverse sounds than their sniffing and panting cousins did.[15] Or, more vernacularly, they had to walk before they talked and laughed. Perhaps song and rhyme evolved to sustain them on their long marches across landscapes as well as to help them identify and commemorate special places along the way.

Being bipedal arguably saved as much as 35 percent more calories than knuckle-walking and allowed humans surplus calories to supply the body and the brain. As science writer Jay Ingram puts it, "Each stride of normal walking involves a cascade of little tricks that we perform unconsciously."[16] It requires spending three-fourths of one's time on one foot or the other. By striking the ground with one stiff leg after another, all of one's weight is set against a descending heel, only to be transferred to the big toe as one rotates their hips and redirects the plane of the foot and leg. (To keep erect when climbing, one tightens the buttocks.) In effect, through the ages, humanity has tortuously walked on two feet with a skeleton designed originally for four-legged travel. Flat feet, swollen feet, distorted toes, blisters, bunions, hammer toes, trick knees, herniated discs, and bad backs, not to mention hernias, hemorrhoids, and other maladies associated with our bipedal locomotion, remain the price of standing proudly erect.[17]

Afoot, humans could carry a myriad of objects across immense distances, especially as they learned to use their heads, necks, shoulders, backs, and waists. With daunting effect, they could hit and throw, smash down, and kick. They also could reach and pick more efficiently, especially as their species developed a thumb that could be used in opposition to the index and middle fingers. Free hands enabled them to examine objects, make and utilize tools, and start, set, carry, and control fire—the latter a discovery presently credited to *Homo erectus*. Each of these functions, according to Richard E. Leakey and Roger Lewin's *Origins* (1977), supported and reinforced one another.[18]

Humans sacrificed an arboreal life to become bipedal earth dwellers. Afoot, humans could better exploit the environment, climbing hills, traversing wetlands, wading ponds, and fording streams, plus—weather and terrain permitting—travel, as walking man perennially has, up to three miles per hour. Being able to transport significant quantities of food, water, and goods, they could sustain themselves over considerable distances. This mobility, which included the ability to carry children, haul tools, transport provisions, and later lead and ride animals, gave humans great migratory powers. However, worthy of noting, walking brought to humankind, women, in particular, the calorie-using burden of lugging children who have not yet learned to walk or cannot keep up.

Liberated hands leaped ahead with the use of tools and the shaping of the environment. In *The Hand*, neurologist Frank Wilson postulated that the brain's development followed rather than preceded the use of tools. Arguably, *Homo erectus* completed the remodeling of the hand, which opened "the door to an enormously augmented range of movements and the possibility of an unprecedented extension of manual activity" and "the redesign, or reallocation, of the brain's circuitry."[19] In turn, sometime during the last fifty thousand years, human thought permitted a great revolution in control over the environment, allowing humans a choice of the paths they would travel and the places they would inhabit.

With a rotating periscope head, strong legs, and unbounded dreams, the walking human became lord of the earth. As a mean and glorious microcosm, the walker stood between earth and heaven, among trodden dust and glittering stars. Walking provided his first hold on space. At the same time, walking was also the evolutionary foundation of a dominant eye, hand, and brain. Subsequent complex historical cultures that crossed great seas and dreamed of flying did not acknowledge the humble feet on which they stood and their earthly gait.

OUR PACE ACROSS TIME

On foot, humans crossed the earth, experienced life, and defined their relationship to the environment. On foot, they carried their children, supported their old, hauled their tools and goods, and herded their animals. Similarly, they fled, chased, killed, hunted and gathered, sought food, water, fuel, and habitat, traveled, played, courted, and enacted, often with the elaborate and fancy footwork of dance to define their rituals. For millions of years, our proximate and distant ancestors moved across history on foot, rendering truth to the notion that we have walked our way toward abundance and fulfillment.

With easily as much as half of our human time and bodily energy dedicated to walking and other supporting modes of locomotion such as running, jumping, crawling, and climbing, changes in the conditions of walking altered lives and societies. Many such changes occurred in the vast period of prehistory, reaching from the first steps and early migrations of our first bipedal ancestors to the Agricultural Revolution and the emergence of sedentary river valley civilizations of ten thousand years ago.

The civilizations in the Indus, Tigris and Euphrates, and Nile river valleys marked a profound transformation in elements of human walking. Hallmarks of these civilizations—being fixed places, having an annual food supply, domesticated beasts of burden, specialization in tool making, utilization of the wheel, command of a river, and dominance of major trails and routes—were all factors that shaped how, why, where, and who went on foot. There, first and dominant lines of status and class were drawn between those who sat, received goods and offerings, and commanded, and all others in the kingdom who walked, worked, carried, traveled, fought, and served principally on foot.

Of all early civilizations, Rome's control at the apex of its thousand-year history reached furthermost in space. Its marching legions, use of horses, animals, and carts, and roads built principally to project its army's power and state authority, formed a system of movement that defined the measure of good surfaces, carrying capacity, and unified routes of travel. Its system of land travel, which relied on ships but was based on and principally required walking, was not surpassed in Europe until the eighteenth century. If walking set the common but variable standard of local human locomotion, the marching speed and distance of Rome's legionnaires set the upper limit of prolonged land travel and defined an order of domination unrivaled since humanity first trod this earth. Who we were and what we became was defined by our bipedal walking.

WE SAW OUR WAY FORWARD

Walking frees our eyes and hands to see and touch afar and up close. With our heads up and noses off the ground, we simultaneously examine the world telescopically and microscopically. We espy in the distance and draw close, pick and examine with our fingers, and scrutinize our find.

As I wrote in *Everyday Life* (2016), "Primates are visual animals, and we think best in pictorial and geometric terms."[20] "Words," wrote the paleontologist Stephen Gould, "are an evolutionary afterthought."[21] Daily life was, in large part, first visual.

To give a poetic genesis to human eyes: they were mothered by the skin and fathered over 500 million years by the light which Apollo doles out day and night and across the seasons. The sun joins us with all the other species classified as phototropic, phototactic, and heliotropic. Contemporary theories of neurobiotaxis affirm that individual nerve cells grow in the direction of stimuli. Some scientists dub the eye "evolution's great invention" and leave us contesting theories about the forms and dates of the eye and brain.

Vision thrives on visual surfaces. Surfaces are the vision's feed and nectar. Without denying the importance of the other senses—touch, smell, sound, and taste— sight makes the stuff of minds. We discern foregrounds and backgrounds, identify objects in context and movement, and set objects in juxtaposition by contrasts of light and shadow, stillness and motion, proximity and distance, and contrasting colors. All of this, which sounds so philosophical, constitutes ordinary common life like blinds and shades that we open and shut to passing traffic.

Eyes deliver people to their first encounters and the most elaborate and delicate sensual experiences. The very eyes that follow the flight of a dragonfly pick up the path of a flying hockey puck and distinguish the brushstroke of a Manet from that of a Monet. Ever-blinking eyes frame and reframe all that comes to them and classify and file some small part of which yet a much smaller part might be turned into words. Visual acuity occupies one-third of our cerebral cortex; a million nerve cells are dedicated to vision—which forms a constantly rotating kaleidoscope of detailed richness in patterns, shapes, colors, brightness, and movement.[22]

Confirming that everyday life is visual, Paul Shepard, in *Man in the Landscape* (1967), conceives of sight as throwing up a constant barrage of changing and even opposing streams of images. Contending that animal binocularity arose from the needs of predation and jumping, he extrapolated that the human eye (significantly similar to a monkey's) resulted from living early life in the crown of a tropical forest where our primate ancestors jumped and grasped as they went from limb to limb. Predatory eyes are never at rest.[23]

We treat sight as identical or nearly identical with consciousness, though we praise its ability to penetrate hidden connections, relations, and meanings of things and people. Eyes see into motives and hearts and penetrate Heaven and coming times.

Christ praised the eye as the lamp of the body. In Matthew 6:12–23, he said, "The lamp of the body is the eye. If your eye is sound, your whole body will be filled with light; but if your eye is bad, your whole body will be in darkness. And if the light in you is darkness, how great the darkness will be."

CHAPTER 5
WE GO BY THE
TOUCH OF THINGS

Bipedalism, the subject of my *On Foot: A Cultural History of Walking* (2004), liberated our eyes and hands. It freed us from being captives of our noses and the ground like our ever-sniffing and scenting four-legged ancestors, as every dogwalker is reminded on their daily walk. Walking on two legs allowed us to not only get our heads up but also freed our arms to embrace the world and our fingers to touch it. Adding to our bipolarity, our arms were free to fall at our sides and reach out, forward and back, up and down, and take the world in hand. Bipedalism afforded us a moving platform for our senses and to become a creature of mind and metaphor who thought in space and time—and *infinities great and small,* and *far and deep.*[24]

The platform of our being is our legs and feet. They create an operetta of movement, pace, rhythm, grace, health, and sexuality. They can be seen, read, and heard to declare who it is that stands before and goes by you. Foot size, barefoot or shoed, and if our shoes are dirty, muddy, manure-laden, scuffed or new, spit-and-polished, and expensive, they all have tales to tell, as do neat ankles, and repelling knees and thighs. Rural peasants used stomp and stamina shown at a dance to judge an eligible young lassie's capacity to be a good and enduring wife—to bear children, work hard, travel up and down the country paths, and carry water and milk cans. Grace and beauty were one thing; strong biceps and thighs were another!

More universally, as a two-legged walker for hundreds of thousands of years, the bipedal human was distinguished from other mammals. Bipedalism meant getting one's head up with their arms free to reach and touch, a nose relieved from capturing smells from the ground, and easily see landscapes and things afar while examining by sight and touch what was at hand. Bipedalism freed us to move, query, quest, and plan across environments—to simultaneously participate in thought and action in macro- and microcosm. It launched us into being a metaphorical creature of space and time. And, I conjecture in street talk, the body and its movements made us *bodyists* for millennia before we were racists, sexists, and other *ists*.

As our eyes are our father, so our hands are our mother. Hands birth us in the world. They guide and serve our body, make and complement our brain, senses, and thoughts, and are the source of our experience. In conjunction with the formation of a muscular and skeletal structure, hands grew as appendages to skin. With skin forming thick palms, sensitive fingertips, and protective, cutting, and penetrating nails, hands become a primary guide to life. Hands make our things, form our landscapes, and build our homes and communities.

It is hard to grasp everyday life without understanding human reliance on the strength of a push and a shove, the adroitness and caress of hands, and the intricacy and delicacy of the fingers' touch. Arms, hands, and fingers acquaint us with the wealth of interior and exterior worlds. Shaking, pounding, and touching are the ordinary way humans validate the substance and form of things. They give measure to soft and hard, receptive and repulsive, what is to be taken in and cherished, and what is to be cast out. Hands, doing and gesturing, enact our relations, transactions, meanings, and conversations with others.[25]

Hands classify and make things and people "handy." We are members of the crafty and inventive race, the heirs of Daedalus. We are ever poking, picking, and manipulating things, and adjusting and readjusting our everyday life. It is no accident we claim tools, machines, engines, and industry and probe into the deepest spaces far and near.

Hands, then, are the models and instruments that make the tools that extend human use in the world. They account for our versatility as a grasper and clasper. The earliest human makers pounded and shaped with wood and stone hammers and threshed and weaved with needles. We raise our arms in praise, and, with our fingers, we pick the darkest recesses of the body's orifices. Fingers make our pleasures and caress our wounds.

Hands are the self and world they make. Hands care for us, our skin, scalp, hair, legs, feet, torso, and each other's bodies. They dress us for necessity and appearance. They serve our aggression and defense. They play a major part in obtaining food, staying warm, swimming, and taking and controlling things large and small. In act, purpose, and results, hands reach beyond what we can name; they are more of us than we can explain.

Hands, which are, for most, a wonderfully harmonic and versatile two, make a wealth of symmetric and asymmetric things. In *The Hand* (2003), Raymond Tallis offers this intriguing comment on the relationship between the right and left hands.

> It is perhaps an overstatement to say they have knowledge of one another or that what passes between them is knowledge rather than experience. But in their interaction, a distance is implanted at the seeming immediacy of a touch: we have a touched toucher touching a touched toucher—and vice-versa.[26]

Tallis goes a step further by suggesting that this tactile interaction of hand with hand magnifies our use, knowledge, and imagination of our own body, self, and the world. Tallis provocatively writes, "we truly touch the world only if the hands that touch are self-touching."[27]

Hands, then, make our many worlds and tell us of ourselves. They are self-confirming, declaring, world-making, and acknowledging. When they quickly grab, they know what the senses excite, and the mind learns and validates.

As we learn from Tallis' *The Hand*, hands are the principal agent of our consciousness, thoughts, and actions. As the primary organ of touch, they establish the great middle ground as negotiators and validators of perception, sense, thought, action, exploration, wonder, necessity, and invention. Hands apprehend, deal with, and underwrite the relations of things and selves. They account for experiences and changes in our landscape. Hands give human meaning to matter, spaces, places, and times. They straddle the material and the spiritual, the rough and the refined. They afford a deepening context and sense of being while accounting for the breadth of our experience and our work in the world. Hands are the agency of crafts. Do not think of magicians and pickpockets unless you wish, but do think of tailors, conductors, cooks, jewelers, craftspeople, sculptors, and artists of all sorts who represent and offer a vision of our world and selves with the handwork of a pen, brush, and chisel.

In *A Natural History of the Senses*, Diane Ackerman specifies touch as the key to the gifts and powers of the hand. Touch tries, tests, selects, picks out, declares fine, and proves healing and therapeutic.[28] With touch, humans bless and designate a chosen one. Fingers link bodies and express anger with a pinch and love with a squeeze. Fingers also scratch an itch, pick a nose, and rub sore feet. Hands, which define all that humans do in common ways and days, from salting their pork to buttering and slicing their bread, also make them brainy, smart, if you wish.

In *The Hand*, neurologist Frank Wilson argues that the brain's development followed the active hands and their tool-making. Freed arms and hands "opened the door to an enormously augmented range of movements and the possibility of an unprecedented extension of manual activity." Their activity led to the "redesign, or reallocation of the brain's circuitry."[29] In the last 100,000 or so years, active and tasking human hands completed the reorganization of the brain of *Homo sapiens*. "Through manipulating by hands and thinking through the brain, the world became incorporated with will, knowledge, and design." Making things made new brains and minds and a consciousness that imagined and willed a new world and self.[30] Arguably, man's capacity to create symbols had its origin and resided in an ability to convert the hands' activities with things and tools into objects of the mind, descriptive words, and even metaphoric language.

In unison with eyes and legs, arms and fingers underwrote hominid advances across the world and led to power and control over things and tools. Rotating arms, moveable elbows, fully flexing and sensate fingers, and opposable thumbs provided humans with power and precision grip.

From the workshop of hands, and their progeny, analytic, synthetic, aesthetic, and fashioning minds, came somatic, material, and social foundations of everyday culture. In the last 10,000 or so years—beginning with settlement and agriculture, towns and cities—*Homo sapiens* established indisputable but not unquestionable dubious dominion over much of the world.

As already partially explained, we live our lives by the play of two hands consisting of five fingers and two palms. With hands and fingers, we accept or wave off an offer, a line on a surface, point to near or far, and count to a lesser number or suggest a number greater than our ability to enumerate, as I learned from a child. Learning to climb and descend a tiny knoll, this child opened her hand finger by finger to count the steps she took. One! Two! Three! Then she opened her whole hand and looked up at the sky with a beaming smile as if she had just achieved much more beyond the numbers she and her hand could count.

Each of our fingers, which have multiple and even singular uses, has won an affectionate nickname: from the pinky that hooks small things and cleans ears, all the way to the ring finger, *the bird* finger, our most versatile index finger, and our thumb which profoundly strengths our grip and, when turned up or down, signals approval or rejection. We use our thumb to hitch a ride, flip through the pages of a book, keep hold of the bat we swing, or prop up the harmonica.

Of all fingers, no finger wins the plaudits of our multi-functional index finger. A close companion of the thumb, hands, and reaching arm, the index finger works in close correlation with our scanning eyes and inquisitive minds. It goes where they direct and reveals what they must see and think. For us, it serves as the first and deepest explorer of the world of the small. For it, no fruit is too tiny to peel, pick, and poke. As the essence of touch, it leads and mirrors our interests and thoughts.

In *Michelangelo's Finger*, Raymond Tallis makes the pointing index finger the hero of our arms and hands. In "the pointer," he finds proof that the finger is "a conscious agent" and joins all the evidence suggested by gesturing that the body talks and is one with the mind in points beyond encapsulating givens of matter and life. As when we affirm and negate, separate, and synthesize, pointing gives special attention and sends us in a direction toward an object that is not visual. The finger points beyond objects, and the head must think more. Tallis writes in his preface, "Pointing is a means of indicating a transcendent world—general, hidden, and shared—and takes us decisively out of our solitary transient bodies, subject to the laws of nature."[31]

Hands and fingers run through everyday life. They make it. They warn, protect, direct, invite, bless, curse, and counsel. Hands and fingers greet, reciprocally agree, and mutually reconcile with a handshake. The base of the fingers is the palm, which gathers, hides, and clinches a person's findings and emotions. The palm of one hand is the board and map of the other hand and its index finger.

Hands and fingers constitute children's and adults' games—marbles, dice, knives, and cards are a few of them. They range from choosing who's *it* in tag to playing *morra*, a game dating back to the Greeks and Romans—and I suspect games based on guessing the sum of concealed fingers long before the Greeks and Romans. In Pennsylvania and elsewhere, *morra*, known as "fingers," involves leagues, drinking, and the test of accelerating speed and guessing the sum of one's thrown-out fingers and his opponent's. Outside Italian clubs in which *morra* is played, men roll bocce balls that show the intelligence of the hands and arms, as do their cousin games, like the French *boule*, the Belgian game *rolle bolle*, and American bowling.

Hands and fingers are at play in many other games. I can think of cards as being literally and figuratively played out in hands. Curling, to take a different example, while so dependent on legs, feet, and arms, also requires hands to simultaneously synchronize an arm's extension and swing and lift with a hand and a finger's measuring in heft, direction, distance, speed, object placement, and aim of the roll.

Hands amaze us with their dexterity and even trick us with their sleights. They bless us and mystify us. (Their dexterity is shown in contrast by the slow and awkward scrawl of a carnival foot writer. No matter her colorful sequins and pretty legs, she writes worse than I did when I was in the second grade.) Chinese calligraphy involves the art of line, color, form, and movement. Hands curse and ward off curses. They reveal fate and fortunes. Palmistry, or call it Greek-rooted *chiromancy*, can offer diagnoses, prognoses, and cures. As the king and priest have a magic touch, so do healers with special touches, such as chiropractors and masseuses. Almost everyone enjoys a rubdown.

HANDS CREATE OUR BIOGRAPHIES

Hands do crafts; *they are crafty, so to speak*. They stitch, sew, tailor, clamp, saw, and hammer down, as well as shape, mold, and build. Hands go with skills, crafts, and arts.

Lovers and married couples know one another by their hands and fingers. They initiate confession and accompany intimate talks. Taking hands for the first time can lead to taking vows and walking side by side for a lifetime.

Hands and fingers tell the world who a person is. They explore, signal, wave, greet, vow, agree, gesture, pantomime, and even ironically mimic. With variance by age and differences by culture, hands confess belonging to people, places, and times. They create seen and touched things, many of which turn to words, language, and joining metaphors. At the same time, hands and fingers, singularly and in concert, connect and converse with inner and outer worlds, as doers become speakers, social, and thinking beings in a community.

As I handled the world with my hands, so hands handle me. They take me into their custody by imagination and language. Here are a few made-up examples: He should be *handed over* to the arm of the law. The police were quick to arrive and took him *in their hands*. They arrested him, saying, *"Open your hands, hands out, up,* and *behind your back."* At an imagined police station, he was called a *pickpocket* and advised to keep his *dirty paws* to himself. He had *blood on his hands.* They put him in a *handsome* prison uniform, and in prison, he *sits on his hands, twiddling his thumbs.*

As legs and feet stomp our lives and ways, so arms, hands, and fingers, which add to bilateralism, write our biographies. I could even see them write chapters of an autobiography titled *All Hands On Deck.*

I certainly could inventory all members of my family by the age, size, skin, use, and mannerism of their hands, *manos* (Lt., sing. *manus,* hand). Everyone in my family had different hands and gestured differently. There were the ways each of my uncles held his cards, my aunts served sweets, and my Sicilian grandmother pounded and breaded veal.

My mother's hands were quick and adroit, and my father's were those of a lifelong white-collar worker at Western Union. His hands were always kept clean and were precise with a pencil and paper. I remember my father only slapping me once when I was under the card table and bothering his and my uncle's serious card game. I also recall the time my mother turned her wooden whipping spoon into a hitting stick and chased me around the dining room table.

My grandfather's skillful hands, which ran metal shaping machines at the Hudson Motor Car Company and made the slingshots we shared, had large knuckles and were visibly veined. My grandmother, who was brought up poor on the banks of Wisconsin's Wolf River, had hands that were skilled at making delicious pies and sewing—which she first did for a living—and once caught and held my escaped parakeet.

However, her hands were not big enough to hold her cards in double-deck canasta.

Hands went with, even made a person. I wrote a poem to my father at work at his tool bench, even though I think of him more often sitting in his easy chair, fidgeting with the lead for his mechanical pencil, doing a crossword puzzle, or helping me with algebra and accounting.

THE HEFT OF A HAMMER

With it he fastened tacks and brads,
And pounded down shingles spikes
And clinched rafters.

Sometimes in the evening,
At his tool bench,
He clawed and pried out nails
And straightened them,
With sparks
On a chunk of a streetcar track
He salvaged when a boy.

He did everything lickety-split
His whole life long.
He finished crossword puzzles,
Cheered for the Detroit Tigers, win or lose,
Prayed and cared for the dead,
But never looked back
To his parents' homeland of western Sicily
With its barren hills
And the twisting meander
Of the Rio Torto.

His hammer,
Which I still touch,
Carries the grip of his hand
The swing of his arm,
The heft of his life.
He missed two days of work in forty-three years.

Am I to empty him
From my memory?
Throw away his hammer,
Which, the spirited swing of his arm,
Nails us together, forever!

As my parents probably instructed me about my hands—not
sucking my thumb, scratching and picking at myself, washing
my hands, and giving *a firm handshake* while looking into
the person's face—so teachers, too, instructed us, their young
students, how *to hold and dip an ink pen, raise our hands to*
be called on, keep our hands on our desktop and *at our sides*
when walking.

Teachers were not always up to disciplining their own
hands. I had a music teacher who tried to slap me. And I
am sure many of my third-grade classmates still remember
a theater teacher, young, tall, thin, blond, and good-looking,
who picked his nose and constantly ran his "boogers" up and
down his pants as he talked.

I measured other boys by the strength of their grip, and
experienced girls having small, soft, and even delicate hands,
nice for holding.

Certain classmates were known by their use of their
hands. Aside from those "toughies" who doubled their fists
for a fight, there was one kid who liked to see who could grab
each other's crotch, and another who constantly gave the
finger—the erected middle finger—concealed in the palm to
teachers and others, while flagging a pointing index finger
and a little finger to identify statements and their source as
bullshit.

I did not gesture, swear, curse, or joke with my arms
and hands much—at least, I don't recall myself doing that.
Nevertheless, my hands were often on my mind. I was an
unresolved ambidextrous boy. My Aunt Mabel, my mother's
younger sister, claimed me as "*a fellow leftie*" at the outset of
each of my visits with her.

On one occasion in the second grade, I copied
assignment numbers off the chalkboard and into my

76

notebook in the reverse order, right to left, making, say, 86 become 68. Being a whiz at math until then, a string of zero scores caught my father's attention when he found all my additions and subtractions were correct and all my answers marked wrong by the teacher. Only at a parent-teacher conference did he and the teacher get to the bottom of the problem, which I remedied thereafter by simply doing as I was told by copying from left to right. In the same grade, I changed my writing hands from left to right. The prevailing argument of my parents and teachers was that I was so bad at writing left-handed that I might as well try writing with my right hand.

I continued to use my left eye, as I still do, as my aiming and shooting eye rather than my truly dominant right. I also used the strength of my left arm and hand to play a better game of golf and occasionally to beat even the toughest right-hand opponents in arm wrestling by challenging them: "Now, let's try left!"

As a Boy Scout, from eleven to thirteen, I painfully labored to tie knots and bandages. More significantly, every time a troop meeting was called to order or a special occasion arose, the Boy Scout oath was recited, and try as I would, I could not manage to tuck my little finger under my thumb and fully straighten my three other fingers. While faking each and every pledge as best I could, I felt myself a secret non-avower.

As a young golf caddy and later as a driving range manager and high school star (at least in my own lights), I forever fidgeted with my grip and arms. They went to the heart of my swing and my pride. I used and even taught the Vardon grip method with the details of the position of each of the fingers and their relation to the wrist, arms, backswing, and ultimately in the hitting of the ball and follow through. I also was proud of the proper and growing calluses on the last three fingers of my upper left arm. When the calluses broke open and bled, I took this as true proof of the sincerity of my commitment to the game, like boyhood exchanges of *blood oaths* made by the prick on one's finger.

A TALKING HEAD AND A TELLING FACE

Skin wraps every person in a telling cover of flesh. If you know a person's skin—and, to a lesser degree, his or her hair—you probably know something about their age, race, health, sex, hardship, work, and even accidents. Skin is a banner in that it can be seen, touch a chronology, and reveal many days and seasons in the sun, or a pallid life indoors. I don't believe I am an exception. I could tell a part or at least a number of stories in relation to itches, rashes, blemishes, infections, wounds, and scabs. I was severely allergic to poison ivy, and for two years, I suffered from acne. From each decade of my life, I have a scar or two from an accident or operation, and today, in my eighties, after a soft life as a teacher, I have new folds, wrinkles, blotches, and thin skin that murmur and shout: I am mortal!

However, after waving at arms, hands, and fingers and wishing to be more than skin deep, I close this chapter with the head and face. I leave it to others to write of eyes, ears, nose, and mouth, different and telling tongues, lips, and irregular teeth; chins, too, reveal selves and make gestures.

As arms, hands, and fingers direct us both to what is at hand and what is beyond us, what do we make of heads, their bones, and brains, ever so much on the surface and buried deep beyond our thought? Is the head a battering ram or a sacred vault of our intelligence, memory, imagination, and spirit? With all science has told us, how do we know what goes on or doesn't go on in our heads? While crowning the body, the mind is a composite wonder of inside and outside, hard bone, sense organs—ears, mouth, teeth, tongue, and eyes. Truly it is a marvelous unity and uncontestable diversity of parts, another earthly sign of the *many* and *one*.

Heads have within them a brain with connections, thoughts, feelings, projects, plans, loves, and deceits. Exteriorly, heads are the top commanders of our person and life, yet on many counts, they do not know what the body does to give us life. Lowered, bowed, and decorated heads display triumph and confess discouragement, contrition, and even despair.

In *Severed: A History of Heads Lost and Found*, Frances Larson offers us this succinct definition of the head:

> A huge number of different components are packed into our heads. The human head contains more than 20 bones, up to 32 teeth, a large brain, of course, and several sensory organs, as well as dozens of muscles, and numerous glands, nerves, veins, arteries, and ligaments. They are all tightly configured and intensely integrated within a small space. . . . It is adorned with various features that lend themselves to ornamentation: hair, ears, nose, and lips. Thanks to an impressive concentration of nerve endings and an unrivaled ability for expressive movement, our heads connect our inner selves to the outer world more intensely than any other part of our body.[32]

A head's misfortunes, as the old know well, can bring instant death or loss of the mind. The head, as bone-hard as most of it is, also is vulnerable and mortal in many ways, by choking, gagging, or being pierced. Death punishments often turned to the neck and head. Hangings, the common man's prerogative, occurred on town squares and large-limbed trees. Nevertheless, chopping off a head with a sword or axe, merited by the nobleman for death by speed and blade, was an imprecise art of depending on the executioner's experience and craft, strength, and aim. A unique chapter in French history came with the invention and perfection of the guillotine. The new blade, designed to be more efficient and less painful, found its public role in the French Revolution's Reign of Terror, 1793–1794. It filled basket after basket with decapitated heads, including King Louis the XVI and his wife Marie Antoinette, and, with equality, almost twenty thousand others deemed anti- and counter-revolution.[33] So, in France, the guillotine desacralized and equalized all in its own *sharp way* by affording an efficient and swift death.

Nevertheless, the frozen backward stare and blush of certain severed heads raised the ghoulish question in the minds of some reflective commentators, how long does a detached head see and think after its severance? Does it look back with a blush at its missing body?

In whatever way the owner of a head meets his or her end, his detached skull, more than any of his bones, retains a certain power. It evokes the spirit of the dead. Whether freshly killed, dug up, collected in a catacomb, or preserved in a museum, the skull is a sacred crypt, retaining and pulsing the essence of a dead person.

The face, however, distracts our attention from the skull, which in the case of most, is disguised by hair. The face is whole and composed of attention-grabbing features, like beaming and concealing eyes, a majestic and comic nose, a busy and frozen mouth, and matching and contrasting ears. While these organs drink in being, the world sees and queries them for what person and spirit lie below the face.

At the same time, these composing elements and vessels of the face project us out into the world. Eyes glisten and move with what the self perceives, thinks, and chooses to reveal. The mouth, with movements, gestures, and sounds, declares the body's internal workings and the mind's perceptions, suspicions, and intentions.

Still and in motion, the symmetric, asymmetric, unified, and multifaceted face inventories, disguises, and declares the person as a harmonious unity, engaging, attractive, off-putting, or an inscrutable complexity. Smiling faces can accompany glad-handed salespeople, while in the poet's eyes, faces shine angelic luminosity or emit evil pulses.

Faces—ours and others'—tell of age, sex, vitality, and beauty. They are a front for personality and character. At the same time, captained by eyes, they can be the suns and moons of communities. They are the headlights of the self. They light up the world.

A face can hold choruses of conversations motivated by suspicion and curiosity. Accented in concert with or in contrast to postures, gestures, and looks, a face talks to our senses, instincts, assumptions, and presumptions, confirming or calling in doubt what we think. Theodore

Dalrymple remarked that the Russians say Putin has "tin eyes."[34]

Lips alone, bitten and dry, or smeared with lipstick or food, say much without uttering a word. Aside from idiosyncrasies of radically protruding teeth or fears that wiggle, faces declare countenances. A face can be a prologue to a comedy or tragedy. It predictably, or with surprise, can burst out with sarcasm, satire, and irony. It can typify a character, personality, and culture. Doesn't he, we ask, shout like a commanding German as seen in dozens of movies—to mind comes the 1953 film *Stalag 17*—or holler like Archie Bunker in the 1970s situation comedy, *All in the Family*, a play to stereotypes. Novels often limp forward on jilted descriptions of faces and bodies.

In the Preface to *Surfaces*, I wrote,

> As the fanning movement of a bird's colorful tail feathers attracts potential mates, so a single glimpse of Beatrice's face won Dante's life-long devotion, and poetic ramifications of great refinement. More prosaically, people speak about a subject as being "as plain as the nose on your face." They read fates in the lines on their palm; talk about "laughing on the outside and crying on the inside"; or make circular motions with an index finger around an ear to describe the loss of an inner screw and outward bearing. Surfaces give out and off, and take on metaphoric meaning: The German word *Blatt*—or similarly the Russian word *list*—first indicates a blade or leaf, but becomes with use a name of a plate, lamina, or yet a newspaper. The French word *taille*, a cut, comes to mean edge, hew, or yet the slim figure of *une personne bien taillée*. And, in a reverse direction, we first trim a hedge or a head of hair but end up trimming a messy budget or sloppy sails.[35]

With winks, gestures, and glances, a face is like a lighthouse signaling a port or bay, shallows, and rocks to an approaching ship. Faces seek ties and can erect walls. A face signals a multitude of meanings from self, group, or culture. A burp, a head scratch, or a sharp, abrupt glance can interrupt a meeting.

Face, to use another metaphor, is the porch of a person. It confesses, in plain air, a body and soul, or is the mask of a skilled liar.

For the poet, painter, and lover, a certain face is a river that runs deep in meaning. Through the ages, artists have looked on faces to dowse and divine souls and fates.

CHAPTER 6
CARVING OUR NICHE IN LIFE

The body forms the means and heart of life. The interaction of body and things writes the text of human evolution and history, from bipedal human beginnings to first settlements and, for the majority, up until today. It makes the means and substance of well-being, work, and play and forms the core of the give and take of society. As I wrote in *Everyday Life*, which I extensively paraphrase and cite in this chapter, "Body produces the kernel of everyday life."[36]

Anthropologist Tim Ingold calls this ecological approach to human life "a dwelling perspective."[37] The sentient body in movement—expressive of our biology—is, as Ingold wrote elsewhere, "fully interactive with a sentient environment from which the body learns and fashions skills."[38] He noted in *Lines* (New York, 2007) that biology, learning, perception, and imagination, do not form antitheses. As humans walk, see, and act, they perceive and represent the world of experience with lines and traces which connect things with maps, drawings, genealogies, stories, and even music.

Over the ages, the body places humans in situations and affords them experiences. As human groups learned, made things, and built environments, they transformed and defined their lives. The body, the living and moving hub of life, forms habits with and around a set of repeating individual and shared actions. Habits meet the needs of the body's own physiology and the community's survival. The way a group of humans hunts, gathers, moves, and dwells establishes relations with waters, soils, plants, and animals. Habits establish a material, social, and cultural way of life, language, and thought.

The body centers us and incorporates us in life. Humans join us to the natural and human bodies around us. Bodies account for our niche, space, and place, which we know as home, neighborhood, village, and, eventually, city, world, and even universe. Our niche, however much it changes, begins, and is centered on where we eat, sleep, meet, live, and intimately know others.

THE BODY PUTS ITS STAMP ON THE MIND AND THE WORLD

The body roots us in life and thought. It underwrites our intelligence with comparisons, distinctions, unities, and affords us metaphoric entrance into life and being.

Besides its bilaterally matched pairs of hands and feet, legs and arms, eyes and ears, the body has form and shapes the forms around it. With such ambivalently symmetrical and non-symmetrical juxtapositions as those between the pelvis and buttock and the face and back, the body also conducts and expresses itself and the world. Of these asymmetric notes, as the critic, Jed Perl explains in his book on early modern painter Jean-Antoine Watteau, *Antoine's Alphabet*, "The back is both carapace and core."

We assume our bodies are us. We adhere within them, and we also go and ooze out of them with glance, touch, and presence. Our very bones hold and retain our essence. Ghosts and spirits (often considered one and the same) dwell in our skeleton and make ominous graves and burial sites.

In any case, our body, with its senses, emotions, and memories, gives us a sense of complexity and intricacies, the depths and heights of the elements, oceans, and innards of the earth. The body, which judges things both common and out of the blue, declares transcendence and mystery and baffles the paradox that the more we discover it, the less we know it. The body defies our claims to be the creator, emperor, or savior of the self and world.

As we showed in the preceding chapter, the body also has poetry. We call and write transcendence in its name. It polyphonically sings and dances. It purrs with contentment and cries out in pain. Blatant and sly, rude and discrete, the body signals its quotidian intercourse with things and others.[39] Sometimes, the body, like a telegrapher who has lost his code, sends out confusing signals about its interaction and discourse with the self and world.

The body's dialogue with the world has attracted a rush of thinkers. This includes French philosophers and object-focused museum designers intent on constructing the history of a people and a place's material culture. A looser metaphor says those thinkers were shoved off in vessels without a captain or ballast master and into the open seas of the body under such flags as "Stuff" and "Things."

EVER AMONG OTHER BODIES

As much as we spend our lives responding, caring, and interpreting our own bodies and their internal functions and external experiences and actions, our individual body always exists and finds its place and meanings among, with, and through other bodies. As much as we belong profoundly to our self, we inescapably are linked to the bodies of others.

There are multiple ways to state this premise. The bodies of others, starting with our mothers, fathers, families, and "tribes," account for our beginnings, changing position, and disposition in the world. Our very beginning as mammals sticks us as body to body in action, emotion, and experience. To say we are social beings is to say we participate and depend on one another for life and meaning.

As profoundly different from the bipolar contemporary individualistic and collectivist society, primitive and traditional peoples shared a commonality in their repeated daily seasonal activities and their passage through history. Communities grew out of interactive bodies and minds as they experienced and defined a common life and culture. From birth to death, individuals lived both mutually and dependently in all aspects of their lives. From our domestic beginnings in small groups in families, villages, and tribes, we lived cheek to jowl, birthed and buried one another, and were reciprocal mirrors of our bodies, situations, and lives.

Even though men, at times, traveled alone for a dozen reasons and shepherds stayed and slept alone for seasons, human life, from primal beginnings to advanced civilizations, principally played out as bodies among bodies. So, men,

women, children, and the old belonged mutually and
reciprocally to one another. Small groups lived, reproduced,
and traveled while dependent on one another's efforts and
works. Exchanges and gifts of food and things, work, care,
help, and services—the ligatures of community—turned
principally on what bodies and persons did for and to one
another. Reactions to exchanges, constant, diverse, and often
uneven, were based on estimated capacity, expected duty,
habit, tradition, a show of respect, as well as fairness and
past exchanges.

In small and dependent groups, all those who came and
went, were born and died or injured and killed, mattered.
Strangers posed dangers. They could be unknown, alien,
or hostile, of different lands, spirits, and gods. Their
appearance, manners, gestures, and comportment must be
earnestly read.

Religions, to generalize the thought of Mircea Eliade's
Cosmos and History: The Myth of the Eternal Return
(Princeton, 1949), identified their spirits and gods with the
springtime rituals of rebirth. Saving and communal rites
acted out springtime rituals, which, including the living and
dead, called on their gods to re-awaken nature and plants,
bring fertility to animals and the community, and initiate the
rebirth of the dead. Dancing, gesturing, and singing bodies
enacted these first and primary springtime rites, which
enacted nature's and the community's creation.

New and renewed bodies were at the heart of these
rites. The sacrifice of animals and humans became the early
peoples' exchanges with the gods. Though debated and
rebuked, sacrifices (etymology: *what made holy*) operate as
a currency of victims in Judaism and, as already suggested,
were central to Christianity, which teaches that Jesus Christ,
God, becomes incarnate and offers Himself on the cross for
man. Christian martyrs responded by offering themselves
for their faith. At the same time, starting with Socrates,
reverence was established for those who sacrificed their
lives for their beliefs, while heroes of the Trojan wars and
Medieval knights offered themselves up for the causes as the

first and founding heroes of the modern nation-states. They offered their young bodies—their lives—for the birth and defense of the nation.

Indeed, traditionally, religiously, individually, communally, and collectively, we know and value the self, others, and the world by the presence and gift of our bodies. We miss one another, we miss a body, what they do, claim, and represent. As I began writing this chapter, I realized I had affirmed this in two poems I had written.

O GOD, WHERE IS MY BROTHER?

The story of a surviving brother, Jeremy Bush, Seffner, Florida, as reported February 28, 2013.

I threw open the door
Of my brother's room—
No more, empty, a vacuum.
Only the corner
Of his bed protruded
From the earth,
From the hole in the earth.
I jumped in
And dug by hand,
Then shoveled
After his body.
The earth has swallowed
The brother
From whom I was never apart.
Sorrowfully, I continue to round the rim
Of that night's sink hole,
Suspended
In his continuing fall.
Though days pass,
I still trudge in mind
Through limestone caverns
Towards a primordial sea,
The bottom of oblivion.
With head bent down,

I kick and shuffle
Along the path
Of an old truth:
That the soul is the image
Of the body,
And the body resides, dwells
In flesh
Pressed close,
Fused
One
In this life.
Even from the tip of my toes
I can't peer beyond
The chasm of his fall
And the abyss
Of my sunken heart.
The black and white maypole
Of memory,
Born of the same bed and table,
Boiling pot
And ember-filled hearth,
Has been pulled—
Wound, rusty, barbwire tight.
And so
I circle this crater,
This empty Jericho,
Lamenting, supplicating:
"O God,
Where is my brother?"[40]

We can't let loose of other bodies. We hold them in memory when they are long gone. They float in our minds as shadows of familiar things—the bodies of the dead pop up by coincidences and connections.

Bodies, especially those of a wife, parent, and friend, and even those of strangers taken by unique and hideous deaths, burrow in the body's and the mind's memories. We see, count, know, value, and cherish the living and the dead as bodies. Bodies form the threshold and heart of social and ethical beings. In the following poem, I recount how my uncle kept his dead buddy's body afloat all night and into the morning until they were rescued. He could not relinquish his hold of his buddy's body, and I cannot quit the memory of his long grip, first taken in November of 1942 in the North African Mediterranean.

A BUDDY AFLOAT

1

Pearl Harbor
Woke the fiery passions
And ignited the latent forges
Of this nation.
Two months after,
My uncle Bill,
My mother's young brother,
Who taught me to skate
Free and fast
The frozen canals of Detroit's Belle Isle,
Enlisted in the Navy.

Before taking Bill downtown to board a bus
For boot camp at Great Lakes,
My grandfather
Made the whole family form a line,
Stand at attention,
And salute his only son,
Young Bill, the sailor.

2

In the fall
Pharmacist's Mate Bill
Went up the gangplank of the USS Tasker H. Bliss,
A refit passenger ship from the 1920s.
The Bliss's first assignment
Was to deliver troops
To North Africa,

Where a novice army
Would learn to fight.

In November 1942,
With its troops safely delivered to shore,
The Bliss,
Along with two other U.S. Navy ships
At anchor off Casablanca,
Was sunk by German U-boat 130.

With floors, stairs, and decks collapsing,
The breaking, splintering, and exploding Bliss became
A hull of death.
Individual acts
Of stooping, merciful kindness
Did not cancel
The fumbling frenzy of its abandonment,
The mixture of leaping, bolting fear.

But over the pitiful human din
That accompanied the solemn sinking of the Bliss,
My uncle's words
Of eighty years ago
Give compass
To an event
I cannot chart.

"I took my dead friend Simpson
Overboard with me,
Into the late afternoon sea
And kept him close by
Until rescue
By morning light.

"For all the powers within me
For that single love
That makes family and friends one,"
My uncle,

Peering in and out of the past,
So close, so far,
Confided to me,
"I would not relinquish him to tugging waters,
To the dark deep.
With all the buoying grace within me
I kept him afloat.

"But this,"
My uncle said pausing,
"Is only a half-truth.
I was not his keeper
Any more than he was mine.
If I abandoned him
I would be taken down
By the swallowing depths,
Night's blackness,
The open jaw
Of what is not.

"In the burnished light of the ship's dimming fires
My only company
Was him.
In the long groaning surrender
Of the descending Bliss,
I clung to him
Ever so tight
With all my youth and fear
Until morning light
When a bobbing craft
Picked its way towards us.

"Two of its crew.
With the help of a boat gaff,
Pulled us aboard.
I don't recall
Whether exhaustion
Or soothing words

Dissolved my grip,
Pried apart my clinging arms.

On shore,
I was first cared for in a luxurious casino
Converted into a hospital,
And more serious wheels still spun,
Cards were turned,
Doling out greater fates and fortunes.
I found my therapy among dates, palms, and moonlight,
And grew well enough to watch
The masked and swaying land ships
Of North African beauty.
Yet inwardly I wouldn't let go
Lest all that was and might be
Would be surrendered to the beating swell
Of the dark sump
Below.

"When the war was over,"
Bill completed his confession,
"I did not return home to Detroit,
Instead, I found yet another new body
For clinging tight.
I took my fresh bride, Margaret, to Boston
To live in a small upstairs apartment
In the house of my buddy's widowed mother.
Where in the watery round of my grieving mind
I still treaded and circled
The sunken Bliss."

3
In the summer of 1947,
When I was seven,
I drove with my father and mother to Boston
To reclaim Bill and Margaret
And their new infant daughter, Mary Ellen,
For our Detroit family.

All the way home,
Every time Mary Ellen saw a body of water
She cried out
The first and only word she knew:
"Gungha!" "Gungha!"—
And we laughed.

And now, a half-century later,
What seems a flood of time ago
Since the trip of reclamation,
With my beloved grandparents Bill and Frances long
gone,
And my very own, Joe and Ethel,
And even Bill and Margaret dead,
I keep them,
Together and afloat,
In the dispersing seas of time.
I do this
With the buoying grace of memory
And the treading kick of word and story.[41]

FIRST NICHES

First niches fit and were formed by and for the human body, man's first companion, medium, and instrument. Daily existence is a corporal matter; the quotidian is never far from bread and pain. The body is our first tool and container and the primary agency of our actions. It guarantees connections and interactions with things and constitutes a condition and goal of our projects. The body anchors the individual in space and time, and it is the corporate guarantor of the community. The body compares and classifies what we see, encounter, take up, and ingest. It affords a binary measure of what is like and unlike, and attractive and unattractive to us—and with the heterogeneity of eyes, hands, and other parts of the body, it tells us what fits and pleases. The body constitutes the everyday judge of friendly or adverse, useful or obstructing. It makes the art in which we see, invest, know, and idealize ourselves.

The body places humans in action, thought, and wish. Bodies move about. They take us to the labor and gardens of our days—along the troughs, ruts, and up onto the roads and highways of everyday life. While eating, sleeping, and mating, humans take and assume their place. Habits underpin settlements and communities across generations, while gestures, traditions, and metaphors keep societies in orbit.

The historian of the everyday must begin with the materiality of life, which is the centrality of the body, and, as we will see in the following chapters, things, tools, energy, and machines. Things and habits tie the knot of everyday behavior, and everyday life spawns needs, wishes, conjectures, and dreams.

Everyday life grows out of tasks and goods—the peasant works and belongs to his land and the village, the merchant lives by goods, travels, salves, and books, and belongs to his guild, and so it is with other forms of work and communities.

The body enters us in the world and into action, to paraphrase the anthropologist and sociologist Marcel Mauss.[42] Historians of the quotidian realize that the everyday is rooted in activity and in the things we do. In this way, the body in motion, movement, accomplishment, and satisfaction ignite and fill our senses and our consciousness.

Humans constantly identify and weave themselves into the things they use, do, make, need, and in modern and contemporary societies, consume and wish to possess. Groups and cultures, which encapsulate individuals, weave selves and things into one fabric. Their use and work with things and tools make and form distinct landscapes and communities, defining home, village, places, and environments. In the words of the art critic Leo Stein, "Things are what we encounter, ideas are what we project."[43]

MAKING HOME AND RAISING WALLS

The home was where humans stayed, lived, and survived. It had, at its core, a space for mother and child and a place for sleep, reproduction, and cooking. It afforded security from enemies and animals while giving access to food, water,

wood, and materials for making tools and containers. It
was made of roofs, walls, and interiors. From home, men
hunted, sought out resources, gathered materials—and even
kidnapped women to perpetuate their own group.

Groups survived and even took root in homes and villages
where they were born, grew, and died. Their place or places
were their entrance into their individual and communal
life. With burial and building, they located the center of
their cosmos, and with dance, song, myth, and ritual, they
entered into relation and communion with higher, protective,
and beneficial gods and spirits. With praise, offerings,
and sacrifices, they looked to higher powers for health,
purification, and rebirth of the living, dead, and nature itself.
Spring ceremonies were the most vital and religious.

With bodies and things, and cultures of rituals and
stories, people encapsulated themselves in homes and
villages as hunters, gatherers, and workers in the field and
as servants, slaves, and craftspeople for those who amassed
wealth and controlled the land. As they took to living in
houses and villages, they wove reeds into baskets and
thatched roofs, found and shaped wood for a hundred tasks,
molded mud and clay into vases and pots, pounded rock, and
chipped shells into tools.

The origins of agriculture in the Near East,
approximately twelve thousand years ago, put whole valleys
and their plants in human control. Agriculture created
surplus food, required and permitted large concentrations of
populations and the specialization of crafts, and ultimately
accounted for the beginnings of cities and civilizations with
great reaches of power, commerce, and culture. This new
control of the body and things grew out of the knowledge of
seeds and tillage. It rested on increasing the control of water
as cities and fields depended on deep wells, lifted waters, and
channeled water in troughs and canals for the building and
sailing of ships. Indeed, our bodies and the control of things
projected our control over nature, terrains, waters, people,
and communities. On an unprecedented scale, we became,
for better and worse, each other's companions in time,

condition, and work—and each other's rulers, lords, bosses, bookkeepers, census takers, priests, and teachers.

This history can be understood as having its source in locating "home," finding a niche in nature, and forming a community. Since the late Neolithic age, first in the Near East and later in China and the Mediterranean, humanity incorporated itself in dwellings and enclosed settlements. Within created spaces, humans lived their lives and incubated new minds and hearts in established places and routines. The "everyday" was self-built.

The house with walls—be it a refurbished cave, a heaping of clay, a gathering of brush, or a mounding of snow—became an extension of the body, a primary encapsulation of life, and a nest of security, privacy, and intimacy, if one wishes. For those with means, homes designed and made of mud, brick, wood, stone, or plastered walls became even more. They came to constitute organized small and interior worlds that could be conceived as man's place in nature and as a human nucleus in the cosmos. In *The Poetics of Space*, Bachelard wrote: "Our house is our corner of the world . . . it is our first universe, a real cosmos in every sense of the word."[44]

The archaeologist Ian Hodder sees the *domus* of the classical house as uniting and making one hearth and home. Beginning in the early Holocene (which began twelve thousand years ago), it furnished a sense of place and became a prime ground for increasing human entanglement with things and, what cannot be overlooked, also a symbolic vessel for holding and treasuring self, family, and things, and a means of establishing a unique form of life.[45]

The center of the ancient home was the hearth. In the hearth, fire lives, giving out warmth and light. The head of the house had their legitimacy as the keeper of the fire. For classical peoples, the hearth, as explained by historian Numa Denis Fustel de Coulanges (1830–1889) in his *La Cité antique* (1864), was where the dead and the family spirits resided. From underneath the hearth, the emissary of the dead, the snake, came forth. As the parental bed biologically centered the living family, special corners and niches in the bedroom, if separate, and in the main cooking room, furnished alcoves for powerful holy objects and saints. (I think of the Orthodox believers' "Holy Corner," the *krasnyi ugol*; in the Eastern European hut, the *izba*; or the west room of an Irish country home, where the old man and wife live out their last years among the family's few but cherished heirlooms.)

Lewis Mumford, the pioneering writer and American historian of technology and the city, pertinently wrote, "House and village, eventually the town itself, are the woman writ large." He noted "In Egyptian hieroglyphics, house or town may stand as symbols for woman."[46] As a biological platform and spiritual agency, to borrow a phrase from archaeologist Colin Renfrew, the home allows us "to appropriate the cosmos" and make it center and anchor our everyday rituals and their actions in the cosmos.[47] "In many domesticated societies," as Peter Wilson wrote in *The Domestication of the Human Species*" (2009), the house is appropriated to mediate and synthesize the natural symbols of both the body and the landscape. The twentieth-century Welsh poet Glyn Jones did this in his poem, "Goodbye, What Were You," making the kitchen the place where a mother and fire are one. Her cooking, metaphoric and metamorphosing, is the cauldron of birth and sustenance.[48]

Walls define human space as home and community. Walls, which make bodies of homes, villages, and cities, are the footing of a place in the surrounding world and the cosmos. They mark off a metaphoric space of the inner and outer, below and above, and secure and vulnerable. Material and ontological walls establish us in being and time.

In the Near East, starting approximately twelve thousand years ago, walls flourished in the building of dwellings and other structures, as the protective and sheltering ring of settlements, and with pens for animals, sheds for crops, and in homes—temples of a sort—for goods and sacrifices. The explosion in walls and their encapsulation of human bodies, things, and groups, and the redefinition of the everyday, marked a phenomenal revolution in human history.

Walls popped up with growing populations, the
taming of space, the ordering and cultivating of fields,
the domestication of animals, the storage of goods, the
organization of communities, and the delineations of profane
and sacred places. "The domestication of plants and animals,
the domestication of man and the material landscape,"
for Mumford, "all went hand and hand."[49] These enlarged
settlements, located principally in fertile river valleys,
dwarfed the largest hunting settlements of the Neolithic
era.[50]

Within walls, humans stored their harvests, protected
their livestock, practiced crafts, exchanged and stored
treasured goods, and accumulated their past. By defining
home, community, and landscape, walls delineated a place
in society and on the landscape; they were primary and
indispensable in defining everyday life as a condition of the
body, movement, and mind.

Humans became, by the force of towns and the
expansion of empires, intramural beings. The built world
not only secured man's core biological needs and embodied
and protected social orders but also ringed off the arenas in
which humans lived out their daily lives and concentrated on
their most advanced crafts, and honed their language, arts,
philosophies, and religions. In summarizing the dimension of
this revolution, Trevor Watkins contends that amid these first-
built architectural frames and settled communities, humans
established social orders and sovereignty, consolidated crafts
and skills, and formed "symbolic orders of meaning."[51]

Between the walls, cities, and civilizations, human
advancement incubated in the social order, technology,
building, goods, and decoration. In their confines, and by
the reach of their extended grasp across lands and over
the sea, humans moved outward in their body and with
things and increasingly went inward with thought, language,
and expression. At the pinnacle of thought, their religious
thinkers and philosophers sought not only to define man's
place in being but also the foundations and reach of their
consciousness.

As increasing populations drove developing agriculture, humans, with great security and abundance, incorporated themselves into places and the routines of fixed settlements. Therein, greater specialization and leisure encouraged human advances in discovering, making, and trading objects. Multiplying objects wrote diverse narratives of their creation and place in everyday life.

Humans literally made themselves into different types of beings as groups mastered different crafts and advanced in canvassing the heavens, inventorying animals, harvests, and goods, accounting transactions, interpreting the law, and reading and writing. With differentiated statuses of royal and religious classes and cultures, humans, largely one, distinguished themselves outwardly in appearance and inwardly in feelings and thought.

Abstract social orders developed from the division of labor and specialized crafts. Writing and auguring priests advised sacred kings, whose agents and armies commanded cities that dominated their immediate landscape and reached distant lands where their merchants and armies went in search of materials, goods, and slaves. Cities and civilizations influenced and even enfolded the countryside and everyday life in their needs and designs. The body had carried humanity far into what we might call abstract and distant relations, which then fell to the mind to give meaning and expression.

Cities, which lived off the fields and people of the fields, carried mankind further in its relation to the realm of things and the self. Cities defined the new, unusual, and extraordinary for the great majority of people who belonged to fields, countries, and villages until recent times. Work, habits, traditions, and cultures defined people by distinct places in their body, mind, and community. Place made everyday life and doled out daily necessities, seasonal and religious beliefs, and celebrations.

Cities were extraordinary in all they did, represented, brought about, demanded, and made manifest. Cities split the atoms of villages, countryside, and rural places. They did it with the lure of goods and freedoms, the disciplines of money and work, as well as taxes, public amenities and services, schools, conscription, armies, and networks of laws, officials, and growing bureaucracies. At the extremes, cities, hand in hand with central states, overran the traditions and cultures of country folks and rural and village inhabitants. They abducted local lands and children and diminished and annihilated country spirits and gods.

Whether a matter of despair or even hope, cities constituted the extraordinary in the countryside, which was perennially subjected to landlords and fixed systems of exchange, laden with the body's labors, tied to long-practiced technologies, and harnessed to the cycle of life and seasons. The urban novelties of education, leisure, and mobility dangled alternative and softer lives for individuals and families. At play was nothing less than the confrontation of two distinct ways of life: that of the enduring, static, isolated, and autarkic peasant life and that of the changing, free, independent, bountiful, innovative, and consuming life.

In his *The Structures of Everyday Life: Civilization and Capitalism, 15th–18th Century* (Berkeley Calif., 1992), Fernand Braudel judged the court and middle-class life to be born of a superfluity of goods, elaborating itself around ample space. Baroque court life of the seventeenth and eighteenth centuries crowned itself in gold canopies, offering heaven on earth. This world used manners to tell how good it was to all who looked. It offered its participants full-length mirrors to decorate their homes and celebrate their places and selves. Dressed as a woman in the flow of embroidered silk and as a man in high, polished leather boots, it was a society on a permanent parade with things and clothes. It went up and down curving staircases, featuring gowns and delicate feet soon to be put to work in elaborate dances on parqueted floors at court balls.

The Baroque court life of the seventeenth and eighteenth centuries thrived in decorative displays. With a superfluity of goods, it featured selves on easy chairs, with instruments, books, and pets, in opulent palaces and gardens. With white, marble, and golden churches crowned with gold canopies, the society celebrated their God, church, and themselves.

THE BODY, VESSEL OF OUR INDIVIDUALITY

Seeing life as the interaction of the body and things opens the door to considering the genesis of individualism and intimacy as a consequence of increased goods, spaces, and privacy and the subjectivity that was nurtured and grew out of them. In the quiet and comfort of a bed and bedroom of choice of only one or two, it became possible for individuals to foster the privacy of the body and its acts and consider them as the intimate and unique possessions of one's own.

This makes it possible to demarcate two historical worlds, "a world without and a world with intimacy." The prior, as I outlined in an essay titled "A World Without Intimacy," was, for the vast majority of all times up to the unfolding of the centralized and materially revolutionary world of the nineteenth century, a world when dwellings were huts, cottages, and shacks, and were small, with only a single room or two, occupied by many and often seasonally shared with animals.[52] Space was minimal, heating sparse, and furniture little, with, commonly, a single table and bench for eating. The surrounding grounds, which may have held gardens, were rough and rutted, and surfaces belonged to the weather, seasons, traffic, and tracks.

From this as ground zero, it becomes possible to roughly chart the history of the growth of wealth, things, comfort, privacy, intimacy, and thus individuality and subjectivity. This growth was pioneered in the high Middle Ages and early modern Europe by the well-off bourgeoisie. They equipped themselves with beds, bedrooms, and space for comfort, hobbies, and display. They even nurtured their children with rooms, things, and dress to become young individuals with lives, interests, emotions, and secrets of their own. In opulent private quarters, with space, comfort, and warmth, families could collect goods and keepsakes, read, write, kill time, cherish and pamper their own body, and elaborate his and her lovemaking. Arguably, wealth and space and the bed and bedroom hatched the modern private and intimate individual.

In this way, individuality was spearheaded by the advancing diffuse aristocracy and the growing upper-middle class. Out of their beds and bedrooms, from their bodies, emotions, and presumed right of privacy, individualism became a brow of advancing modernity. A history of the nineteenth and first half of the twentieth century could be written as the arrival of the great majority, urban and eventually rural, to the presumption of having a bedroom of their own.

Bodies flourished in advancing material society by being pampered with space, things, comfort, leisure, and the presumption of rights, public concern, and medical treatment. With this came the culture and commerce of the body around the concept of the body as a whole, healthy, attractive, and sexual being.

Sexuality, culturally assumed, commercially and pornographically developed, and medically and clinically diagnosed, became a multifarious source of self and identity. In Michel Foucault's lecture at Dartmouth, "About the Hermeneutics of the Self: Two Lectures at Dartmouth," published in May 1993, he set a goal: "I wish to study those forms of understanding which the subject creates about himself. These forms of self-understanding are important . . . to analyze the modern experience of sexuality." For many, beauty, health, and sexuality define the self. Arguably, the body, pampered and cherished, birthed the modern individual.

CHAPTER 7
MIND OVER FOOT

Over the ages, the body taught and continued to develop the brain and mind to think and talk; and after (choose a very big number) millions of years as an ape, and then hundreds of thousands of years of bipedality, conscious thinking, and talking, the mind claimed the body as its own. It sublimated and, to a degree, subjugated the body's signals, emotions, reflexes, and instincts to its conscious experience, language, faculties (intellect, imagination, will, judgment, and memory), and its ethics, aesthetics, and individual social traditions and cultures. In a nutshell, the subordination of the body to the self, which I call "mind-over-foot," underlies but does not entirely shape and determine this chapter. In other words, the mind's directorship of consciousness and claim to transcendence does not hush or deny the voices of the body that sing in the chorus of the self, denying Descartes' modern supposition, from his 1662 *Traité de l'homme*, that "body is nothing but a statue or machine made of earth."

Surely, traditional, folk, peasant, and village cultures, which in ever fewer numbers have continued to exist until our times, had their foundation on the primacy of the body, its functions and needs, and the interactions of bodies with things and other bodies. In traditional villages, the needs, actions, as well as conditions, and characteristics of the body were imposing. The most important concerns, prayers, and rituals sought abundance and good health.

With considerable cultural variations, the body and the spirit of the dead lived on. They were incanted with words, dance, song, or ritual. They could never be put away easily and forgotten. Manifesting their old traits and characteristics, the recognizable dead appeared and even commanded the living. They, in so many ways, shared and even dominated, for better or worse, the lives and worlds of the living.

Village censuses were taken by body and genesis: who was linked to whom, who was the child and grandchild of whom, and who were the aunts, uncles, and cousins. Likewise, villages recorded where a person was from and when they came. Of course, in constant play were references to his or her physical traits.

Descriptions and nicknames derived from a person's size, height and width, parts of their body, and his or her uses of their senses—eyes, ears, noses, mouths, and hands—were alive in stories, jokes, and gossip. Never forgotten was the quickness of tongue and wit—and, often left to talk of the clandestine, there were suppositions about sexual prowess and powers to charm, curse, and perform magic.

Neighborhoods and villages flowed with nicknames that were familiar, succinct, indicative, and, of course, judgmental of character. Common last names were even derived from villagers' bodily pejoratives, such as the deaf, crippled, illegitimate, and stinky.

Traditional and village attitudes about the body didn't die out with their arrival in the city. Rather, they continued on to constitute popular and, if you wish, vulgar neighborhood cultures of ethnic families and newly formed urban masses. They formed part of everyday street talk and conveyed the range of people's feelings, expressions, and characterization of individuals by sex, body shape, and parts. Out of certain mouths, the aim of the vulgar could be no more or less than a good joke about a person's clumsy step, crooked (witch's) pointing finger, a woman's flat or generous chest, a man's barrel chest or immense stomach, or flat backside, "a satchel ass."

THE MIND WINGS UP THE BODY

As traditional life and popular and everyday life continue to express and value their lives in terms of the body, and the body in industries, commerce, and fashion supply and profit from bodies served and sold, we should not overlook our primal disposition to treat our body as individually and collectively ours. We assume—really take for granted, except when pain, illness, and death intrude—to claim our body as a companion, servant, and agency of all we think, imagine, and will our lives to be. It is ours to work, comfort, treat, accommodate, and reproduce ourselves. It belongs to us to place and decorate ourselves as individuals and groups among others and in nature. It is our raft and our vessel for the mind to decorate, elevate, and define and value the self.

Tribal rituals, myths, and masks show and suggest our most elemental uses of the body as physical, visual, cultural, and religious ways to project selves. Dance, tattoos, jewelry, and dress, along with posture and gesture, show the body as a way to tell ourselves who we are and talk to the living and dead, spirits and gods. The body enacts the self with and even before words.

With the beginnings of cities and empires, the mind of those in power and with control stands above the body and lives of slaves. Ten to twelve thousand years ago, as we learned to control fields and waters, utilize metals and trade, build ships and fashion wheels, we expanded in numbers, concentrated in places, extended our power over and uses of lands and waters, increased our wealth, advanced specializations and crafts, counted, recorded, and wrote. At the same time, those on top, enhanced in command, status, and individuality, advertised their self and position with goods, buildings, temples, luxuries, and decorations. Royal priests divined the heavens to synchronize the beginnings and ends of orders of rule with the movement of cosmic orders. Royal ceremonies sought to preserve rulers for eternity. At the extreme, Egyptian pharaohs prepared their preservation by building hidden chambers in pyramids and making plans to take with them their treasures, pets, and multiple virgins for their abiding pleasure.

Positions in the imperial hierarchies and especially the new cities, colonies, and political centers around Greece, Sicily, and the shores of the eastern Mediterranean, elevated and beautified the body to serve public status. They did this through speech, rhetoric, and gestures, manners and dress, sculpture and idolization of heroes, and personalization of the gods. At points, the representation of the bodies of men and gods was not to be told apart. Greek and Roman idealizations, representations, and enactments of the beautiful, athletic, and healthy body formed an enduring element of Western culture.

In multiple ways, those with means in the Middle Ages also celebrated the body with its song, dress, and art. The palace and court elevated warriors with ornate armor and the courtly women with the best linen, silk, and cotton. Sculptures of mortuary set in stone images of royalty and the church. As knights glittered in metals and ladies in cloth and jewelry, the majority knew their days by work and their nights by being huddled in humble quarters around fires.

The core of the medieval views of the body was found in the Christian faith, the Old and New Testaments, and in the church's theological and doctrinal development. Faith placed the body at the heart of being. The body was joined to the person's soul from birth and went with the person's soul through life and death on to resurrection. God's very Creation, Grace, and Revelation worked through the body.

The body was not only the housing and animating energy and motor of the person, but it placed the person on earth and in a human community. God not only specially created men and women in body form, but calls, tests, rewards, and saves them in their bodies. The body incorporates us in matter, place, and time and also makes the human narrative from the beginning to the end of time.

In Chapter Two of Genesis, we read of the tie of body and Spirit in the story of Creation: Lord God formed man in His own image from the dust of the ground and breathed the breath of life into his nostrils. Then God's singular concern for man's solitude leads Him to fashion a woman for lonely Adam from his rib. In the garden of paradise, they commit Original Sin by eating the fruit of a forbidden tree. Their punishment becomes shame in their nakedness and expulsion forever from the garden. Man will wander and live forever in the shadows of toil and death: "By the sweat of your brow you will eat your food until you return to the ground since from it you were taken; for dust you are, and to dust, you will return."

For Jews and Christians, the mortal body holds and joins our biology and souls, our minds and spirit, and acts on and receives Grace. At the same time, the body is the vessel and agency of our experience, knowledge, will, and freedom. In our body, we have pleasures, pains, and satisfactions and know the true, the beautiful, and the good. In it, we make our exchanges, recognize gifts, and offer sacrifices. As earthly and blessed, the body sinks us to condemning sin and carries us into sacred and resurrected form, transporting us, according to Christian belief, to everlasting communion with the fathers, the dead, the saints, and ultimately God himself.

EARTHLY BODIES IN HEAVENLY EMBRACE

Based on the Old Testament story, the New Testament story reties Heaven and Earth, God and man. In a cosmic reversal of the Jewish foundational story of Abraham—father of the Jews, who was asked, and positively responded, to sacrifice his first and long-awaited son, Isaac, to show his faith—God Himself chooses to sacrifice Himself in the form of his Son, Jesus Christ—the second member of the Trinity—to become an incarnate being who will be crucified for the redemption of man from sin and death, man's eternal salvation and incorporation of body and soul in the kingdom of God.

In every sense, Jesus Christ was incarnate. He was birthed by a human mother and grew up embodied in family and with friends. He was tempted, fasted, and prayed. He selected apostles and, in their company, traveled, taught, and prophesied. In every way, he entered fully into the worlds of human experience, minds, words, stories, and society. As the word made flesh, Jesus Christ was taught with parables and prophecies, and He was tested, mocked, persecuted, suffered, and died agonizingly on the Cross. He was buried in a tomb. He arose from the dead, visited Hell, returned to the Earth to further instruct his apostles, and ascended bodily to Heaven to his Father. His sacrifice freed Christians of the consequences of Original Sin, subjects all to the last judgment, and, for the saved, opens Heaven, body, and soul to everlasting communion with the risen dead, the angels, and God.

Christ's ministry to the body of earthly men and women runs through the New Testament. He couples his teachings with bodily cures and miracles. He multiplies fish and loaves, fills nets with fish, transforms water to wine at Cana, curses a fruitless tree, calms seas, expels demons, and even resurrects the dead. On the fifth Sunday of Lent, the first reading from Ezekiel 37:12–14 tells of God, His Father, binding Himself to the well-being of His people,

> Thus says the Lord GOD:
> O, my people, I will open your graves
> and have you rise from them
> and bring you back to the land of Israel...
> I will put my Spirit in you that you may live
> and I will settle you in the land of Israel.

In Christian teaching, God makes us, individually, the Israel of his Providence: from the depths of body and heights of consciousness, we belong to his concern and salvation. In the Gospel of John 14:18–20, Christ, Son of God and Redeemer of men and the Earth, says prior to his death and resurrection,

> I will not leave you orphaned. I am coming to you
> In a little while, the world will no longer see me, but you
> will see me;
> because I live, you will live.
> On that day, you will know that I am in my Father, and
> you in me, and I in you.

In Romans 8:10–11, Paul declares that "the Spirit of the one who raised Jesus from the dead dwells in you, the one who raised Christ from the dead will give life to your mortal bodies, through his Spirit dwelling in you."

God enters incarnate man in life through his Son. God creates, judges, loves, and saves men and women in their flesh, bone, and blood, in their actions, thoughts, and conscience. For Christians, God himself takes incarnate form in the person of Jesus Christ, who, in the words of the fifth-century Apostles' Creed, was conceived by the Holy Spirit, born of Mary, a Virgin, suffered and was crucified, and was buried. He then descended into Hell, rose again from the dead, and, after forty days, ascended in spirit and body into Heaven and is seated at the right hand of the Father, and He will come again to judge the living and dead.

Seeded in the Virgin Mary by the Holy Spirit, the third member of the Trinity, the Son, Jesus Christ, became God in flesh. He gave his life to ministering not just to the spirits of the people he met along his way but to their bodies as well. He made the deaf hear, the lame walk, and the blind see. He even resurrected the dead. In one instance, reported in Luke 8:33, Christ expelled the demons from a madman into a herd of pigs that ran off a cliff to their destruction.

Culminating his earthly ministry in the garden of Gethsemane the evening before his death, Christ *sweats blood* in fervent prayer. The following day for the sake of mankind's sins and the reopening of the gates of Heaven to His Creation, Christ allowed himself to be tortured, whipped, spit on, and nailed to a cross. His self-sacrifice opened Heaven to an individual's bodily resurrection and the communion of the living and dead.

The body, as the essence of being and the highest and irrevocable gift of a person, takes us to the heart of Judaism and Christianity. There can be no Covenant lest Abraham proves willing to sacrifice his long-awaited son, and there can be no eternal life and reunion unless Jesus Christ allows Himself to suffer and die on the Cross in order to renew and eternalize his new covenant. The church's major sacrament is Communion, the taking of the Eucharist and drinking of the wine, which are the body and blood of Christ through the Eucharist.

Christian communities grew up around the sacrament of Communion, the Eucharist, which duplicates Christ's invocation at the Last Supper to eat his body and drink his blood, which in the Latin mass proclaims, "Take and drink ye all, for this is the Chalice of My Blood of the New and Eternal Testament: The Mystery of Faith: which shall be shed for you and many unto the Remission of Sins."

The body and blood of Christ symbolize and embody his total sacrifice to God on behalf of man, and the consecration and partaking join man by faith and dedication of his life to the suffering of the Cross and the way of Christ to God. The sacrament of sacrifice forms a compact with God and believers that promises eternal resurrection and lasting among the heavenly body of believers and God's Grace.

This vision, which I do not elaborate on, is the antithesis of the contemporary views of body, individual, and self. The body becomes a vessel of all of God's Grace given and received from nature, among others, and through one's freedom. The body enters life with a God-given soul and the body, in realizations and ordeals, leads us to the boundless gifts of God as Creator and His Son as Savior. By faith, the body is the given form through which humanity lives in and beyond time.

As the Lord's body enters the body of the believer, the believer responds by giving themselves totally to God, which, in the first Christian prayer, the "Our Father," petitions "Thy will be done"—not mine. Paul envisions the *one* as *many* and the *many* as *one*. "For just as the body is one and has many members, and all the members of that one body are one body, so also it is with Christ. For by one Spirit we were all baptized into one body, whether we be Jews or Gentiles, be bond or free; and have been made all to drink into one Spirit. For the body is not one member but many," (1 Corinthians 12: 12–14).

Again, in 2 Corinthians 4:12, Paul encourages the faithful, his brothers and sisters in Christ, to take into account, no matter their plight, that they are not abandoned and destroyed, but they are in the body of the dying Jesus. "Constantly given up to death for the sake of Jesus so that the life of Jesus may be manifested in our mortal flesh. So, death is at work in us, but life in you."

As central to the faith and practice of the Old Testament, repentance, purgation, and self-sacrifice likewise stood at the center of Christian belief and ritual. Ever on their knees, lying supine, anointing themselves with the sign of the Cross, Christians prayed that they would find and follow the path of the Cross, which meant the renunciation and purification of the body for the salvation of the soul.

In this framework of faith's metaphors and church teaching, Christianity mixed customs, folklore, and superstitions and disciplined and chastened their bodies following Christ on his path to the Cross. They entered the Lenten season of the forty days of Christ's passion by being anointed by a cross of ashes on their forehead and vowing to limit their food, drink, and activities. Lenten abstention, which symbolically joined the hold of sin and winter's grip of darkness, births and anticipates the bright colors of the church, altar, and its liturgical Easter dress.

In the Middle Ages, Church authority translated the forgiveness of sin and granting of miracles with Lenten regimes of fasting, praying, donations, and pilgrimages of varying distances and types. Additionally, the prodding of authorities exhorted surplus and troublesome knights to undertake crusades to purge heretics and win back the Holy Land. Believers, themselves of mixed interests, passions, and characters, entered different monasteries and orders of the priesthood and sisterhood, requiring lives of obedience, poverty, and celibacy, and monastic lives of work, isolation, and solitude.

From its beginning, Christian saints and martyrs dedicated and gave up their lives for Christ, thus watering the Church as Christ did with his suffering and blood. The shedding of innocent blood established holy sites and evoked reverence while it formed pledges and unions throughout

secular cultures. Some Russian tsars, as elaborated by
Michael Cherniavsky in his *Tsar and People* (1961), were
declared holy not for the reason of dying a holy death but for
having simply been killed by violence.

THE CHURCH INCORPORATES US BODY AND SOUL

The corporeality of the early Church and Medieval theology,
manifest in the suffering and miracles of Christian saints,
disseminates itself through the mixed lens of ages, societies,
classes, and cultures. It forms the heart of the orthodoxy and
mediates man's relationship with God. As a young Catholic
in the 1940s, faith, Catechism, and the sacraments of
Confession and Communion put Christ's body as Eucharist
and His image at the center of my faith and formed a
view of my own body, which, by thought, will, and action, I
could either make myself holy and pleasing or sinful by my
freedom. I assumed, or better said, never doubted, that my
body was the meeting ground of the Holy Spirit, Grace, and
my own impulses, desires, corrections, and chastisements,
for it came with life, was the seat of my being, and integral to
my salvation or damnation.

For me, a Catholic and member of a sacramental and
symbolic faith, a church was a singularly imposing and
intimate place, with images that elicited a sense of mystery
and holiness, awe and transcendence. Sanctified and risen
bodies decorated church ceilings. A crucifix hung from the
ceiling over the altar and acknowledged the very presence
of Christ, Mary, and saints; believers genuflected, bowed,
and knelt in prayers while the clasped hands and mumbling
lips of women dressed in black prayed their rosaries. The
changing seasonal liturgical colors in covering cloths and
vestments declared the purple of six weeks of Lent's sorrow,
the white of joyous Easter Resurrection, and the red of
Pentecost's fiery revelatory tongues. Around both sides of
our church, there were the sculpted and etched Stations of
the Cross. The fourteen stations told the story of Christ's
final hours, from his condemnation to the painful and
humiliating steps of his suffering way, to his death on the

Cross, lying in a sepulcher and placed in a tomb. The center of the church, which upon approach called for a lowered head, a bent knee, and the sign of the Cross, was set off by a long Communion rail dressed in white, with stone stairs leading up to the Lord's table, on which, as we were taught in First Communion class, the Last Supper was reenacted with each Mass. On the table sat a golden tabernacle, behind whose doors and within whose curtains there was tucked a golden chalice that held the consecrated body and blood of Jesus Christ. The altar constituted the holiest of places and a center of time and being. Here earth and God, the sacred body of the Eucharist, and my body met in the present and forever.

Of course, at seven years old, I could not articulate this. I was not prepared in language or theologically for the meaning of taking Christ's body into me as his last earthly and eternal promise. Nevertheless, the preparation for the holy Mass and Communion gave me an elemental sense of my body as a whole and pure vessel, one with a soul, and carried with it the first sense of sin as self-contamination and damnation. I learned I could lose my soul when yielding to impulses and pleasures.

Preparing for my first Confession underlined Communion's gravity. I learned of my capacity to commit a mortal sin, a sin so grave which, unacknowledged and repented, would separate me from God and land me in Hell's torments forever. Among the most serious of sins would be to not confess or to lie about my mortal sins, which would have the effect of taking the Eucharist, Christ himself, into my impure and sinful self.

Preparations for Confession, which proceeded the Communion and the Eucharist, taught me that I was capable of mortal sin and the rejection of God. It introduced me to the examination of conscience, which brought awareness that little sins lead to big sins and that the roots of venial sin arose from bad impulses, wishes, habits, and acts. Though so young, I learned to examine myself by self-reflection and see the body as a source of temptations and sin.

My body was divided then. It could be felt as fresh, light, pure, and sanctified as God, his Grace and forgiveness could make it, or it could be as dark and heavily laden by sinful thoughts and acts. As thoughts and impulses passed in my head, I recognized the sacred, profane, sinful, and sanctified body.

The sign of the Cross became my self-blessing, my self-given entrance into life and prayer. It started and ended any serious act and introduced my prayers for meals, was made before an open casket, throughout the church, when passing a Catholic church on foot or in a car, and even as any thought or impulse that deserved thanks, glory, or forgiveness and purification crossed my mind. So, my body, a seeing eye and a vessel of thinking and doing, proved a kind of middle ground of good and bad, sacred and profane.

Communion, the partaking of the sacred, amounted to taking the elevating and saving body of Christ into me. The Christ of Heaven and Earth, Cross, Crypt, and Resurrection, was in the Eucharist. He was the Eucharist, the *good Grace*, to stress its Greek etymology. In Catechism, which was held once a week at church for we public school students, I was repeatedly drilled on the notion that our body can be purified and Graced or corrupted and damned by selfish desires, acts, and bad habits. I later learned, as I suppose all or almost all young people do, the confessional agony of admitting to someone else the telling of lies, swearing, and the sin of masturbation. In this way, theologically and personally, my body, both of God's creation and my power and responsibility, was a matter of unremitting self-reflective consciousness.

DEEPENING AND REFINING

Reading early church thought and medieval theology, coupled with the study and visit to English and French Romanesque and Gothic cathedrals, made them and the Middle Ages my symbolic and metaphoric earthly well of Heaven's forms. I incorporated their reaching ideas and architecture, with great glass windows, towers and roofs, and symmetries, into my thoughts and emotions. My Christian faith fused my

body and soul, faith and revelation, and creation and last
things. Christ's birth, death, and resurrection spoke with
icons and through rituals and sacraments. With its promise
of resurrection and communion, therein remained, to use my
favorite metaphor, the spring of springs.

Christianity centers on God, our Creator, whose care and
Providence work in and through our bodies. Differentiating it
from the Old Testament, Christianity centers on Christ, both
God and incarnate Son. Finally, the gifts of the Father, Son,
and Holy Spirit come not just to the soul and spirit but also
to the body and acts. Love and charity lead and accompany
us to eternity through the body and soul.

The body, thus, transcended and symbolically enhanced,
establishes our tie to God and the dead. The body is
generated of images, metaphors, prayers, and hopes that link
God's design, will, and ends. In Psalm 23, metaphor follows
metaphor, beginning with "The Lord is my Shepherd."

> He maketh me to lie down in green pastures.
> He leadeth me beside still waters. ...
> Though ... I walk through the valley of
>   the shadow of death...
> Thou preparest a table
>   before me in the presence of mine enemies
> Thou anointest my head with oil
>   my cup runneth over. ...
> I will dwell in the house of the Lord forever.

In his poem "Come Ye Disconsolate," Thomas More coaxes
those who languish,

> Here bring your wounded hearts, here tell
>   Your anguish.
> Earth has no sorrow that Heaven cannot cure. ...
> Here see the Bread of Life; see the waters
>   Flowing.

Of all earthly things linking work and nurturance, *bread* is the bridge, the metaphor that crosses in words and prayers between earthly substance needs and fulfilling heavenly gifts of Grace. The manna of Heaven spares and feeds us as we cross the wilderness during the long seasons of life. Transformed into Christ's body, the Eucharist opens the door to Heaven. The sanctified cup of wine, representing Christ's blood that circulates in us, becomes His passion and salvation.

CLEANING UP THE BODY, CIVILIZING THE SELF

Earthly well-being, power, and status opened other paths to happiness than those of transcendence through philosophy and religion. Royalty, aristocracy, and the highest ranks of the upper bourgeoisie of state and service made earthly life a pleasure and an end in itself as afforded by leisure, goods, luxury, style, association, individual taste, and subjectivity. They of the upper class found themselves with the means and in the settings for the cultivation of bodies, lives, and selves.

As I wrote in *On Foot*, which is the source of much of this section, the royalty, nobility, and the highest ranks of the bourgeoisie of governmental service and wealth, fashionably walked, danced, pranced, and rode their way into *the good life*.[53] With manners, fashion, good taste, and etiquette, or what the French called *civilité*, *politesse*, and *honnête*, they expanded the control of the body—how it appeared and moved, where and how it walked, promenaded, and danced. The body, and its appearance and movement, told the world of a young person's beauty, charm, grace, importance, and sexual powers, and, echoing what once was told of the old's underlying and enduring nobility, their composure and character.

Since beauty and manners are largely skin deep, gesture and clothing covered the inner self, which, for most, was more fragile and ambiguous than certain and confident. The steps toward elegance in Europe, as no doubt elsewhere in the world of elites, involved many human artifices. They included perfumes and make-up (powders) of one sort or another and wardrobes of ornate clothes, headdresses, canes, umbrellas, and—not least—footwear and apparel for riding, strolling, and being on display at the palace. Indeed, the slick slipper and the high leather riding boot defined the feminine and masculine poles of noble perfection.

Changing styles shaped and constricted the woman's body in a hundred ways. Conforming to taste, the graceful woman pinched her steps, altered her gate, drew in her stomach, and curved her shoulders back to realize the era's prescribed image of beauty at rest and motion and to accommodate the clothes she wore. Corsets, stomachers, crinolines, hoops, trailing skirts, rising embroidered collars, garters, gloves, fans, parasols, elaborate wigs, bonnets, and preposterous hats supporting exotic plumage or model ships, all played their part in giving birth to Venus and caused the goddess to walk with a stiff neck, stilted posture, and restricted walk. Not only did corsets, hoops, long-training dresses, and layers of skirts and petticoats weigh the elevated woman down, shorten her stride, and diminish her maneuverability, especially in the face of doors and entrances to sedan chairs, but they also offered proof that she was beyond manual work and that she, her husband or father, and the estate had servants to maintain space, monumentality, and beauty. An overview of French fashion from 1500 to the French Revolution shows how it placed walking, standing, and sitting women, and, for that matter, their escort, in stern bondage.

Footwear served nobility's ascendance. Literally elevating them above the mud and muck that engulfed contemporary country and city lives, upper-class women relied on pattens and clogs of one sort or another whose heels could lift them a foot or more off the ground. As late as the nineteenth century, these pattens and wood shoes sounded on city streets. At one point in *David Copperfield*, their sound returns Dicken's theater-struck protagonist to the reality of their surrounding "muddy, miserable world." Indoors, however, nobles dared not wear their loud and clumsy pattens, lest they track mud over shiny floors and be like the lower-class hobnailers, whose heavy, awkward shoes made their very name a synonym for a boorish and churlish individual.

With their shoes as important to the impression they created as the hat they doffed, the ringed hand they extended, or the parasol they carried, and, on formal occasions, as the ornate language they spoke, one put their best–heeled foot forward. The aristocrat and upper bourgeoisie's shoes carried their wearers on select, smooth, and crafted surfaces such as parquet floors and carefully combed estate trails— and rarely across the uneven lands and on the rough paths trod by the majority.

Conspicuous refinement and extravagant ornamentation ruled in the seventeenth century with the wearing of silk-soled shoes, mules with floral or silver embroidery, and silk ribbon latchet shoes with silver embroidery. Shoes were further refined in the eighteenth century with shaped heels, the use of buckles, and printed leather. And in a pinch, one could always speak of the exclusivity of one's shoemaker or, better yet, casually refer to one's very own private shoemaker. Inadvertently, they also testified to a simple fact: those with means were up and out of the mud and up and off rough surfaces. They went where their fancy shoes glided on smooth surfaces. The transformation of Cinderella's original leather shoes into glass slippers suggests how far polished and inlaid wood led the imagination to retreat from bumps, filth, rock, and stone. And even those noble officers, who rejected slippers in favor of big, black, shiny boots, did so to call attention to their higher and dashing calling in the service of the king and sword. Boots also declared ownership of a horse and stable and came with a servant to shine one's boots (which set one at the other end of the universe from a *boot lackey* and *bootlicker*).

The evolution of the stylized and *effeminate* cane (the British walking stick) revealed how increased travel by the upper urban classes generally found its way into a tamer environment on more negotiable surfaces. In aristocratic hands, the diminished and stylized cane—made of ebony or sturdy oak—still retained the lethal potential to strike humans or animals and replaced the taller, stronger, homemade country-traveling walking staff. The light bamboo cane first appeared around 1500. No doubt, a product attained by foreign trade, its development—including the use of ivory, ebony, and whalebone, as well as highly decorated and jeweled knob handles—depended on the increasingly regular surfaces of courts, gardens, and cities. Though still used to prop up the gouty arthritic rich or draw attention to a war wound, the cane—with rare decorative samples made even in glass—principally served as a clothing accessory. However, its hidden history reveals the cane could disguise a sword or, with the rise of street crime in the early nineteenth century, a gun. It could also provide pen and paper, conceal medicine, hide a needed drink, or serve the peregrinating walker in other ways.

The umbrella also underwent a transformation and, at points, came to double as a cane. Having disappeared in the Middles Ages, it reappeared in the sixteenth century in Italy, in the seventeenth century in France, and in the eighteenth century in the rest of Europe when it took the form of the fashionable, colorful parasol of the upper-class stroller and became an important dress accessory and lost any significant use as a club or stick. As a parasol that warded off harsh sunlight from fair skin, it remained a standard element of women's fashionable outdoor dress through the nineteenth century. An early symbol of heavenly sovereignty and a preserver of the fair lady, the shading parasol punctuated promenades with twirling and flirting colors.

When waterproofed in the late seventeenth and early eighteenth centuries, the umbrella developed a second utilitarian use for the walker: it would shield the walker's body and clothing from drenching rain. By 1800, this plebian cousin of the fashionable parasol became the common companion of all urban pedestrians to the consternation of London carriage drivers for whose views open and raised umbrellas blocked. Unfortunately for their aspiring owners, the umbrella offered prima facie evidence that its owner walked and, thus, lacked a carriage or means to hire one.

By the eighteenth century, French ways penetrated upper-class Western ways of walking and talking. The British upper classes proved themselves to be the most adept students and disseminators of the French way. Popularized among the nineteenth-century Victorian middle classes, English etiquette—shaped by French manners—was readily adopted by respectable folk throughout the British empire.

As the eighteenth century materially developed, those with means found and chose pleasant places to travel, ride, and stroll. Carriages and coaches had begun the integration of the city and countryside in the most prosperous and populous parts of Europe. Gardens, parks, city walls, and nearby riversides, forests, and villages all afforded a place for fancy and recreational footing. In this period, walking went from being a leisure activity of the aristocracy to a popular pursuit of the upper middle classes. Originally done in carriages (*Promenaden en Carosses*), promenading on foot grew in popularity. For instance, increasingly in Germany, men and women began to see their public strolls as a means to health, wholeness, and community. In this way, walking moved from indoors to outdoors, from tailored garden lanes to tree-lined avenues, from ramparts and city overlooks to the surrounding countryside. The German words revealingly *Spazieren* ("walking") and *Wandeln* ("wandering") remained synonyms until the 1830s, when walking in the city and hiking in the countryside, differentiated in fact, went their separate linguistic ways.

PUTTING WINGS ON YOUR FEET

No one better delivers us to the origins of romantic walking than eighteenth-century French writer and thinker Jean-Jacques Rousseau. Born into the working classes in 1712, much of his early life "was that of a wanderer, an adventurer, the life of a hero of a picaresque novel."[54] Viewing himself as a perpetual outsider even in his recognized but never prosperous years in Paris from the middle 1740s to 1750s, and plagued especially in the final decades with restlessness fed by a growing paranoia, Rousseau, never wealthy and with kidneys that did not tolerate the bounce of the carriage, was a determined and deliberate lifetime walker.

"Of all writers known to history," Will and Ariel Durant wrote, "he was the most devoted walker."[55] Rousseau acknowledged his indebtedness to walking. In his *The Confessions*, he declared his oft-quoted remark: "I can only meditate when I am walking. When I stop, I cease to think; my mind only works with my legs."[56]

Starting in the last decades of the eighteenth century and the first decades of the nineteenth century, Rousseau and his progeny and likes began a transformation in the sensibility of upper-class and literary Europe. With more leisure and a turn to self-cultivation and reflection, increasing numbers of educated individuals sought themselves, their inner selves, while out on foot. Walking afforded both inner solitude and communion with the countryside, nature, and the inner and hidden self.

Arising out of improved material circumstances and leisure gave the means to travel and a choice of places to go. More than a handful of the educated and privileged took to scouring the countryside and exotic locations. With a choice of what to see and do and where to walk, they made their pleasure an occasion to discover, *botanize*, and commune with nature and country people. It allowed these privileged county walkers to individualize and romanticize themselves. Bodies, with gestures, travel, and walking, confessed hearts and professed new ideals. When catering to individual choice and personal style, the stage was set for new poets whom we characterize as the children of Jean-Jacques Rousseau, as they dramatized their inner feelings as he had in his autobiographical *Confessions*. Against backgrounds of wind-blown land and seascapes and identifying with distant causes, ways, and dress, the romantic poet could confess with dress, face, and verse his courageous, sensitive, and torn self.

121

Walking was transformed for select elites as a path to a new self, art, and science. It validated the countryside as a fresh source of human feeling, knowledge, and experience. Fostered at the backs of gardens and along the edges of promenade grounds, Romanticism set hearts on more distant places. Associated with global exploration and the early nineteenth-century origins of folklore and anthropology, it allowed the rambler to embrace surrounding peoples, their customs, and beliefs. Romantic artists, as they took to the seaside and mountains, and followed early settlers to the west in the young United States, celebrated nature as beautiful, rich, and awe-inspiring.

WORDS ALONG THE WAY

Continuing to rely on my *On Foot*, in the 1770s, the Flintshire naturalist Thomas Pennant, Britain's first great tour guide, left the main-road travels to discover "the authentic natural-born Briton," the descendants of the earliest tribes that had survived "the onslaught of modern civilization."[57] Those bored by the Grand Tour could search for the real Britain on donkeys, ferryboats, and by foot and arrive at true adventures along the lakes, mountains, and precipices, experiencing encounters with the wild, the picturesque, and the awe-inspiring. By going on foot, they could enter the heart of enduring Scotland and Wales, where ancient lyrics and epics resonated. By walking, one swore his allegiance to the past. To be a true patriot, one went on foot.

English romantic poet William Wordsworth sealed his devotion to the country by walking incalculable miles in the Lake Region and Europe. Affirming his allegiance to place, step-by-step, verse-by-verse, he affirmed the local and rural character of England's true life.[58] Wordsworth's poetry formed the trailhead of a tradition of poetic pedestrianism that reaches from English Romanticism to the Americans, Whitman and Thoreau, to the Japanese poet Basho. Wordsworth's poetry disencumbered walkers of their polite and mannered selves. He substituted country freedom for courtly stricture and urban constriction. As aesthetic vagabondage, his walking was on a continuous pilgrimage. It set body, flesh, words, and hearts against the restricted gardens and parks and the emerging congested city. Wordsworth's poetry predated the transportation revolution by at least fifty years, which made fast and cheap travel available and, thus, stripped walking of its perennial claim to be one of life's necessities and assumed part of the poor and vagrants' way of life.[59] In *Walking, Literature, and English Culture*, Anne D. Wallace conceives the peripatetic as a response to the aesthetic problems generated by the transport revolution and enclosure. She argues that the improved speed and reduced cost of travel between 1750 and 1850 transformed the place of walking in society.[60] As Robin Jarvis shows in *Romantic Writing and Pedestrian Travel*,[61] her argument depends on predating the popular development of a transport revolution as articulated by Philip Bagwell in *Transport Revolution*.[62]

Reflective walkers offer written testimonies to the discovery of forgotten peoples, villages, and the epiphanies of nature. With a variety of projects and passions, they put themselves on the side of the wild, pristine, exceptional, and eccentric side of things. Such thinkers as the poet, scientist, botanist, naturalist, traveler, and writer Johann Wolfgang von Goethe (1749–1832), the continental explorer, geographer, and naturalist Alexander von Humboldt (1769–1859), the philosopher of history Georg Wilhelm Friedrich Hegel (1770–1831), and the American philosopher and traveler Ralph Waldo Emerson (1803–1882), sought what lies outside and beyond the French Enlightenment's quest for a rational and universal explanation through unique encounters and reflections.

As much as any romantic walker, the American thinker and naturalist Henry David Thoreau (1817–1862)—who was a keen reader of Wordsworth, Rousseau, Goethe, and Humboldt, and a student and friend of fellow Concord townsman, Emerson—stood in opposition to expanding Boston and the nation's rapidly spreading railroad. Across decades, he walked daily, exploring, collecting, botanizing, and writing as he crisscrossed Walden Woods, circumambulated Walden Pond, canoed rivers, and hiked Mount Kata while he suffered the path of hegemonic technological civilization. At the end of his life, dying of tuberculosis, Thoreau traveled to western Minnesota for a last glimpse of the West before it was consumed by national expansion.[63]

Diverse and conflicting in its impulses and forms, Romanticism outfitted the minds of nineteenth-century western walkers, especially hikers, mountain climbers, and countryside ramblers, with uplifting reasons for setting out on foot. With feeling, sentiment, passion, and nostalgia, romantic walkers could idealize their walks, rambles, and hikes as a means to have direct contact with nature, authentic natives, and the populace of urban streets or country lanes. As a sweeping cultural revolution that influenced the writing of history, literature, and philosophy, and the making of arts and fashions, Romanticism changed walking. It elevated it from being a lower-class necessity and a way of being to a select upper-class leisure activity and a means to experience nature, the world, and the self. The body became a vehicle for the mind's wishes.

These poetic pedestrians of the upper classes left off strolling in courts, squares, gardens, and places where promenading carriages assembled and took to walking alone or in small groups in out-of-the-way and even sublime places. In early generations as individuals, and in subsequent generations as groups of adventurous tourists in remote landscapes and forgotten places, Romanticism encouraged walkers to ramble and explore. For romantic natural scientists, walking was the best means to study the earth up close.

Casting themselves in opposition to the fixed and sedentary confines of the court and city, romantic walkers made going out on foot an act of repudiating those whose walking amounted to safe and routinized strolling and promenading. They used their rambling, hiking, exploring, and even mountain climbing as a means to encounter unique and uncharted landscapes and traditional peoples. Walking opened paths and won scenes and intuitions of transcendence for the mind and the self—its senses, feelings, and experiences—without reliance on formal religion and theology.

PATHWAYS FOR THE MANY TO INDIVIDUALITY

The great majority who were, in the course of the nineteenth and twentieth centuries, to become workers and citizens of national and democratic societies, and beneficiaries and masses of the urban, commercial, and industrial world, did not travel the pleasing and chosen paths that their aristocratic, wealthy, and elite predecessors had traveled. They moved across oceans on steamships and across continents on railroads. They followed the goods, means, and dreams that skirted mass production, transportation, and communication. They were invited by the doors of open immigration and the possibilities of work, money, and a place of their own. Their trails led onto paved surfaces, into worlds drained by sewers and offering running water, with public schools, health, and equality in market and polity.

With work and money in their pockets, a choice of multiplying goods, and increased safe and private spaces, they could be individuals with fates of their own making. With the exception in North America of the majority of children of slaves, Blacks, and Native Americans, and in Europe of certain ethnic and remote peoples, for the majority, this movement to self-consciousness and self-definition increased across generations. Freedom and independence came with choices about and improvements in how, where, and why one lived. These new citizens, workers, consumers, and individuals—in sum, modern selves—were youthful and optimistic. A common premise of their societal lives was: one's body was secure, free, and a matter of one's own care, indulgence, and pleasure.

For this revolution to occur and be sustained over decades and across generations, several other coinciding revolutionary transformations had to take place. The

Industrial Revolution concentrated populations and capital, astronomically accelerated production and commerce, and made money the source of profit, the medium of exchange, and the key to family savings and self-discipline. Clothes, the first product of the Industrial Revolution, meant not only a shirt on one's back but also a choice of style and identity. More than dressing the masses by class, sex, and age, the clothing industry used fashion to conjure dreams. Window shopping sold potential looks on streets, at home, on the beach, at play, and in the bedroom.

On smooth, clean, lit, and policed streets, the nineteenth-century West formulated public codes of dress, behavior, and cleanliness. By the end of the nineteenth century, cities began to furnish public toilets and urinals. As censuses recorded, ever more completely, the names and addresses of residents and citizens, so sectors of society prescribed and even required manners and dress. While certain public agencies had uniformed employees, and early department stores regulated their employees' dress and comportment, military service drilled its uniformed members to get in step. Increasingly, national and democratic societies taught yeses and noes of public movement and appearance, as twentieth-century society and cities wrote laws against public nuisances, and rural society divided its lands, controlled and drained water, fenced in animals, and battled weeds and unwanted plants.

Legislation, laws, and codes, as well as regulations of work, health, and sanitation, became a principal activity of the growing state. They determined behavior in civic places and increasingly turned society at large into one collective and regimented society. Increasingly, bare feet signaled poverty and backwardness. The loud clomping of wood shoes echoed the passing of backward *rustics* and ignorant *rubes*. Paved roads, sewer systems, sidewalks, and public transportation, although slow in coming and never arriving in large parts of the countryside, shaped traffic flow and imposed a certain order and direction to lines and "waiting for one's turn."

Stores were prohibited from turning road fronts into storage warehouses and salesrooms. Manure piles were carted out of town. Sewers, sanitation, and even public urinals and bathrooms, along with increased police, municipal waterworks, city lighting, and even traffic lights, brought new order and conformity to the civic body. As crowds learned to queue up in lines and respect the distance, senses, and sensibilities of those around them, politeness became a norm of being civilized.

By 1900, Western Europe and North America moved, marched, and were surveilled with a certain order and respect in contrast to the mudslinging and angry crowds of earlier centuries. By the mid-twentieth century, with running water in homes and apartments, citizens increasingly became polite, clean, and even respectable. Spitting was prohibited. Common decency required underclothing, muffling one's farts and burps, carrying a handkerchief, and not blowing one's nose in one's hand. All that, and a dozen other bodily non-conformities and indiscretions, were judged at home, in schools, on streets, and buses as *pee-YOO, gross,* foul—impolite.

Bodies of citizens were increasingly counted on as a measure of national strength, source of labor, and consumer of goods. Taking up the work of religious and private charities, modern governments cleaned and straightened up their people with prisons, hospitals, poor houses, and asylums. Nations praised those and the families of those it called to service and venerated and commemorated those that had served and sacrificed themselves for the *sacred national body*, contending there was no greater love than that of the wounded and killed in service of the nation.

The First and Second World Wars called nations to sacrifice bodies by the millions and stacked-up bones in great, great numbers. Patriotism filled military cemeteries at home and abroad and left generations empty of all but tears and sorrowful memories. From the wars of the nineteenth and twentieth centuries, new orders of national saints arose and created sacred sites of war battles and left-over burials.

The war dead became the polar star of patriotism. No sacrifice was held greater than theirs, as I wrote in this poem about the Somme, one of the great battlefields of the great First World War in northern France.

THE SUM OF THE SOMME
ANOTHER CENTURY'S GETHSEMANE

1. A Cemetery
In a cemetery in Picardy,
Airy words float adrift.
"Their Names Live for Evermore!"
"Their Glory Shall Not Be Blotted Out!"
"To Live in Hearts
We Leave Behind
Is Not to Die.
Good Night,
Daddy."

This cemetery
Holds yet more chaste stones,
"A Soldier of the Great War,"
"A Lancashire Fusilier."
"Known to be Buried here."
"Thought to be Buried here."

2. The Somme
A battlefield in the great bend of time,
A mere season's pull of oars
Along a river
Through a hilly landscape
Populated with towns like
Ginchy, Guillemont, and Vimy,
Where the Canadians burrowed, tunneled, and battled
Below torn, shredded, but sheltering earth.
And then there was Delville Woods,
Where on July 14 South African troops went out
3,000 strong
And returned on July 20
At 140.

3. Counting the Past Dead

Invite the living to conjure the past,
Tell them about messages sent by
Pigeons, drums, telephones, signal flags, and telegraph.
Help them imagine No Man's Land.
Chew every metaphor into mind's cud.

But see now in the fields
That cows graze around stone crosses,
The mounds of sugar beets heap up at the end of once
  blood-bitter fields.
Listen to the whine of power mowers cutting memory
  lanes among grass-covered knobs and knolls,
And do not be too harsh with yourself
For your flitting, speeding empathy.

Remember that, like a great nervous shutter,
The mind's eye opens and closes with a blink.
It is hard to stay awake counting the fallen sheep
Of another century's Gethsemane.

As announced by the First World War, the twentieth century incorporated bodies, spirits, and lives by the millions into national needs, drafts, and official rolls of the dead and heroic. In war, the good of the nation depended on the bodies of the nation and prevailed over individual minds and consciences, and a community's traditions and loyalties.

Twentieth-century totalitarian regimes, ever on a war footing at home and abroad, dealt with bodies in mass as deployable and disposable. They carried out their *censuses* in terms of class and race, ethnicity and nationality. Nazi Germany judged the Jews as filthy, impure, corrupt, and subversive. Soviet Russia defined, depicted, and treated the enemy as the exploiting capitalist and decadent and individualistic bourgeois. Defining the antithesis of the unwanted, Nazi, Soviet, and Fascist poster art of the 1930s projected a new social order of vibrant and youthful health.

Totalitarianism enacted the state's control of its people as one body and mind. It married marching and thinking, state and people, communities and values. It opposed the transcendence of religion and constitutional and traditional rights that inhibited the state's will. It battled all forces of market and culture that rested on freedom of movement, thought, and conscience.

Even though totalitarianism did not prevail in the Second World War, all contemporary states, democratic or not, have come to use government, laws, and bureaucracies to direct their people in mass during peace and war. In varying degrees, all public plans, ideals, and ideologies are predicated and hinge on directing and subjugating citizens' bodies and minds.

No doubt, this is the increasing cost of collective progress. Industry, market, and government, each in their own way, make us one. In great measure, contemporary medicine, public health, and legislation call for uniformity. Individual rights of freedom, choice, privacy, and intimacy cannot suspend the laws of the market and government. Materialism and secularism, too, have their insistence on a common way. Only on *wax wings* can individual citizens fly free of engulfing society, technology, economy, and state. The shared premise of new times is "we are in this together, body and soul, Heaven and Hell, now and hereafter. We are of our own making."

CHAPTER 8
THE BODY IS OUR FATE

The body with the mind makes us a multifaced being in a multifaceted world composed of many other bodies, things, places, situations, experiences, thoughts, beliefs, and wishes. Our interactions and communications with the self and the world are multiple, I dare say infinite, for we are a set of surfaces amidst a world of surfaces, a body, which is a multitude of bodies within a world of bodies, and a mind of many minds and ways.

We encounter the world with our body, senses, feelings, and images, so the world enters us with sights, touches, sounds, smells, tastes, solids, and emotions that arrive with immediacy, familiarity, and sheer surprise, evoking sensations, feelings, moods, thoughts, questions, reflections, needs, wants, and wishes. We go out into the world with our bodies and mind, and the world enters us with its elements and things, animate and inanimate, plant, animal, and human, and things dead and alive. In this way, we, individually and collectively, become our experiences of worlds and selves.

Our ongoing conversations pour through our skin and flow through our senses, though far from uniformly, clearly, and even understandably. Our own body and the bodies of others arrive with bumps and caresses, inviting and warning, pleasurably and painfully, blatantly, subtly and ambiguously mixed. Our first outdoor hikes bring new and different encounters with the freshwater springs, edible wild berries, as well as thorns, prickers, burrs, and mosquitos that pierce our skin. I remember the terror of my first encounter with an insect called a "walking stick." It clung to my arm, moved, and was alive!

Bodies, the self, and the world are in a reciprocal state, as explained in the preceding chapter. Our bodies make the paths we travel and the places we settle and dwell. This makes our lives and selves. As we will see in the following chapters, humans, over great stretches of time and with considerable variation by periods and places, turn things into tools and, ultimately, machines that make and remake environments.

Indeed, our bodies, in contact with other bodies, have an infinite and ongoing history. This history reaches from our deepest biological roots to transcend our most ethereal and abstract thoughts, from our recent global expansion and dominance of resources and energy to the increasing control of minds and societies.

This history is revolutionary for the body and mind, the self and world. The differences between a woman's and a man's body define the poles of feelings, thoughts, cultures, and our very senses of awe, terror, and beauty. As the woman's body can suggest birth, sharing, sustenance, nourishment, and the sacred temple of life, so the man's body expresses strength, will, autonomy, and purpose. Earliest cities and civilizations made the body the metaphor of first sources, whereas, in our modern democratic, commercial, and industrial times, bodies are collectivized in images and representation for the sake of mass communications, advertisements, ideologies, and propaganda. At the same time, the body and the self are increasingly collectively, individually, politically, and aesthetically manipulated, elevated, and even venerated.

The body, as we noted in the conclusion to Chapter Six, is equated to the individual as belonging to a unique, independent, and free person with spirit, rights, choices, and goods. Entire majorities of nations are ideologically caped by public weal, constitutionally endowed with rights, and made the primary object of commerce, medicine, and psychology. With the boost of popular literature, fashion, style, sport, photography, and the movie screen, individuals identify with the self through the body's claim to privacy, intimacy, and identity, along with an expectation of security, comfort, abundance, and choice.

BODIES AND SELVES IN SOCIETY AND HISTORY

From the earliest times, people incorporated themselves into daily life through the bodies of groups. By belief and rite, myth, culture, and religion joined the living and dead in one body, which was recognized as such by the earth, elements, seasons, and gods.

Societies of multiple groups defined their members more abstractly by cultures, laws, roles, crafts, and wealth as wholes and parts of society. Ringing themselves with walls and official religions, they set down principles and laws for the self and corporate control, ownership, fairness, and exchange, commonly reserving the highest praise for warriors who risked and sacrificed themselves for the body and life of society.

Tradition, the law, education, bureaucracy, armies, and ideologies molded or at least sought to unify society and its members into a single body of the same mind, words, and heart. Monarchy and royalty elevated the body to a sacral sphere. To paraphrase Kantorovich's *The King's Two Bodies* (1957), the sovereignty and transcendent political good radiated from the king's body in the late Middle Ages, which was derived from Christian theology's idealization and veneration of the body of Christ as human and divine. The Middle Ages incorporated the sacred body, the *Corpus Christie*, into the Eucharist, the first sacrament and highest ritual in the New Testament.

As society differentiated itself militarily, politically, and religiously, select individuals grew in power and prestige. Their positions registered recognition. They sat at bigger and higher tables and fed more people at their castles. Their entitlements registered on their estates, lands, and the number of serfs, and villages they controlled. Court bards sang their lords' deeds and glory.

The idealized queen and courtly woman was made the pinnacle of grace, a temple of beauty. Poeticized, she was the true jewel of the court. Her body showered the court with grace and light. She merited the knights' greatest act of heroism and the court troubadours' best verse and song.

The labors and bondage of one's serf redounded to one's status and assured leisure, and a life of choice—one free of repetitious and tiresome necessity. With traditions, laws, institutions, and religions assigned higher obligations, lords and ladies by station, dress, and refined life became one another's companions in presence and action, taste, behavior, manner, and conscience.

Starting in the high Middle Ages and spreading in the Renaissance and Reformation, members of city-state, and princely and territorial politics lived the higher life. Philosophy, realistic art, and science secularized body and life—or more precisely defined, differentiated, transformed, and idealized the body, exteriorly and interiorly, and its movements, functions, intricacies, development, and evolution. With great concern for line, light, and color, the Renaissance, while still moved by Biblical and theological motifs, offered a new page of graphic realism with the depicting line, detailed sculpting, and studied anatomy, which some, like Leonardo da Vinci, based on the careful dissection of cadavers, or like Rembrandt, expressed with sculpted life-size and giant idealized bodies.

Across the Renaissance and early modern Europe, the political polity as sacred, holy, and authoritative displaced the king's body. Secularism increased across seventeenth and eighteenth-century Europe into what R. R. Palmer called *The Age of Democratic Revolutions*[64] moved by the Enlightenment's belief in rationality and law, increased by the centralized administrative state, and strengthened by national competition and censuses of peoples and territories. Ideology, enhanced political and technological powers, and improved well-being and goods spread the belief that the body and soul of the world were for progressive human making.

Aristocratic cultures, which were built on family, deeds, possessions, and even proximity to royalty, beaconed an enviable superiority born of access to goods, leisure, luxury, and space. They radiated their members' bodies in dress and goods. Outdoors, they framed themselves in carriages, gardens, and parks. Indoors, they positioned themselves on estates and filled their rooms with rugs, metals, furniture, and mirrors for self-reflection and self-projection. They did the same with the portraits they hung. In them, they posed, men in their way and women in theirs, standing straight and tall, sitting behind pianofortes, resting on divans, strumming a guitar, or holding a lap dog. From their elevated porches, they surveyed manicured lawns and gardens with ponds and statuary. They strolled on even surfaces and rode on smoothed roads. In dance, etiquette, and all modish things, they showed their stature and stood their ground with body gestures, movements, and well-chosen words. They were superior.

In the closing decades of the eighteenth century and the beginning decades of the nineteenth century, the commercial and industrial revolutions overwhelmed the aristocracy and upper bourgeoisie with tides of the new middle class. Dwellings with furniture, goods, and beds, along with money, education, newspapers, and citizenship, became within the generation's reach. Work yielded cash and afforded individual and public advancement. As innovations and goods spread across the European continent and the cities of the world in the first half of the nineteenth century, the middle class began to shop the windows of new arcades for fresh and stylish clothes and goods.

The public eye of imitation, want, and achievement became a many-eyed Argos. The first lens of this attention-seeking eye was none other than Napoleon. Though short of stature and of common birth, he sired an unmatched individuality won not by blood but made by deeds on the public stage. In contrast to status and inheritance, fame on the public stage won an enduring halo of glory. Office, money, business, manufacturing, and accumulations also won attention. The writing of literature offered another select door to earthly immortality. Working from the inside out, Romantics made a profession of their hearts, their suffering, and simply their dress and stylized gestures as bids for distinguishing notoriety.

THE TRANSFORMATION OF THE
BODY AND MIND OF THE MANY

The fullness of the revolutionary transformation of body
and mind lay in freeing many from the imprisonment of
muck and mortality. The majority had come to believe that
they, too, would be free of place and bondage, dirt, scarcity,
and the daily threat of disease and death. Or, the majority
had to believe that they, too, could join the world of having
things, comfort, independence, opportunities, and respect. In
tracing their path to becoming modern citizens, we learn the
stories of our grandparents', great-grandparents', or parents'
boldness in migration, pride in work, and belief in their
own struggle. We also learn of the rewards earned by their
progeny as they purchased the family's first home, received
an education, were, at least on Sunday, clean, neat, well
dressed, and wore a second pair of shoes—all in all, appeared
as a respected person with a private, intimate, and chosen
life of their own.

Their path to becoming the new majority of a mass
democratic society, which I wrote about in *Everyday Life*
and draw on here for the next several pages, reveals the
historical genesis of the modern individual, liberated body,
and independent spirit.[65]

At ground zero are the peasants, who lived under the
sway of the curvature of the law of Malthus, which contends
that population increases geometrically (2, 4, 8) while food
supply increases only arithmetically (1, 2, 3, 4). Across a
lifetime, the majority lived by toil, obligation, and bondage
to their landlord and the seasons. The condition of their
everyday life in the not-too-distant past tests the imagination
of the contemporary historian who eats cake while the world
he studied suffered obtaining its daily bread. The peasant
world teetered on the year's grain yield, for it meant food for
today and seed for tomorrow. In good times, French peasants
would respond to an inquiry about how they fared by saying,
J'ai du pain ("I've got bread!"). In bad times, peasants made
bark and moss bread, dug up roots, hunted nuts, and ate
birds, rats, and insects. With their survival measured by what

they ate and could scrounge, the smallest things could sway lives and fortune, especially during famines, which stalked European peasants until the nineteenth century. The potato came as a savior crop to northern Europeans but could betray those who depended on it, as happened strikingly to the Irish with the four-year Irish Potato Famine, also known as the Great Hunger, that began in 1845.

Peasants who lost their place on the land, be it to increasing populations, the penetration of the cash economy, or disease, scarcity, and famine, became wanderers. They scavenged the countryside for food, migrated to nearby lands, sought refuge in the woods, and flocked to the cities where they lived under bridges, in piles of straw, or even in manure heaps. Beggars in tattered rags were everywhere—at the door, outside churches, in the marketplace—and come bad times, they died like flies. Although their macrocosm, fleshed in by the Church, magic, and the most ancient metaphors and fantasies, reached the stars, peasants' lives and hopes revolved around small things. Without photographs or heirloom objects, medieval people saved fingernail clippings and locks of hair from the head of a deceased family patriarch in hopes of preserving the *Domus'* good fortune.

In *The Silhouette of a Civilization*, twentieth-century French historian Lucien Febvre wrote, "Concrete man, living man, man in flesh and blood living in the sixteenth century and modern man do not much resemble each other. He was a countryman, a rustic; in all this we are far from him."[66] Modern leisure, abundance, choices, and sensitivities were as alien as could be to the rustic caught up in "a perpetual combat to be waged against man, the seasons, and hostile and ill-controlled nature."[67] He knew life to be precarious. "The very things which are nearest and dearest to us today—home, hearth, wife, and children—seem to have been regarded by the man of the sixteenth century as merely transitory goods, which he was always prepared to renounce."[68]

The Medieval European peasants lived mired in muck. Even the medieval city, according to Febvre, wallowed in mud: "The sunken road leading to the gate was muddy. Past the gate, the street widened as it followed the capricious route of a filthy stream that alongside the street and was fed by rivulets of liquid manure seeping from nearby manure heaps. It was a muddy slough in the rain in which urchins, ducks, chickens, and dogs, even pigs, in spite of repeated edicts to control them, all wallowed together."[69]

Only a small part of the population knew leisure. Travel was for all, as it etymologically reveals, a matter of travail including likely dangers and one-way finality. Goodbyes were taken to be once and for all.

Houses, if they were not cottages, shacks, huts, or caves, were composed of few rooms, often two—one as an attic room and one as a backroom which wintered the animals and helped heat the dwellings and forced individuals to live elbow to elbow and hip to hip. As in ancient and primitive times, the hearth (later the oven, stove, or furnace) commanded the house and made the gathering of wood the first of the chores.

There was minimal space for privacy for all except parents, while children slept several to a bed. Aside from a kitchen table at which the wife rarely sat for a meal, a bench, and, just possibly, a chair, furniture of any sort was scarce. People leaned against walls and trees or sat on their haunches. Their dwellings were devoid of rugs, chests, religious keepsakes, or any sort of art. They rarely saw, touched, knew, or imagined a world of fine and intricately crafted things.

Privacy in homes and villages was scarce. Intimacy proved unknown. Conditions suppressed tenderness and care; circumstances fostered harshness and indifference. Misery, hurts, hunger, illnesses, accidents, and death tramped emotional claims and individual rights. Little counseled individual feelings and happiness.

Outside their dwelling, peasants did not find individuality or privacy. Communities were small, and though each historian must run his or her own calculations for a place and time, most medieval and early modern communities numbered fewer than two hundred inhabitants. Communities frequently stood across the river from each other, and a few, perhaps only a handful, made their recreation by cursing, signing, and mooning their cross-river rivals.

Everybody's affairs belonged to everyone else. Families, headed by patriarchs, commanded the order of necessity, while lords and landlords ruled the landscape. Fortunes distinguished, suspicions scrutinized. Little could be disguised in a village of fifty souls, and whatever good came someone's way was subject to jealousy and envy. A blanket of superstition covered wishes and fears. Anything could happen to one's body by an accidental fall, the crush of work, the blow of another, or the whisk of spirit.

Magic furnished diagnosis and, along with home cures, served therapy. No end of proverbs and folk stories reveal legions of invisible helpers. The devil, too, supposedly, had many nearby abodes and workshops. While demons and troublemakers messed up, saints answered prayers of all kinds. Grace made bread, and the devil, some explained, shat on it.

In this world, women were reduced to being *une machine aux enfantement* ("a baby-making machine"), and children were often too plentiful in number to be sheltered and fed. A mother's touch healed only so much, and infants and children died in large numbers; those who didn't die were drafted at an early age, even as early as four, for work and had no hallowed childhood. Necessity spared nobody. Women and men were meant for reproduction and work. The mother, truly the heart of the family, was scrutinized for disloyalty; and the village examined the father for flaws of laziness, stupidity, and faults of character.

Friendships were rare and not long-lasting. Friends had few gifts to give and neither private space nor time to share themselves. Relations, whatever they were, were vulnerable to and broken by death in this world of finite things and scarce advantages. To lose a mate, as it remains today, was to suffer the loss of one's companion.

Getting old instructed all in their expendability. Survival for the old meant keeping one's place on the land and in the family, and this determined all else. The old knew that to lose their ability to work and their grip on things made them vulnerable to starvation and a last trip to the woods.

The glance, rub and touch of another body, and romance, were lifetime magnets in the world of yesterday. Infatuation and dreams belonged, at most, to youth for a year or two in a lifetime, if at all. The poorest knew that their children married out of chance or necessity or possibly through a pure heart, but that almost never gave any long-term advantage. All parents knew and dreaded that when marriage was left to their children, much was risked. After all, to cite an old French proverb, "A good-looking face is a fool's mirror!"—and youth was ever prone to choose appearance over strength, health, and an earnest heart. Love's infatuation forsook cunning about wealth. When calculated, marriage counted such important goods as a new set of clothes, bedding, a good animal or two, or even a little money to procure a good match.

The poorest, who were many, barely clung to their place in society. Like my Sicilian great-grandparents, they were the in two lines of a poem I wrote about my Rosalia and Antonino, ". . .were without land for tillage /and a donkey for the mortgage." In traditional society, almost all were without place, means, and money. Beggars were everywhere—at doors, in the market, at the top of the stairs of a church, and at the crossroads where bandits lurked and beggars, lepers, and the abandoned gathered. As cities grew, so too did the crowds of the homeless and insane. Whores, thieves, drunks, and bandits made the night dangerous. Punishment and hangings provided entertainment. Their expulsion was the regular civil broom, while the Church's charity, showing the other side of the human hand, welcomed orphans, the sick, and the insane into its care. In bad times, hungry people envied their fed pigs and successfully scrounging dogs; and in the worst of times, they ate bark and rats and dreamed about cannibalism to assuage their hunger.

Peasant and folk tales reveal a harsh world. This world was not invented by subconscious fears and desires but learned from everyday experience. In the early nineteenth century, the Brothers Grimm collected folk tales that were truly "grim." Hunger, poverty, death, danger, fear, and chance lurked all around. "There are," according to the historian of France, Eugen Weber, "many orphans; there are wicked stepmothers, stepsisters, and mothers-in-law; there are poor children who have to go out into the world; there are forests inhabited by woodcutters and charcoal burners but also wild animals and outlaws and frightening spirits—forests that provide a refuge, but whose darkness breathes dangers, where it was easy to lose one's way or to run into trouble."[70]

In the words of historian Robert Darnton, folk tales voiced a Malthusian world:

> Most Frenchmen lived in or near a state of chronic malnutrition and offered little resistance when plague and famine sliced through the population. Of every ten babies born, two or three died before their first birthday, and four or five died before the age of ten. Marriages usually lasted only about fifteen years, terminated by early death rather than divorce. The old regime was a society of widows and orphans, of evil stepmothers, and innocent Cinderellas.[71]

Folk tales left out the closing line of "happy ever after." Certainly, happiness could not be enacted in a village or family except on the occasion of feasting. Everyday life essentially lacked a personal and intimate side. Again, to rely on Weber, it was a world opposite our own and the ones of which we dream.

These stories are full of greed, envy, and exploitation: stepmothers are terrible, of course, and stepsisters are awful, but you cannot really trust your friends either or your spouse. Husbands beat their wives or condemn them to horrid ends, wives betray husbands, and blood relations are no better: it is brother against brother, sister against sister, and parents against their children.[72]

Piero Camporesi, the Italian historian of literature and anthropology, puts readers in the gut of the past. He probes the biological condition of everyday life with references to bugs, itches, scratches, diarrhea, maladies, and warming piles of manure. Placing his work at the opposite pole of commanding ideas and high metaphors or the predictable rhythms and movements of peoples and classes across time, he directs us towards minute things and biological conditions that go with having a body and being human. His narrative turns on anecdotes about a time before indoor water and light and public sanitation and health.

Camporesi writes of peasants:

> [They were] dirty, almost always barefooted, legs ulcerated, varicose and scarred, badly protected by meager and monotonous diets, living in humid and badly ventilated hovels, in continuous, promiscuous contact with pigs and goats, obstinate in their beliefs, with dung heaps beneath their windows, their clothes coarse, inadequate, and rarely washed, parasites spread everywhere—on their skin, in their hair, and in their beds—their crockery scarce or nonexistent, often attacked by boils, herpes, eczema, scabies, pustules, food poisoning from the flesh of diseased animals, malignant fevers, pneumonia, epidemic [cases of] flu, malarial fevers . . . lethal diarrhea (not to mention the great epidemics, the diseases of vitamin deficiency like scurvy and pellagra, the convulsive fits so frequent in the past [of] epilepsy, suicidal manias, and endemic cretinism).[73]

Hunger was real, remembered, and feared, goading and even driving peasants from youth to the grave. Hunger kept them working and living in dirt and dust well into the eighteenth century, making life for the majority, as Camporesi comments, "the antechamber of death."[74]

Peasants did not doubt that they were members of the biological kingdom. Mites, lice, ticks, fleas, and mosquitoes

142

had their sting and bite, and all made human beings their food and spawning grounds. A southern Italian peasant of the twentieth century described the peasant's community as full of small and hurting things when he said, "We peasants are poor earthworms; we live with the animals, eat with them, talk to them, and smell like them. Therefore, we are a great deal like them."[75]

The French historian and prominent member of the third generation of the Annales School, Emmanuel Le Roy Ladurie, encouraged historians of daily life to examine sixteenth-century skin and its diseases. The conditions included "the itch, ringworm, scabies, leprosy, St. Anthony's Fire, and St. Martial's Fire." Even peasant insults and curses referred to "scrofula, fistulas of the thigh, ulcers, and abscesses." "Villagers," he shared, with "a new order of intimacy, much like that of chimpanzees and other monkeys, carried around with them a whole fauna of fleas and lice. Not only did they scratch themselves, but friends and relations from all levels in the social scale deloused one another. (The mistress deloused her lover, the servant her master, the daughter her mother.)"[76] The thumb was called the "louse-killer" (*tue-poux*).

Most simply, "peasants were dusty, dirty, smelly, and near or in the manure pile. They were fodder for bugs and vermin. They belonged to a world of small, nasty, and invisible things."[77] They lived in a world without the intimacy of space, private things, delicate flesh, or the possession of delicate feelings, cultivated affections, and conditions and rituals to celebrate nudity and sexuality. Love was not uttered in poetry. To our refined spoiled eyes and our touch, nose, and sensibilities, the peasant was a rough, injured, broken, bent, and prematurely-aged creature.

Peasants lived intimately with the smallest living creatures—bugs, spiders, and worms. Peasants knew dust and dirt. Worms occupied their fly-covered compost piles, maggots generated in rotting meat, cockroaches were born from scraps of food that fell to the floor, and mice sprang out of dirty boxes left in undisturbed darkness. And they knew throughout their days that they belonged to the kingdom of dust to which they would return. It accompanied them on their skin, in their clothing, throughout their fields, and within their houses; it was the smallest and finest thing they saw.

Peasants grasped intuitively at what contemporary people strain to imagine: the eternal cycle of all living things. It made sense to them that God used spit and earth to make humans—after all, what else was available? And they had no doubt that they, along with mighty monarchs, made good food for worms.

With brooms, shovels, taboos, and rituals, they struggled against contamination and pollution. With elevating conceptions, they made themselves a superior order of souls and spirits to transcend the body and biology that dragged them down into darkness. If culture were to do anything, it would be to insist that humans were not just the dust-grovelers, dirt-eaters, excrement-makers, and shit-kickers they knew themselves to be. It would allow men and women to think—believe, hope—that they were, somehow, more than beings to be cautioned by the Church's stern Lenten warning: *Memento, homo, quia pulvis es, et in pulverem reverteris* ("Remember, man, you are of dust, and to dust you will return").[78]

These peasants continued to occupy the villages, towns, and cities of the nineteenth and even early twentieth-century western worlds. They surely occupied a place in everyday life up to 1900 and possibly until the First World War. The majority of pedestrians in Paris, witnesses testify, continued to appeared and smell as they did when they first arrived in town. They didn't bathe or change their clothes regularly. Nor did they brush their teeth or visit a dentist. They did not live in the blush of a new opportunity or thing.

In those days, when fashionable people had taken to wearing white shoes, the majority wore their only pair of worn brown or black shoes. As barefoot children still enviously peered through shiny, glass shop windows, workers and newly arrived immigrants from the countryside still trudged their way through Paris without a *sou pour le Métro* ("a penny for the subway").

In the city, the majority were still deprived of space and things. They inhabited small, damp quarters without access to running water and indoor toilets. (Even hospitals did not have an abundant supply of running water, and Paris' richest people, who had indoor toilets, did not have bathrooms and had only a single tap of running water on each floor. Many streets still remained without sewers. "By 1903, only one Parisian house in ten was connected to the [sewer] system."[79] Also, to be noted, until the turn of the century, European and North American city streets still belonged to horses and drays (low, heavy carts without sides). One of their many uses was hauling the city's tons of *horse manure* to nearby suburban farms and market gardens.

In the countryside, the walking speed of man, that bipedal beast, measured out in steps the distances between home and field, village and neighboring villages and market. For much of rural France, where in 1891, two-thirds of the population still lived in small rural parishes of fewer than 5,000 inhabitants, adjacent provinces were as remote and mysterious as other continents. In contrast to the quick-footed, scurrying, and unencumbered city pedestrian, their country cousins were peasants who trudged the land as their ancestors had, weighed down by tools and materials for and from their fields. Walking and working the land still constituted the duty of being alive.

Everyday life in the countryside remained precisely what it had been for centuries. Streets there were often unpaved, barely lit, narrow, and winding. There was only, if that, a short walk to promenade and a small square where a newly formed local band—commonly, a military band—might play on Sundays. There were few stores and minimal social interaction between classes. Only market day interjected a sign of life into what seemed static, impoverished, and misery-producing towns.

VILLAGE AND OLD WAYS ABIDED IN BONES AND HEARTS

Rural ways remained in the countryside and in the minds and hearts of immigrants to towns and cities. Surviving, though tattered, traditional cultures remained alive in isolated regions and small groups well into the twentieth century. They furnished complete moral and practical maps for being in and having a body. As much as traditional peoples were individualized by their own bodies, their bodies still belonged to the beliefs, precepts, and even spirits of myth, religion, and culture. Their reality was not divided and segmented by specialists, class, politics, and ideologues who came with a city, gathering commerce and political, cultural, and educational centralization. Many still saw the self and community as connected in life and spirit.

Material abundance, personal space, and public standing fostered individuality with the growth of privacy and intimacy. In small, closed, and relatively static traditional communities, all hunted the same forest, worked similar fields, drank from the same spring, walked the same path, ate the same meal, and were exposed to the same weather and events. They knew one another with daily familiarity. They knew one another by size, traits, injuries, and aging, as well as speech, gesturing, and clothes. Bodies often won nicknames and became last names, such as the Italian name *Gambino*, "little leg."

THE BODY AS REFINED AND ELEVATED, GLORIFIED AND STUDIED

Of course, the body is the first way to know, represent, identify, and glorify ourselves as types of people and individual persons. We can touch the body, dress it, declare, and mask it. As perennially true of humans and animals, the body is what is recognized, cared for, and put forth.

Religions, the arts, and sciences affirmed the body. They studied, defined, and idealized it. They recognized its movements, functions, intricacies, development, and evolution. The Middle Ages incorporated the body into its rituals and sanctity and its metaphors, symbols, rituals, and theology. The body gives life and vitality to the peoples of the Old and New Testaments. The books spoke and taught God's words.

With great concern for line, light, and color, the Renaissance, while still moved by Biblical and theological motifs, offered a new page of graphic accuracy and realism with the depicting line, detailed sculpting, and even detailed anatomy of the body.

Court and city life made the body a matter of public appearance and identity. Aristocrats, burgers, and craftspeople adopted a defining dress. Metaphorically and often literally, they were associated with bigger buildings and higher staircases. Off the street, they acted themselves out in more spacious, elevated, and decorated spaces. Even when dead, they commanded more respect for their bodies with tombs and statuary that would speak to the ages of their stature and deeds.

As early high European society differentiated itself militarily, politically, religiously, and aesthetically with painting, sculpture, and public and private architecture, its members made shows of themselves, places, and goods. They insisted on recognition. They sat in carved and ornate chairs and at bigger and higher tables in castles, estates, lands, villages, and farms. In all ways, they were unlike peasants who were jammed into cottages and huts with one or two rooms and who felt blessed with a stove, table, bed, a nearby well and garden, and a cow and pig.

The commercial and industrial revolutions of the late eighteenth and nineteenth centuries swept away the cultural dominance of aristocratic and upper-middle-class life exclusivity. As innovations and goods spread across the European continent and the cities of the world in the first half of the nineteenth century, so, individuals in growing numbers walked in the new arcades and were drawn to streets that invited window shoppers to graze and gaze at what they could have and dream of having. To an increasing multitude of consumers, better dwellings and more property, furniture, goods, and beds became accessible. This revolution of industry, commerce, wealth, and wages brought respect, leisure, and dreams to the new majority, creating an individuality rooted in senses of choice, privacy, and intimacy. It advertised and made many with the slightest means potentially special and loving beings. Bodies were treated, elevated, and idealized as wholesome and healthy, attractive and athletic. Bodies became the commercialized, promoted, and aestheticized vehicle for a popular, fun, and love-filled life.

Politics and the arts shone new paths to earthly fame and immortality. Romantics, as discussed earlier in this work, worked inside out, casting their heart and appearance on the stage of singular and even exotic singularity. With eighteenth-century Jean-Jacques Rousseau as their patron saint and his *Confessions* as their catechism of the sensitive and ever-questing self, novices made sensibility and appearance their confession. As the nineteenth century crowded the world with diverse individuals, places, communities, and classes, romantics chose long walks in the countryside or sought to fuse themselves to the democratic causes of their idealized democratic brothers and sisters in the struggles and on the barricades. Delacroix's painting of 1848, "Liberty Leading the People," puts handsomely bare-breasted Marianne atop the street barricade, pointing the tip of the Tricolor flag towards the advance of *le peuple*.

As realists and naturalists, artists captured the people in the decades after 1848 and the ascendancy of Napoleon III, in their labor, grime, and daily necessity as they emerged from basements and attics not as well-dressed carriage-riding middle-class shoppers, but as the democratic masses who emerge in the maze of manure-filled and congested streets and tunnels, on occasion marching for rights and causes.

In the second half of the century, Paris and other metropolises began to widen, become clean, contain police, and bring lighting to its streets. Ditches were fed into sewers and joined to great networked sewage systems. Here and there, along public routes, municipalities erected public urinals, turned on electric street lights, built parks, and even began to supply running water to innovative indoor plumbing systems. As the condition of the human body was improved and idealized, meriting a full place and life in society, so the public body, the face of streets, and the appearance of the passerby were undergoing a cleanup. A half-century ahead, there would come a time when "all the girls in France will wear underpants."

The masses who arrived from the countryside, drawn by the magnets of work and money over time and generations, improved their condition and appearance. Their situation was not just their own but that of the government's commitment to sanitation, public health, and medicine. Like members of respectable families, their children went to public schools, learned to read, and participated in their nation's new civic life and civilization's mounting prosperity. Democracies and nations promised that everybody would become somebody. In France, each and all were to become *un vrai citoyen d'une vraie démocratie!* ("a true citizen of a true democracy!"). The proof of this became clear as more were fully dressed, washed, and even perfumed and mannered to take their place in line with proper society.

Bodies underwent a great renaissance in Western society from the Revolution of 1789 to 1960. Everyone merited a photograph. At work, in the market, and at play, all, or almost all, became fellow beings and citizens. Increasingly, individuals appeared as best they could afford to. The youth got their hands on money and enjoyed the pleasures and adventures of sexual bodies. They left their homes and sleeping quarters dressed to join their changing times. With increasing goods, space, and even a degree of privacy, their parents entered ever more fully into their dreams of public and private life.

After the Civil War in the U.S., the Franco-Prussian War of 1870, and especially the Great World War of 1914–1918, nations officially learned to bury and commemorate their dead as well as medically, surgically, and institutionally care for their wounded. Victory and defeat were counted in casualties and mortalities, while nation-states consecrated their fallen dead as forming the sacred host and enduring body of the nation.

In the post-war world of the 1920s, with a return to peace and prosperity, one witnessed the Age of the Flappers, young women noted for their energy, dancing, and immorality. They dressed in short skirts and flaunted themselves disdainfully in the face of the surviving Victorian authorities. They danced, smoked, and even drove cars, declaring freedom to come and go. At the same time, Bolsheviks, Fascists, and Nazis advertised themselves as peoples and parties of a new body of vitality, youthfulness, and health. Their spirit would triumph over the old, decadent, and corrupt.

Bodies came out of the shadows. The young strolled and trolled to catch the eye of the opposite sex. Healthy and beautiful bodies hooked the interest of nations and commerce and made therapy and self-transformation the ideal. Bodies in full bloom filled newspapers and screens and added new dimensions to sports, recreation, and vacation. Fun became the new goal. Liberated from older traditions and conventions, the body at rest and play sinned no more. Sexuality and romance were crowned queen and king of the new days.

The body became the tabernacle and Eucharist of modern life. Growing numbers were summoned on health and beauty crusades of diets, exercise, and concern, despite the Charybdis and Scylla of anxiety and anorexia, to make themselves all they could appear to be. One was to stay young at all costs. These newly shaped, dressed, and styled young bodies sought other matching bodies. Young, healthy, and sexual bodies were the magnetic face of the protean individual. They were equipped to play a multitude of public roles. A lasting prescription from the last half of the twentieth century became, "Young, showered, and ready to go—a world to do, make, and be."

Already the new men and women of my parents' generation, born prior to the First World War, owed the self a body that had ambition and energy for a date, a good job, and eventually a car, home, family, and career. A young woman's success depended, as it still largely does, on a wholesome and attractive body and choices of marriage, reproduction, or independence as she saw fit.

Industry and advertisements found good commerce in producing for and selling to the young who aspired to have healthy and attractive bodies. The body's images, appearance, activities, health, leisure, desires, and dreams spawned profits. Clothing, shoes, cosmetics, leisure, sport, and exercise populated the well-off world with industry and shops, while the seasons and stages of life stimulated research, therapies, and treatments for all functions, parts, and actions of the body.

Hundreds of articles of clothing and shoes tell the history of our times. Take the example of the tennis shoe. The single superstar of twentieth-century footwear, it involved a revolution of materials, design, and use. As a child of the soft-soled canvas boat shoe, the tennis shoe became the king of athletic, recreational, informal, and stylish casual wear. The tennis shoe also became the therapeutic shoe of choice for its strength, flexibility, overall comfort, and even balance for all, especially the tottering old.

It is therefore not surprising that modern mass culture, which fused the material and spiritual, high, literate, popular, and commercial cultures, imbued and draped the body to foster and fit the individual's needs, choices, and ideals. The body was depicted and dressed as bold and striking, even suggestive and seductive. The body's appearance followed the sensibilities of literature and arts, the contours of the most recent fashions and styles of the known and famous. Fads and fancies highlighted different aspects of the body at work and play and in leisure, travel, and relaxation.

From a historical perspective, starting in the last decades of the nineteenth century, mass culture (truly a mix of commercial, class, popular, national, and ethnic factors) turned away from the traditional, classical, and Christian selves. It neither focused on discipline and soul, cast and order, nor remained in tow of Victorian manners, rules, and ideals. Rather, popular and mass cultures highlighted the body as natural, sensual, youthful, and healthy and as a vessel of feelings, choice, and freedom. To a degree, mass culture gave the unrestrained body dominion and sovereignty over the private and public self. Victorian virtues, as historian Gertrude Himmelfarb underlines in her 1995 *The De-Moralization of Society: From Victorian Virtues to Modern Values*, went out the window.

In modern times, a composite of cultural leaders and makers began to preach that our bodies are our own. They belong to our will, use, pleasures, and happiness. They do not belong to tradition or God's order, Christ's incarnation and sacrifice, or the Holy Spirit's illumination and guidance. They are ours to choose, value, live around, and live for, lest our health and mortality dictate otherwise.

Indeed, two other orders of secularism, which make this world our reality and end, came with politics and political ideologies, science, and medicine. The first, starting in the late seventeenth century, across the Enlightenment and into the first decades of the early nineteenth century, were schools of philosophy that collectivized us, joining us by body and soul to the state and idealized humanity.

In the nineteenth century, political thought and ideology perpetrated and glorified the democratic nation-state, making it our parent and family. In a word, we belonged by body, life, and action to the sovereignty and spreading hegemony of the many.

Sciences broadly fed a second revolution for the body and the self. Our bodies were increasingly intellectually deeded over to the laws of science and materialistic explanations and mechanisms and physical development and biological evolution. The person, by the body, brain, and mind, is not just made by our thoughts and choices but by an evolutionary chain of life, stretching from the smallest molecules and cells to plants, animals, and mammals, then to apes and early humans.

This view of the body and the self, grew out of theory and laboratory, chemistry and pharmacy. It grew out of careful observations, experiments, and medicine's intervention in the body and mind. For some, the body and the mind belonged to ages and stages and the inner probing of psychology and psychotherapy. Assuming the secrets of life were to be discovered in the smallest elements and the micro-processes of the body, science began to focus its microscope and other penetrating and atomic devices on the minutest life in Petri dishes and what might be discerned within the smallest units of our body—even those cells which straddle the greatest gulf between the material and unconscious, and the spiritual and consciousness. So, chemistry and biology, married by molecular and cell theory and the nervous system and the brain, crowned the person and life with self-awareness and, at the same time, saw the body and self develop atomic scopes and discover cell division, replication, individuation, DNA, and RNA.

In the last two hundred years or so, science, technology, and medicine have laid a platform for our expanded knowledge and treatment of the body, brain, mind, and self. Across the same period in the world, improvements in nutrition, sanitation, and public health have redefined life around the statistics of improved birth and survival rates and increased well-being and longevity. Nevertheless, confounding this view of progress for the body and self, the modern age has not spared us accidents and wars, famines, diseases, pandemics, waves of mental problems and drug abuse, and increased real and feared ecological catastrophes. For some, the growing body of humanity threatens the Earth, its lands, waters, air, and climate.

As the sciences plunged ever deeper into the infinitely and theoretically complex body to explain us as living creatures and thinking beings, so the great majority take our body as wholesome and pleasure-giving vessels in life, unless we have chained ourselves in self-destructive habits, or have been imprisoned by pressing maladies, medical diagnoses, and promised cures. Our bodies are us. They are free and mobile, open to interact with other bodies, and follow their own choices, pleasures, and personal plans.

This secularization of the body and self has made us self-identifying individuals who are self-satisfied even though we take medicines and advice to avoid an itch or ache, to lose a pound or two, to help along a faltering organ or function, run a little better, climb higher, or get a good night's sleep. We also are still that body that, in one way or another, walks by on the street, shows up on the television and media screens, or is snapped in the family photograph, smiling, hugging, posing, teasing, or horsing around.

CHAPTER 9
THE BODIES OF OUR THOUGHTS AND TIMES

The body individuates us. It substantiates us as material and natural. It makes us grow and change, accounts for our birth and death, and shapes us through the stages of life as it bears its accidents. Our incarnate and corporeal body set us forth to our self and world. It places us in life and makes our experience. Our body is our instrument for action and reproduction, along with a means to gather, make, give, and take. It joins and marries us to others in flesh and conscience. It accounts for our independence and dependence.

Inseparable from who and what we are individually and communally and, in modern times, collectively and politically, the body makes us who we are. We see, enact, and define ourselves through our bodies, or, in the words of two of my prefatory quotations to this work:

> The body makes us the one and the many we are. The body, a multitude, is the fragile, mortal instrument and vessel of our single given lives.

> We may be sexists. We may be racists. But surely, we all are "bodyists" who know each other by our walks, noses, resolute chins, and gapping mouths.

Since we first projected and represented ourselves in nature, with others, before the gods, in birth, life, and after death, we have identified ourselves and our place as beings with feelings and thoughts and through images and words of ourselves as being and having bodies. Cultures, traditions, and arts represent, depict, and even value our bodies as alive and dead and in the form of gods and animals.

As societies differentiated themselves by power and wealth, so cultures and arts, including dress and manner, elevated, magnified, and even glorified the rich, powerful, and handsome, while degrading and even profaning and vilifying the bodies of the poor, powerless, homeless, awkward, and ugly. Workers and serfs were described in images as rough, coarse, and rude, if not dirty and gross. Slaves were chained to a task, place, and master. Without freedom, they could even be denied the rights of marriage and family.

In the nineteenth century, democracy, with its professions of rights, goods, and choices, revolutionized societies' assumptions, discourse, and conception of the body. Depictions of bodies were incorporated in polar and diverse directions.

Naturalism, realism, and social critique depicted entire groups bound by necessity or as victims of unjust distribution and exploitation. In the guise of being a science, Social Darwinism, eugenics, and racism depicted the inferiority of bodies by assigning degrading anatomy and stereotypes to assign inferiority and threat to racial purity, thus justifying subordination, exploitation, and even elimination. Ideologies, opinions, and government ordinances, along with design, illustrations, and posters based on bodily images, attributed reality to stereotypes.

Conversely, with bountiful images and supporting ideas, the body was incorporated into claims of democracy, the production and sales of commerce, and the causes and ends of the new nation-states. The body of the national soldier as warrior-martyr created a national icon. At the same time, the growth in public health and longevity fostered words, images, rhetoric, and sensibility in the service of the progressive myth of "having it all" concentrated in a belief in wellness, recreation, support, and eternal youth. To a degree, the belief in the body has underwritten the modern and contemporary revolution of individuality.

On no ground has this revolution and accompanying war over the meaning of individuality been more diversely and profoundly fought than around women's bodies. This is seen in images and portraits of their subservience, bondage, and slavery, and more precisely, their reduction to a sexual object, a polite and mannered being, or a lifetime servant of self-sacrifice and giving.

Women's battles have been waged for political emancipation, civic equality, and full participation in politics, sport, and leisure—to no longer be passive, a come-in-second Eve, an adoring and tearful witnessing Mary, a mere matter of a man's eye and wish, or at the family and work's command. Women no longer wish to play the roles men have written. They wish to take full command of themselves and have their full share of the world and the future. Their new self-image, language, and ideology seek a liberation beyond corporeal, emotional, or intellectual boundaries. Sisterhood carries them beyond tradition to a new community.

A woman's body, so rich in images and projections and not without confusion and anger, becomes myriad as it enters cultural, political, and ideological discourse and arguments about rights, freedom, and activities. It goes to the heart of being an individual and having one's own identity. It can seek liberation as a mythic door that allows her to make her body and self all she can be, and in the work of some proponents, read as a war against inherited biology, history, and culture.

In her *Unbearable Weight: Feminism, Western Culture, and the Body*, contemporary philosopher of the body, Susan Bordo, wrote, "The body, as anthropologist Mary Douglas has argued, is a powerful symbolic form, a surface on which the central rules, hierarchies, and even metaphysical commitments of a culture are inscribed and thus reinforced through the concrete language of the body."[80] She goes on to say, "Our conscious politics, social commitments, striving for change may be undermined and betrayed by the life of our bodies—not the cravings, instinctual body imagined by Plato, Augustine, and Freud, but what Foucault calls the "docile body, regulated by the norms of cultural life."[81]

I take an easier path than trying to construct the woman's body historically and culturally. I autobiographically tell of the body by the conditions, ages, and stages of my single male body. In youth, blessed with good health, I came to know and accept my body as my trusty vessel—not without confusion, shame, and guilt—and as a close and good companion. In old age, the body has turned fickle, alien, and even inimical. In many ways, it tells me my days are limited.

I could, here, surrender some of *the truths* of my body to my *world and age*, its ideas, culture, institutions, manners, disciplines, and fads. I could even borrow a phrase from Martin Buber's 1923, *I and Thou*, and contend that my body belongs to the *Zeitgeist*, the spirit of contemporary times. However, I choose otherwise. As the title of this work and this chapter suggests, I am a plurality, a multitude, and out of which I became a one, a self, a person, and an individual. My body, ever myself—one body, one mind, one self—makes me a Many, yet one of a myriad of selves, inseparable from many worlds.

We, as individuals, groups, and cultures, are *entangled* to use a favorite term of contemporary British archaeologists. By experience and thought, images and wishes, we are joined to the bodies of others and material substantiality of things. I also am woven into places and times, ideas and ideologies, images, fashions, and fads.

Thus, what follows here about the body and the self seeks no abstract resolution of their relation. Instead, I stick to my notion that the body and the self are a unity and a many. I do not divide or empty self from body or body from self.

We Take Body and Self Apart and Put Them Together

Many have seized and carried off the body as the bride of their intelligence. As suggested in preceding chapters, since early modern history, materialism and secularism put knowledge in control. They made the promise of future happiness the ring of progress, with its, laws, science, and inventions. Progress offered the individual, as part of society, freedom and redemption by reason, device, and choice.

In the last two hundred or so years, science, technology, and medicine have laid a platform to know, treat, and improve the body. Across the globe, there has been improved sanitation, public health, and nutrition. Diseases have been fought and, in many instances, defeated. Hunger and disaster do not stalk all people. Childbirth takes far fewer infants and mothers. Longevity increases, and the people of progressive nations dream of abundance and well-being.

At the same time, modernity, with all its improvements, has not spared us accidents, chemical dependencies, disasters, and wars. Long lives can mean debility and senility. Great fears remain. We worry about what the ever-centralizing state will claim and what markets and communications will invade. We see mass society determining our future. Eight billion people of distinct bodies—the advancing world's population in 2022—claim their individual and collective needs and ideals.

We have shrunk the earth for profits, choice, and power. On the negative side of the ledger, the price of progress has been climate change, the cutting of forests, the draining of wetlands, the exhaustion of the soils and their fertility, the endangerment of the seas, and the extinction of countless species.

As ecological catastrophes prophetically loom, nuclear fingers do not relax their grip on the trigger. Since the launching of the first satellite, Sputnik, in October 1957, competition, surveillance, and national pride have turned outer space into both a junkyard and a launch pad for mutual destruction.

Events still surprise and threaten. As I write this book, Ukraine fights a battle worthy of a free people against Russian imperial expansion. I am reminded of the worst scenes of the Second World War. Nuclear war, which I have feared since I was seven years old, seventy-seven years ago, whispers again of the world, "Ashes to ashes, dust to dust!"

Contemporary physics, astronomy, and chemistry turn what was certain and solid into particles and electrons, waves and charges. Energy itself is swallowed by black holes.

Something and nothing "dances with the stars." The atom has been split, and everything has become divisible. The infinity of the small and invisible becomes, as I argued in *Dust: A History of Small and Invisible* (2000), greater than the infinity of stars and galaxies. The very elements—and the seas and seasons, fall under the sovereign dominion our expanding reach.

As matter goes, so the body and mind go. We have divided, annexed, engineered, and exploited the material world. We have made the body a singular and plural territory for exploration. With all boundaries of God, spirit, or nature transgressed, we have made the body and the self, divisible, malleable, and transformable. We, whoever we are, find ourselves in the service of new wishes, designs, and desired revolutions, whatever they may be.

BODIES ALWAYS ON STAGE

To repeat an earlier statement, bodies, perennially identified with nature, beauty, life, and personhood, underwent a great renaissance in Western society over the course of the nineteenth and twentieth centuries. They were democratized and universalized, made the measure of progress, and the vessel of happiness. Bodies went with the popularization, commercialization, and universalization of the individual self. They accompanied people on streets and sidewalks, on trains and buses, in cars, and at beaches, amusement parks, parades, and rallies.

With the American and French Revolutions, people climbed on the stage of making history and haven't gotten off. They waved their different flags, first in Europe and North America and then in the world. They call for a different and better future for the body and the self.

Nineteenth-century Realism in literature recorded truth as the condition of the body and its changing conditions. Photography, the new art of democracy, focused on the people as seen. It filled increasingly popular newspapers with vivid images. It turned its myriad lens on the people at work, in the market, at rest, and even traveling by steamship and train. Photography presented the American Civil War with diverse scenes. They came to readers and multitudes of non-readers in the form of portraits: soldiers standing in front of tents, among their carts, tents, and horses, marching off to a new battlefield or returning to the home front, wearied, injured, captives, to be repaired and ministered to in a hospital.

Photography, however, did more than capture the old and new faces of war. It took to the streets, proposing a new daily credo for our times: Reality is what you see. The outward situations and conditions of the people's bodies are the *res ipse loquitur* ("it speaks for itself") of the age.

Photography is not alone in telling us who we are. Societies, starting in the late eighteenth century, increasingly began to count and enumerate who was among them and what their status, wealth, and needs were. Censuses and citizenship papers, along with growing official and organizational records, surveys, and statistics, numbered and described populations and their places.

Correspondingly, individuals in our emerging democratic era feel a need to appear publicly presentable as best they can. Some even seek to appear as the photographic version of their idealized selves. By dress, grooming, posture, glance, smile, a tilt of their head, etc., they make themselves into their exterior idealizations.

Youth increasingly dream and mold the body to depict the self. With each generation of improved well-being, youth, in ever great masses, declare themselves fresh, exciting, and epochal—a new face on the clock. They do it with the hour's fashion. With multiple identities to be played out, they pose before their bedroom mirror to imagine who they will be. They posture and dress themselves to multiple roles and situations, subjecting themselves to the imagined glances they will receive.

It is not surprising that mass culture, which fused the material, spiritual, high, literate, popular, and commercial cultures, shapes our image and meaning of the body we have and wish to have. The Argus-eyed "other" sees us as the singular One and Many we imagine ourselves to be. The body of each of us depends on fresh sensibilities and fashions. Fads and fancies take hands with bodies and selves at work and at play.

Starting in the last decades of the nineteenth century, mass culture turned away from traditional, classical, and Christian ideas as enacted by earlier aristocratic and upper bourgeois cultures. It idealized the body and the person as free, outward, and progressive and made the body a vessel of action, freedom, and cause.

ARTISTS GOT THEIR STROKES AND TOUCHES IN

Already in early modern Europe, artists—I think of sixteenth-century Flemish painter Pieter Bruegel the Elder as leading the way—depicted individuals outwardly in groups, villages, and towns, across the seasons at play, dancing at a wedding, or on their way to work in their fields, or even skating on frozen ponds.

By the late decades of the eighteenth century and across the early decades of the nineteenth century, artists give unique worth to their subjects and their settings, moods, and individual poses. With a brush, Romantic artists gave birth to art depicting unique persons, places, situations, and singular landscapes. Seeking adventure and eliciting awe, they selected their subjects from the past or present, from literature or imagined scenes. They dramatized their subjects—which spanned classes, places, and conditions— on a windblown hill, at the seaside in a fog, on a raft barely afloat in a roiling sea, or on an inviting couch.

The Impressionists and Expressionists of the middle and late-nineteenth century chose a multitude of subjects from nature—from beaches, hills, fields, and gardens to Vincent van Gogh's tortured asylum olive orchard, a field of sunflowers, and a starry night. Both Impressionists and Expressionists, limitless in their exploration and depiction of subjects, loved rural landscapes at the seaside and as a pale, tan, pinking, and disappearing cubically drawn field. They found their subjects near Paris, in southern France, among exotic landscapes of the imagination, in crafted gardens with pools of water and stands of flowers, along village streets, in pool halls, suburban beaches, restaurants, and dance halls. Their subjects spanned classes, conditions, and states of mind, and often, their eye was drawn to a woman's body, be she nude and in repose, in a colorful dress with a high lace collar, in dance, or on a prancing horse.

Both Impressionists and Expressionists employed different techniques. They utilized light, color, and shading to experiment with different perspectives and to elicit a new sensibility. Georges Seurat (1859–1891) and Pablo Picasso (1881–1973), a generation and century apart, represented Impressionism and Expressionism and their heirs' Pointillism and Cubism, which spread across the twentieth-century Western world. With its depiction of the body, contemporary artists teach each generation to see, know, idealize, and even dramatize the self.

In an 1884 painting, *A Sunday on La Grande Jatte* (an island in the Seine on the western edge of Paris), Georges Seurat innovated with an experiment in painting based on dots, form, and colors. In this work, clusters of individuals and small groups composed of different women, men, and children, with and without umbrellas, are dressed in an array of colors, standing and sitting on the lawn, in and out of the shade of overhanging trees and the shadows they cast, are depicted sitting before the beaming blue water on which boats sailed and rowed. With remarkable precision and in unity and contrast, Seurat assembled his multiple frames in service of his aesthetic of optical and color theory. He approached Cubism and Pointillism through his utilization of tiny dabs of colors that sought contrast in a field of singular luminosity.

While there are many other artists—Manet, Monet, Van Gogh, and Cezanne come to mind—I find myself before a work of the young Picasso, his 1903 *Blind Guitarist*, a work that culminates the mood and color of his Blue Period. His subject, sitting with his guitar, so thin, so old, with long bony fingers and a neck cast down and to one side, appears with his whole body straining to hear the note he thumbed as the last chord of his suffering life.

By the end of the nineteenth century, the visual arts taught a wealth of ways to see, feel, and think about the body, the world, and the self. No one line of theory could form a circumference around the representation and functions of the body in twentieth-century art. Bodies were depicted as wholesome youth, subjects of the state, factory, and race, or isolated and alienated individuals, who lived in small, empty, dirty, and solitary places.

Artistic sensibilities went to war in the twentieth century. Artists, along with a string of educated soldier-poets like Siegfried Sassoon, Wilfred Owen, and Rupert Brooke, told of their personal experiences in the Great War. They portrayed life in the trenches, mass executions by machine guns, abandonment, and death as they were left dangling from fences, gassed, choking, in parts and bits strewn and scattered across *no-man's land.*

Artists from Goya to Picasso, and young soldier-poets, found death and truth in war. They depicted mutilated bodies—severed, beheaded, mangled, distorted, and left crawling and screaming—which told of the personal and impersonal, and of our and the world's deaths. Even the advance of twentieth-century surgery, prosthetics, cosmetics, and pharmacy, which care for and mend every part of our body, have not entirely disguised the brutal bite of mass chemical and engineered war into our recently spawned youthful society.

Slow-working painters and poets fell behind instantaneous and mass-circulated photography and newsreels that immediately captured the assembling and destruction of bodies—deaths as single and solitary, by whole brigades. The lens captured a war's immediacy and poignancy. The camera's snap vouched for death in contemporary wars.

The visual arts, more subjective, individualistic, analytic, and theoretical, sought to be fresh and creative with exaggeration, distortion, abstraction, colors, forms, and details. Abstract artists sought *a deeper truth*, with reflective, analytic, constructed and even mythic art. They fragmented, exaggerated, and distorted the body to get at their meaning. With wire, sculptures in wood or metal, or images drawn and painted on mixed, curved, and broken surfaces, they voiced their message about individuals and crowds by the transformation of the body.

As multifaceted modern medicine and science described and inventoried the body as internally and externally organic, mechanical, visceral, and conscious, photographs, films, and the arts had a heyday representing, imagining, conjuring, and commercializing images of the body. Literature and stage performances, movies, and popular arts resonated and expanded on the subject of who and what we are. They, too, dressed us in different, even shocking, bodies, presenting us as creatures of different conditions, desires, and potentials. Represented, studied, medicalized, imagined, commercialized, and ideologized, the body became a multitude and plenitude. The body, true to its origin, became multiplying and dividing cells.

The body became the central ecumenical object of contemporary commerce. Hundreds of articles of clothing and shoes tell the histories of the individual in our times. The image of the body as healthy and long-living, free and in motion, and sensual and sexual pervades all. It forms an ethic. All must shape themselves to be all they can be. The idealized body proves the groundwater of the protean self. The dictum on the front door and bedroom door of every aspiring individual, reads, *Be all you can be!*

SHAPING THE FACE OF THINGS

As traditional society with its most therapeutic devices relied on crutches, coarse wood stumps, and arms with hooks, modern medicine has turned to technology for well-fashioned and moveable prosthetics and plastic surgery for limbs and faces. For the body as a whole, we have turned to science, health, chemistry, medicine, and diets.

165

Thanks to this promise and to advances in science and medicine, we are far less often confronted on the streets with crippled bodies, open wounds, and faces injured and burned beyond recognition or pitted and scarred by smallpox. In contemporary towns and cities, noses and mouths are no longer rudely split by hair lips. Electrified lifts, motorized chairs, specially equipped vehicles, smooth city surfaces, and leveled crossings clear the way for the impaired.

The contemporary body increasingly becomes an object of style, fashion, and commerce. It is made ready for all seasons and occasions. Industry dresses us for work and play in formal and sophisticated displays. Make-up, polishes, and varied treatments and manicures serve the skin, nails, and hair. Diets aim at shaping the body for health, appearance, and appeal. Jewelry and tattoos distinguish individuals and afford social identities, be it on the front or backseat of a motorcycle or a weekend on a luxurious yacht.

The bodies of the passing crowd are moving billboards for the self and others. The self has become an open realm for projection, sales, identities, membership, and the stating of loyalties and identities. T-shirts claim and profess all.

A society's well-being is seen on the streets and found in government statistics on health and longevity. Bodies collectively march in a victory parade of contemporary health, nutrition, and mass manufacture. We, of the advanced nations, have food to eat, running water, and places to sleep and relieve ourselves. Work is to be found, money is to be made, and there are places to occasionally go to relax and have a good time.

Industry and advertisement have found good commerce in selling to and producing for young and healthy bodies. The body's images, appearance, activities, health, leisure, desires, and ideals spawned realms of profits. The body has generated multiple industries and shops for clothing, shoes, cosmetics, and exercise. The stages and seasons of life stimulated research, therapies, and replacements for body parts and functions.

A selective list of nineteenth- and twentieth-century medical and public health accomplishments offer prima facie proof of progress. We blossomed, not just in well-being and longevity but also in play and recreation, as evidenced by our numerous public parks, pools, beaches, amusement parks, athletic fields, and stadiums.

Another way to count our improved well-being, to which we will return in closing chapters, is by the measure of accumulating energy, machines, and systems of communication that make us faster and more thorough in all we do. A simple list of inventions demonstrates our accumulating range of powers. For instance, think of canned and frozen food, pasteurized milk, safety razors, hair dryers, deodorants, rubber boots, photographs, movies, plus vaccinations, prosthetics, chloroform, hypodermic needles, anesthesia, antiseptics, and transfusions. And do not forget public works and civil engineering that built drainage systems, tunnels and bridges, smooth and paved roads, sidewalks, sewer systems, and sewage plants. In addition, consider rubber made for inflatable wheels on which cars and tractors, trucks, buses, metros, bicycles, and even wheelchairs run. To take only the first two, as automobiles spearheaded invention, new materials, and individual comfort, mobility, and convenience, tractors and farm machinery, ever subject to continuous invention and powers, opened fields, transformed farm size, multiplied crops, and redefined farmers, who now in the American Midwest and elsewhere, plow, seed, and fertilize their lands with computers and GPS.

ON BODY AS IDENTITY AND RACE

I conclude this section on a dark note. In its advance, progress, in union with science, technology, and the centralizing state, advocates materialism and secularism.

Truth becomes equated to science and know-how, and knowledge becomes equated to power and progress. Induction, observation, research, and applied activity supplant metaphor, myth, philosophy, and religion in modern culture.

One of the worst fruits eaten from that tree were supposed scientific theories that, in the nineteenth and twentieth centuries, endorsed racism. In the hands of many natural and social scientists, moral reformers, aggressive liberals, conservatives, and Fascists, these theories warranted the hierarchies of biological, social, and moral superiority and inferiority, justifying the discrimination, and even elimination, of those at the bottom.

Most coarsely, racism and eugenics based on the body became translated in the proposition: *You will know them by their bodies. Look at the shapes of their heads, hair, and the characteristics of their faces—eyes, lips, nose, and mouth. You also can identify them, your new neighbors, by the way they cluster, act, and live and the way they eat, sing, dance, and play. With more sophistication, you know them by their genealogy, their bloodline, and genes. They also can be identified by their names, both as given and altered to fit in, the place of their origins, and the date of their migrations. Of course, complexion matters, as does association, be it by craft, education, leisure, and neighbors.*

Physical identities by the race of people and groups were underpinned and even thought confirmed by pseudo-scientific theories along with nineteenth-century materialism, scientism, Darwinism, and ideologically underpinned ethnicities. Each of these theories, as quasi-science and active prejudice, came into play in national rivalries and doctrines of imperialism. In the United States, during the first decades of the twentieth century, racial theories justified calls for exclusion and the imposition of quotas on immigration and even the purging of society on the grounds of health, energy, morality, and purity of national life. Despite constitutional rights and inclusive democratic claims, the twentieth-century government in the American south legislated to keep segregation in place, while in the north, self-proclaimed progressives, facing a rush of immigrants from southern Italy and eastern Europe in the period of 1880 to 1914, argued that theories of racial identity accounted for crime and moral degeneracy, and broadly prescribed eugenics as good science with beneficial policies and practices. Selectively distinguishing and cutting out inferior races offered grounds for limiting immigration and forced sterilization and abortion in institutions. In the U.S., some Blacks were subject to medical tests and experiments, while in the name of racial purity and regeneration, Nazi eugenics justified the use of "inferior" people for medical experimentation and the sterilization and elimination of minorities, the weak, and Jews.

Across Europe and the entire West, choruses lauded the young and healthy body. Sports and athleticism attracted players and fans and built leagues and stadiums for games. Cities and towns, villages, and countries found a reason to cheer for their own teams as competitive sports branched out on fields, tracks, ponds, canals, rivers, and roads. At the end of the nineteenth century, sports won a golden crown for itself and history with the restoration of the international Olympics.

Reacting against Napoleonic hegemony at the start of the century, the resurgent Prussian German initiated the *Turner Verein* movement. Imitated across Scandinavia, the *Turner Verein* called for a nation built on strong and muscular bodies. The American YMCA movement and the British Boy Scouts also, in degrees, spoke of rebirth through health, morale, and discipline. By the end of the nineteenth century, Darwinism, racism, and selective eugenics echoed the call for vitality and national resurrection through the fittest. Mussolini's Fascism marched forward under the banner of athletic, harmonized, and energized youth. National Socialism did the same but would eliminate the weak, inferior, and corrupt. It aimed at making the Nordic individual and nation physically dominant. It would prepare itself for victory—*Sieg Heil!*—in the next war.

Enlightened America, which loved its sports and competitions, was not free of beliefs of racial and ethnic purity and subjugation and utilization of one group for the benefit of another. Racism had a head start in its southern states with the long institutionalization of slavery. However, not to be forgotten, Massachusetts soldiers and ships joined Britain and Halifax in the expulsion of approximately fifteen thousand Acadians in 1755. The successive removal of Indian peoples prior to and during the formation of the American nation utilized racist arguments to side with the establishment and defense of white breeds of "Nordic" Europeans with colonial, Anglo-Saxon, and Germanic identities against natives, Latinos, and the waves of new Eastern European, Mediterranean, Chinese, Asian, and Latin American immigrants. This racist nativism was enacted in the 1924 Immigration Act, which limited the number of immigrants allowed entry into the United States through a national origin quota. The quota provided immigration visas to two percent of the total number of people of each nationality in the United States as of 1890, which, de facto, reduced the flow of new Eastern European and southern Italian immigrants who, like my grandparents and relatives from Sicily, arrived in mass at the end of the nineteenth century and the start of the twentieth century. Imaginary constructions and attributes of body and race shaped the mind and the hour of the new world.

THE BODY IS THE VESSEL OF THE SELF

The self travels as sweeping arcs in a certain but ragged course of life and aging. The body underpins our experiences, feelings, relations, and thoughts.

As I have already written, so much tells us in so many ways what our bodies and selves are. Our art rests on contradictory views of the human body. Designed images enter us in space, place, and time, within the touch, feelings, and ideas of others, intimate and alien, and circumscribe us in many situations that unify and separate our *selves* from our bodies.

The body, which puts us in space, place, and time, and, among others, is greater than we can think and imagine. We can glorify and agonize over the thoughts and images we have of it. We can project our bodies into animals, trees, hills, and valleys. Within *In My Flesh I See God: A Treasury of Rabbinic Insights about the Human Anatomy* (1995), Avraham Yaakov Finkel suggests the many ways Jews lived and believed with metaphors and laws saying that their bodies were of God's creation and Providence.

In *Purity and Danger* (1966), anthropologist Mary Douglas (whom I mentioned earlier in this chapter) proposed that dietary laws intricately model the body and the altar upon one another. Catholic and Orthodox Christians venerate the divine in the Holy body of Jesus Christ. They do this with fasting rules, the centrality of altars in the church, and the Eucharist as the most important of sacraments. They contemplate the Immaculate Conception of Christ and venerate the Cross. Christ was in a body as a child, among the people, crucified, resurrected, and glorified. Christ's Holy Body defines the sacrament of Communion and is central to the teachings of the New Testament. In Corinthians 2, 4:10 (King James version), Paul says: "Always bearing about in the body of the dying of the Lord Jesus Christ so that the life of Jesus might be made manifest in our body."

Our secular imagination can carry us, by the body, to be other persons. We project ourselves as a prosperous business person or the fictional failed salesman of Arthur Miller's *Death of a Salesman*, who, in the end, protests his exploited life to the world, exclaiming, "You can't eat the orange and throw the peel away—a man is not a piece of fruit." Our modern sensibilities and imagining, stimulated by images and screens, are ever-roaming. We transmute our protean bodies into those of stars of the screen or athletic fields or perceive ourselves in the form of the old, poor, and abandoned.

At times, we anguish about the fate of our own body and empathically suffer the injuries and die the deaths of others. Pinned down in the finite, in the mazes of our eyes and ears, and earthly words and thoughts, we call ourselves up into the infinite. Imagination and hope make the body the vessel of the transcendent self. We merely hear or read of a physical accomplishment, test, or tragedy of another and internalize it as our own. Offering an example of this, a friend and baseball

fan, Dana Yost, revealed to me how he took to heart the 1958
career-ending accident and the resulting life-long paralysis of
the admired famous catcher Roy Campanella (1921–1993).

> This afternoon, I watched part of a documentary on
> Roy Campanella, the great catcher for the 1950s
> Brooklyn Dodgers. He got into a car accident in
> 1958, broke his neck, and became a paraplegic. For
> about the first seven months after the accident, he
> was very depressed and suicidal but then worked his
> way out of the depression. But for the rest of his life,
> he could barely move his forearms, could not use his
> hands, and, of course, was paralyzed from the neck
> and waist down. He relied on a caregiver pretty much
> every moment he was awake, every day.

Of course, differences in aging, new health conditions,
cultural inheritance, and sensibility filter our reaction to our
own body and that of others, which we can intermingle and
even find confusing. We assume and embrace other bodies
we intimately know and strongly imagine. Their bodies can
compass our own. We take upon ourselves the maladies
and deaths of a parent, and, fearing their death, we wish our
death to short circuit the death we knew and imagined that
our parent suffered.

We cuddle and discipline, love and hate our bodies by
the inheritance of family, place, culture, times, and condition.
Different parts of the body distinctly appeal or repulse us.
We are all aware of the egotistic flap of President Donald
Trump's wagging tongue and the stuttering, whimpering,
mumbling, and muttering tongue of President Joseph Biden.

As anyone who has been associated with young students
knows, the ravages of self-hate can cause severe cases of
bulimia or anorexia and lead to dramatic weight loss and, in
the case of one student that I had, eventually lead to suicide.
Conversely, I have encountered academic narcissists of many
types throughout my life. While at the University of Michigan
in 1957, I had an elementary Spanish teacher who lectured
while continually twirling his Phi Beta Kappa medal on its

gold chain as if to tell us he was truly among the elect elite. In recent years, the very appearance of an older local priest filled me with disgust. He winked and tiptoed, with prancing, darting eyes, clowning gestures, and finger-fluttering hellos on his parades up and down the side aisles of the church while an assistant priest said Mass.

To steal a popular line from a song, "Little Things Mean a Lot," whether picked up and taken in by the body, eyes, or an impression. I remember my teen years when my gaze in the mirror focused on a single pimple, which awoke two painful years of battling acne. A lifetime of constipation left me knowing anger and disgust with my own body.

Today's therapies, popular and scientific, often prove to be boondoggles and boomerangs. What is wanted and willed often does not square with what is at hand. The mind, a mess of knots, does not untie what pain, mood, and thought wove. There is no Alexander the Great who, with one swift slice of his sword, can cut the Gordian knot of our tangles of the body and the self.

Yes, I repeat myself. The body is a multiplicity that exceeds our feelings, thoughts, and understanding. We inevitability vary in our interpretation by mood, situation, encounters, pain, and pleasure. We cannot tailor our bodies to fit our clothes, and often our clothes do not fit the bodies we have or the bodies we want. Diets fail, and prayers do not seem to lead to transfigurations. We often settle with the laws of entropy, informally translated for our bodies and selves: "We are in the game, we cannot get out, and, eventually, we will lose!"

BODIES DISTINGUISH ALL AND ESPECIALLY THE FAMOUS

I return at the end of this chapter to the ever engulfing popular mass society and culture. Films and television paraded before my generation and that of my parents. They threaded their way in and out of our senses, language, and minds. They distinguished bodies—bodies that we knew, idealized, and discussed the world and ourselves. There were not just singularly attractive women and men whose bodies and movements netted attention, fame, stardom, and championships, but there were also comics trained by vaudeville and silent films. I think of Charlie Chaplin's animated rapid movement and face of many moods. I also think of straight men and contrasting pairs. There was the slender and sarcastically smart Abbott and the fat, dopey, but likable Costello, and the duo of the frail and hesitant Laurel and the fat, dictatorial Hardy.

The bodies of popular stars afforded classifications, names, and words for thinking about the world of the self and others by acting, dancing, singing, playing, swinging, and running their way to fame. Media wrote the age's messages about character, style, and meaning with and about bodies. Particularly healthy and beautiful bodies defined the desirable. They filled newspapers and screens and made the world of sports, recreation, and vacation. Fun became the new end. Healthy and liberated from older ways, traditions, conventions, and work, sexuality and romance were advertised as crowning individual lifetimes, and the body at rest and play sinned no more.

Marilyn Monroe (1926–1962) was the 1950s quintessence of the sexy body and the prow of contemporaneity. She was most desired. Her curves of bosom and thighs paralleled the curves of the shapely bodies of cars encircled in chrome. When her skirt blew upward, the world looked in and up.

She was the lighthouse of the luxuriously sensual woman that beaconed the age's leisure, desires, and profits. Clothing, shoes, cosmetics, and exercise fed growing industries and shops. Increasingly the popularity of articles of clothing and shoes offered corporeal histories of our times.

Depicting selves as bodies spawn our age's abundant romantic and commercial troubadours, be they cheap and wordy novelists, platitudinous counselors, anatomists, or pornographers. Obsessions with bodies are tyrannies of minds. Falsified and counterfeited, made malleable to wish, and impervious to the realities of aging, obsessed bodies can kill empathy and destroy an understanding of the body from womb to tomb. They can even blind us to the ample evidence of and testimony to contemporary poverty, starvation, mass migrations, ethnic purges, and death camps.

THE BODY, A MATTER OF DREAM AND CHOICE

Today, for those with money and means, the re-designing, re-making, and re-training of their bodies becomes possible and even a commercially-urged good. Science, technology, and types of therapy offer transformation of the body with a fresh means to envision and enact one's body. Chemists, surgeons, and dentists serve individual wishes and choices for a price.

As of late, proponents of universal choice, be they educators or advocates of sexual transformation, have begun to encourage elementary school children to realize and choose their sex. They offer—even coax—youngsters to consider the proposition, "I may have been born into the wrong body. I can change myself in accord with whom I am and whom I choose to be."

A polar opposite of this radical extension of choice could be seen in the Taliban's restrictive legislation against women's bodies, education, travel, and participation in public life. Through the ages and across cultures, the body came with a sex defined at birth and was treated accordingly by culture, religion, dress, and associations. The body placed one in marriage, family, work, and community. It determined all that sexual definition appropriated, including wishes, ecstasy, and dreams. (Of course, those who fell outside this bipolar world were held in opprobrium.)

As specialties and types of medicine blossom, the body increasingly belongs to our wishes for longevity, beautification, convenience, and our choices. In the United States, Wade v. Roe (1973) subjected the fetus, the unborn child up to viability, to the *constitutional right* of a woman's choice of abortion, regardless of her age, marital status, dependency, or mental condition. In China, birthing was officially reduced to a single child, and the axe fell on newborn females. The depth of their axe still cuts into contemporary China's needed population.

In recent decades, people, especially in developed and developing societies, have surrendered their place, personal well-being, and family for a life of material well-being, pleasure, opportunity, and wealth. Education and specialization promote mobility. Individuality, which supports autonomy and, some suggest, the isolation of the person, rests on the claims of the body, its movement, and happiness. In *The Madness of the Crowd: Gender, Race, and Identity* (2019), British author and politician Douglas Murray sees individuals, groups, and states turn against biology and history. To him, conception, birth, motherhood, infancy, and childhood, along with community and traditional culture, all lose standing in the face of mass choice and secularism.

Against the background of increasing wealth and opportunity, science, technology, medicine, chemistry, and physics enhance our powers and propagate the illusion that we are in control of ourselves and our own bodies. They have reached the inner depths of our body, nerves, brain, and mind. Medicine contests that one's body is one's fate. Therapy, pharmacology, surgery, and psychology suggest the possibility that body can be changed, even transformed.

Therapy plays a game of leapfrog between *the real and the imagined*. We increasingly make the body into our thoughts and wishes. Some medical self-help books make the teaching brain a dream-making cockpit of the body, such as Daniel Amens' 2010 best-selling, *Change Your Body: Use Your Brain to Get and Keep the Body You Have Always Wanted*.

Today, science, medicine, technology, chemistry, and psychology have made the body a matter of choice and revision. In *The Coming of the Body* (2010), Juvin Hervé, a French politician, argued the body is transformed by capitalism and dissected into ever particular and smaller parts. It has become a matter of DNA, cells and atoms, microcosmic entities, and forces. In the tightening grip of science and technology, it becomes too technical and small for cultures. The body, born in touchable skin and visible blood, has vanished in concepts, forces, and numbers.

Hervé elaborated on this great revolution as a detachment and disconnection from the old. He posits that humanity loses its perennial ties to traditional needs, suffering, stages of life, and the passage of time—all the very coordinates of our moral compass. This revolution suggests the possibility and the desirability of a life without work, free of aging, marriage, family, and anchoring roots in home and community.

Journalist, editor, and friend, William Hoffman, at the University of Minnesota Medical School, selected five biomedical innovations that redefined the human body in the past half-century: [82] 1. Magnetic Resonance Imaging (MRI); 2. Regenerative medicine; 3. Immunotherapies; 4. Genomics and genome editing; and 5. mRNA vaccines. Collectively, these five new sciences and technologies can be used to measure how far humanity has traveled from the turn-of-the-century discovery of the atom and x-rays.

These five revolutionary bio-medical discoveries created new understanding and relations to diagnosing and making prognoses of our bodies and plunging us into atomic and subatomic technologies and realities. As I boldly argued in *Dust: A History of the Small and Invisible*, we have made the realm of the microscopically small greater than the infinities of the telescopically vast.

On the threshold of the twenty-first century, we began to create and invent materials and devices with nanotechnology at ten to the minus nine and subatomically explore and theorize at ten to the minus thirty-third. Contemporary physics and astronomy set our imaginations in pursuit of particles, electrons, waves, and charges that vanish down black holes. Something and nothing now "dance among the stars." The body, along with the self, reaches deeply into infinity.

As our science and intellect go ever deeper, we move to a progressive public optimism in light of expanding materialism, secularism, growing industry, commerce, and the caring state. On the stage of invention and medical empires, we live and dance to and by choices about how we appear and what we do with our bodies. Entire careers, dreams, and drives for fame rest on shaping bodies to public fads and fashions. Tattoo artists, who once served primarily sailors, motorcycle drivers, and entertainers now show up nearly everywhere, even in shops along once conservative, rural, and Midwestern main streets. They leave no skin surface, however hidden and intimate, free of a symbol or logo.

We live in a world where many walk fashion's rampways and dream of sensual pristine beaches. Generations turn their backs on high cultures of words and books and, thanks to pervasive phones, project themselves as "*selfies*." Social reality assembles itself on "Facebook." We trade snapshots for symbols, spirits, and gods.

The lens and screen turn us into bodies elevated beyond cultures. The body forms us in the bedroom and hatches out of intimacies lived and imagined. The body carries us into a community and the all-consuming, ever-posing, parading public square. Cameras and the news carry us virtually to temples, churches, hospitals, schools, and stadiums. There our lives play out before our eyes.

The mass of society, which clothes and represents us, also impinges on the choices and freedoms it proposes as ours. Eight billion bodies—the world's population in 2022, up from 2.5 billion in 1950—rub against us, even crush and suffocate us. Day and night, the great and sloshing *many* knocks on the windows of our minds with their needs, wants, demands, doings, politics, and the exhaustion and pollution of the land, water, air, and climate. Markets, economies, states, and political organizations take everything in their rude, grasping, and clumsy hands. Nuclear fingers remain poised while science attempts extraterrestrial escape, and a commercial appendage of space travel offers, to the very few, million-dollar-plus, ten-second rides beyond gravity, with peeks out a small window back down at the Earth.

Events ever surprise and threaten. They recall and evoke deadly possibilities of past and future wars. As I write this, the war in Ukraine returns us to terrible scenes of the

Second World War while awakening the seventy-five-year-long and unrelenting terror of the Cold War. Across the globe, from west to east, massive needs, compounding desires, and hegemonic commercial plans overrun the world. The dream of free and chosen bodies, minds, and lives remains select and utopian, leaving many of us putting our trust in traditional faiths and hopes.

CHAPTER 10
DAEDALUS, OUR FATHER: THINGS AND TOOLS MAKE LIVES AND MEANINGS

The body is man's first and most natural instrument.
– Marcel Mauss "Body Techniques"[83]

To paraphrase twentieth-century master historian Marc Bloch's *The Historian's Craft*, historical evidence is nearly infinite. Everything that man says, writes, and makes teaches us who we are. In hundreds of ways, the body enacts itself and, in so doing, makes and defines itself singularly and collectively.

Then there are the tools, machines, and engines that make and lead us to invent and dream new and multiple things that, over and over again, make our bodies, minds, selves, and societies. This chapter will examine the body's ongoing, developing, generative, and multifarious relation to things and tools.

A premise at play in the last few chapters runs throughout this chapter; that is, we explore, know, and make ourselves the world by our touch, that of body, skin, and things. Reiterating and elaborating an idea found in Constance Classen's *The Deepest Sense: A Cultural History of Touch*[84], preliterate and modern people participate in the interconnected world of touch and things. They do this more than they can perceive, express, or even have language to represent. Nevertheless, this does not void the fact that people still move, think, imagine, and believe that life is by, with, and through touch and things. Things and touch, themselves interlocked, connect us to ourselves, others, landscapes, places, and times. They fill our senses and are platforms of our imagination and representations of the invisibly great and small worlds of contemporary science and technology. They even furnish the language, concepts, metaphors, and symbols that seek lasting meanings. Touch and things make us the explorers and the poets of internal depths and celestial spaces.

———————

Throughout history and profoundly accelerating in the last two and a half centuries, we humans have depended on things and tools and made ourselves with and out of them. Our entanglements with things and tools, as described in Hodder's first chapter of *Where Are We Heading? The Evolution of Humans and Things* determine lines of development but do not assure certain and irreversible progress. In fact, our dependency can increase our vulnerability and contingency.

Things took over what became the first and essential activities in our lives, such as gathering, shaping, cupping, bundling, carrying, protecting, forming, and decorating. Things made of mud and grasses, strings, cords, ropes, sacks, pots, bones, sinew, and entrails are used to gather, carry, and store. Blankets, hides, and rugs, along with kindling, wood, and fire, play a crucial role in securing warmth, preparing food, and establishing a shelter.

The truth of this is illustrated by all the uses Natives of the North American Plains made of the bison. The hide, bone, and entrails were used in gathering, securing, storing, hauling, building and covering a shelter, carrying a child, and making comfortable and portable dwellings. Heads, horns, and bison beards defined the power of shamans, the beauty of women, and the ornate dress of rituals. We might say we used our body to make the bison's body ours.

Edible things were gathered, hunted, and then cooked and shared as food to sustain and celebrate. These things preoccupied the lives, pleasures, and dreams of early people. They were at the heart of the lives of the first groups and tribes, and any king had to give the greatest banquets. Foods followed and made historical changes with trade routes and the formation of food industries and markets that fed ever greater numbers of the world population. In his seminal *Sweetness and Power* (1985), anthropologist Sidney Mintz followed the revolutionary transformation of sugar from a spice from the East to becoming a mass commodity in the West, grown and harvested by slaves on Caribbean plantations and distributed wherever commerce went. As the sweetener of countless products, sugar is the attractive essence of candy bars and sodas. The sugar-frosted cake has become a prerequisite for celebrating birthdays and weddings during the last two centuries. Sugar, in part a popular rival of alcohol, became the synonym for *sweet* with all its luscious associations with taste, affection, sex, and all that urges us to make and declare of life, *How sweet it is!*

Offering and sharing foods, the first act of hospitality, secures community by pleasing the body. A meal can have multiple meanings. It can be a singular act of generosity to a stranger, proof that one has abundant wealth, and even an offering to petition the dead and spirits. Food commemorates occasions and acknowledges a season's bounty, a harvest's success, a good hunt, and a winning season on the sports field. Food is a means by which people get together and participate with one another; through eating, talking, and moving, full and slurping mouths join each other. With banquets, we induct members to our team and celebrate a season's play, a year of work, and someone's retirement. Food also provides a time to get together and take pleasure in being *one* of a *many*. At the table, stories, resources, acts, and lives are recounted.

In his *Entangled: An Archaeology of the Relationships between Humans and Things* (2012), Ian Hodder joins the study of archaeology, anthropology, and early cultures in showing how central things are to every aspect of our being. He also explores things as embedded symbols. From his research on Çatalhöyük, a Neolithic proto-city settlement in southern Anatolia which existed from approximately 7500 BC to 6400 BC, he offers insight into the substantial yet changing connection of things and symbols in the culture of a people.

The relationships between the core and peripheral parts
of entanglement change through time. In the early and
middle parts of the 1,400 years sequence at Çatalhöyük,
the main social interest was in entanglements that had to
do with burial, history-making, feasting, and wild animals.
It is the wild animals that are shown in the art, and it is
their horns that are installed in houses. Art and decoration
are found in houses, often related to the ancestors buried
beneath the floors.[85]

WE MAKE THINGS, AND THINGS MAKE US

To rely again on our prefatory quotation from Marcel Mauss's
"Body Techniques," "The body is man's first and most natural
instrument."[86] We learn and practice how to walk, run, jump,
swim, talk, write, crochet, knit, cut, carve, and cook, even
dance, sing, hit, and throw. The use of our body is an art and
skill which we individually start to develop and practice in the
earliest stages of childhood.

Given that bodies are our first instruments of action,
we cannot separate bodily techniques from all aspects and
consequences of the things we make. Bodies, our vessels
of life and movement, are the principal agency of our self,
social place, and role, and the maker of our environment. Our
works, skills, and crafts become the defining disciplines and
habits of our lives, for they give us bodily powers and control
over things, selves, and, to a degree, others.

Among the earliest things we made were tools that
extended the body's ability to make other things. Our first
tools were hammers, knives, mortars and pestles to make
and crush, and containers such as pots, spoons, bowls, and
cups to carry and cook. Both tools and containers were used
to form the walls and roofs for dwellings.[87]

We incorporate our lives into the things we make, use,
and save. We think, dream, and invent things. We adopt
and design materials. With them, we establish villages and,
ultimately, cities. As born of the activity and discovery of
the body and mind, things account for the domestication

of animals and the planting of fields, for articles like ropes, cloth, and the wheels of ships.

Things place us on the earth and account for our relations to land and water, field and forest. We also use things to commemorate the dead and celebrate spirits and gods. They are our crutches along the road and slings that throw our imaginations toward stars. They help us collect and make things. They inform our language with analogies, metaphors, and symbols. Tools prove instruments of our reason, imagination, and understanding.[88]

THINGS, THINGS, AND MORE THINGS

The body's movement, perceptions, senses, and consciousness went with its use and development of things and tools, and as we entered modern history, the increased use of machines and new sources of energy around which and by which we organized lives. Things, tools, and, later, machines and engines increased and transformed our use of and relation to nature. Specialized tools advanced and revolutionized our assumptions about our place in being and furnished instruments that we turn into words, analogies, and metaphors for understanding, arranging, and making the world and self. They lead us to project ourselves beyond our present place and time.[89]

Historians must conceive how the body, in its movements and functions, affects our senses, habits, speech, and gestures and join us to others making social worlds.[90] "Body," indeed, "is our first and most natural instrument to be and act in the world," in the words of anthropologist Marcel Mauss. As argued in Chapter 9, we are increasingly transformed individually and collectively by our entanglement with things and our dependency on tools. Things satisfy bodies and emotions. They establish our private and public orders, while they can be used to show wealth and abundance, facilitate exchange, and be a source of gifts.[91]

Over thousands of years, things have written the conditions and premises of the body and the self. Through actions, habits, and consciousness, things wove us into life. Things made our first senses of wholes and parts useful and useless, animate and inanimate. In measure, things defined our survival, wants, needs, and opportunities. They defined our lives, body, and self as foragers and rummagers, hunters and gatherers, and, additionally, as tool-using and tool-making creatures, who, since the agricultural and urban revolutions, increasingly made and designed the worlds we have inhabited, exploited, traveled, and dreamed.

In our earliest history as bipedal creatures, we needed and sought certain things. In different places at different times, we discovered and used different things, which we joined together, shaped, and made complex. Things captured our close and far-surveying eyes, reaching arms, and grasping hands, transported by stabilizing and far-traveling legs.

We integrated things into our lives for their use. Tool making shaped our ways and labors and our very environment. Our advantage over other animals rested on the interpenetration of the energy and use of the human body, which was increasingly joined to things as tools magnified our energy and expanded our minds. Our mastery over things registered our claim to the world, which we worked, named, and made our own.

Things formed axes of our experience and power. They formed the rudiments of our consciousness and the grammar of our actions and control. We spoke, named, and acted with things in hand.

Early people learned their world by what they found and made useful. They learned uses for the wood of trees, the grasses of marsh reeds, and the mud of shores. In combination, these materials could make a container, a net, and the walls, roof, and bed of a home. Along a river, villagers could trap and net fish and, on shores, find shells to cup and cut. Wood floated their bodies and things on the water while wooden walking staffs facilitated crossing uneven terrains and streams.

Long before they grew their food and domesticated animals, villagers made complex things and started crafts. Consider the skills involved in sliding or rolling a heavy object and how that led to skids, sleds, and, eventually, carts. Sleds and wheels were pulled with ropes that harnessed animals and floating rafts, which increased trade.

THINGS AND TOOLS, BORN OF THE BODY, MADE OUR HISTORY

As *Homo sapiens*, we did not come into the world naked and empty-handed, but rather we came forth dressed and using tools thanks to our predecessor's inventions hundreds of thousands of years prior to our emergence (roughly estimated to be 300,000 to 400,000 years ago). Things and tools had already sharpened our eyes, hands, bodies, senses, and intelligence, placing us in the world we lived in.

Things and tools knotted the body and mind together and the world around us. With tools, we built homes and established settlements. We chose places and fields and selected plants, seeds, and methods of fertilization, plowing, and planting for them. Agriculture emerged approximately 10,000 years ago in the Near East, and from its surplus food, populations gathered and grew, and villages and cities arose, often along rivers in fertile valleys. In them, crafts, specialization, learning, accounting, and writing occurred. The growth of villages and cities meant the domestication of animals, specialization of crafts, increased water and land travel, and the transport of materials and things. In diverse ways, homes and things fostered senses of individuality, privacy, family, and self-making.

The individual is born into a cradle of material and social dependency and blanketed, so to speak, in diverse and countless ties and relations. He or she knows their self by place, role, and activity. The individual's body, their attunement of senses, and long-term development of emotions and skills depend on imitation, repetition, and support. The individual matures and develops through instruction, discipline, education, and the grids of tradition and culture. Relations, reactions, familiarity, and emotional ties grow out of receiving and taking, giving and exchanging. All humans live by and with a sense of common bodies, things, and senses.

IN CONVERSATION WITH THINGS

Individuals and groups weave themselves into things through traditions, cultures, and learning. The things around us, both animate and inanimate, form voices. They speak to us through the full array of our senses and across our consciousness and subconsciousness. The interconnections of our material and social being mix us as bodies and minds, selves and worlds, things, tools, actions, constructions, and words.

With great variation—and admittedly a license to figurative speech—things and bodies assimilate each other. They account for the habits and grudges that anchor everyday life in affections, resistance, repetition, consistency, and daily routines. Things and bodies relay messages of danger and satisfaction back and forth, evoke emotions, ideas, and dreams, and spawn curiosity, which distinguishes the very genesis of the human species and, most recently, as argued by science writer Philip Ball, prove a great interior spur to modern science.[92]

Things call us to thinking and making—or in the words of art critic Leo Stein, "Things are what we encounter, ideas are what we project. Things provide the substance, which we turn into objects and symbols of our place in being and narrative in life."[93] The interaction of bodies and things writes the main text of human evolution while making the substance and texture of daily life, which is lived out by learning the ways of things and our fidelity to habits.

Anthropologist Tim Ingold follows this approach, anchoring his studies in "real human beings, in specific places . . . embedded in the wider ecology of life," which he defines as "a dwelling perspective."[94] The sentient body in movement—expressive of our biology—is fully interactive with a sentient environment from which the body learns and fashions skills.[95] Biology and learning, perception and imagination, do not form antitheses for Ingold.[96] As humans walk, see, and act, they perceive, learn about, and represent the world of experience with lines and traces that connect things with maps, drawings, genealogies, stories, and even music.

DAEDALUS, TOOLMAKER AND INVENTOR, ADVANCES THROUGH TIME

Over the ages, things placed and developed humans in the world and afforded them experience and self-knowledge. Tools, with variation by groups, places, and cultures, made more tools. Then, starting in late medieval and early modern history, machines were powered by engines first driven by steam and one hundred and twenty-five years later powered by electricity and, subsequently, by other sources of energy. The body's power to make, manufacture, and multiply has increased exponentially. Our reach, grasp, and touch cross the breadth and depth of all things, great and small.

As human groups learned and made things, they built environments and so transformed the contents of their lives. What humans did, made them. A body's needs and skills created the kernel of everyday life, a person and group's habits, ways, wants, and ambitions. With things and tools, humans defined home and their place in groups and nature.

As I traced in *On Foot: A History of Walking* and in *Surfaces: A History*, early civilizations ran on few, short, and rough roads. They had to test river and ocean trails. Smooth surfaces remained unknown. In contrast, today, all phases of life travels are nearly effortless. We move on sidewalks, roads, and tracks beside power and communication lines and systems. Machines and engines run on smooth gears and wheels. The assumption that we can travel far, fast, and smoothly underpins our belief in our improvement and notion of progress. In utopian dreams things have been regularized, obstacles removed, and we travel frictionless and instantaneously. Satisfyingly, the versatile body, free of labor and travail, moves only for pleasure and at its own leisure.

As the modern world advances in its control of material things and the making of tools, machines, and engines, it fosters the belief that we can improve the body and life of the individual and society. As we speed and roll to new frontiers, we believe the world is for our wishing and making, often without realizing how much it is a creation of our body as an instrument and, in extension, with things, tools, machines, engines, and factories. The telephone and the car, two inventions whose origin date from the second half of the nineteenth and the early twentieth century, individualized, revolutionized, and intensified our entanglements with things and others and profoundly altered our movement across places and spaces. They led us to the cables, rockets, and satellites that speed us to imagine, wish, and fear our best and, alas, worst dreams.

To be modern is to travel in new vessels that traverse distances at speeds that require the exactitude of clocks and schedules. The steam engine changed our relationship with space and time. It transformed and regularized water travel. More dramatically, trains established interurban and transcontinental travel and transport. They put individuals, communities, and whole industries and nations on the clock. Their ability to transport and deliver, joined supply and manufacture, goods and markets, and communities and families. Railways crossed mountains and rivers with tracks, tunnels, and bridges. They calculated the most direct and fastest possible routes. Walking, going on foot, our first and perennial way to travel, became essentially a hobby for the well-off and the leisured, and mountain climbing became an adventure and sport for the boldest.

As someone born and brought up in Detroit, I am compelled to mention the importance of the car in making twentieth-century history, similar to how the train shaped nineteenth-century history. Cars, which stand at the center of twentieth-century innovation and design, made whole industries, towns, cities, families, and individuals. Cars, in turn, delivered our bodies, families, and things through space with speed and in style. They were engineered for smooth running, visibility, handling, storage, comfort, and travel. Cars were not mute. They called out for newer, faster, and better-forming engines and tires, wide and open roads with signs and signals, and better intersections and connections. Brands and types of cars served wealth, style, and leisure. And with increasing numbers of owners on their side, the auto industry pressed to reorganize the roads and streets of cities to serve their growing car-owning and commuting population. The car, thus, came to define the movement of the body and the sense and feeling of self in contemporary life.

Trucks followed cars. They, too, were invented towards the end of the nineteenth century. They were diversified by the loads carried, the types of work done, the sites used, and the distances they traveled. Pick-up trucks and vans, half-car and half-truck, or metal hybrids (or centaurs, if you wish) began competing with cars as early as the 1920s. They were first at home in farm country where the flatbed served for small and quick hauling, and the cab afforded quick and comfortable rides to neighboring farms and towns. The tractor, with a gasoline engine, also worked on the farm. It was mobile in fields and between fields with the seasonal and daily tasks of pulling and plowing, as well as with drilling, leveling, and even lifting and pulling specialized implement machines for plowing, seeding, and harvesting. During the last one hundred and twenty-five years, tractors have defined the nation's fields, soils, waters, and increasing farm sizes. More powerful, specialized, and comfortable tractors have increased our energy and techniques and done away with much of the most taxing labor. While increasing farm size and yet reducing farm population, these tractors demanded their place on better roads and quickly adopted GIS (Geographic Information Science) channels for mapping and economically managing their fields.

In the country and the city, we contemporaries live amidst more multiplying things born of new technologies. We fill the inventories of our cars, trucks, tractors, and boat dealers, along with the shelves of our grocery, department stores, and other stores (too many to list), with new things for work, health, leisure, and play. Also, more and more devices are conjured out of electricity, chemistry, and physics to serve our eyes, ears, mouth, touch, and handling. They pave new paths for the body, feelings, mind, and senses. They and what they allow us to make, take us, body and soul, into their custody.

To be a contemporary person is to talk about nuclear devices, microcosmic particles, and electromagnetic waves. The body and mind become recipients and captives of medicine and drugs. Increasingly, the old learn of implanting pumps, valves, devices, and artificial organs. Aortic valve implants offer a choice of calf, pig, or plastic. I read about producing embryos from humans, monkeys, and pigs. The making of artificial wombs excites new theories, materials, and devices. The body and self stand at the entrance of expressways to the beyond.

CHAPTER 11
THINGS HOLD US AND MAKE US INTO OUR DISCOURSE WITH THEM

Things catch our attention and find a place in our words, ways, and days. They ride the tip of our tongue and make our wit. One thing may be of multiple experiences, meanings, and words.

Take trees, for example. They constitute primary materials, furnish our shade, define places, and mark and orient our travel. Do they not evoke density, permanence, beauty, and even awe? How many of the old have a companion tree as a chronometer of our lives? Trees can identify our home. They are the poles around which we often go, and they even mark the starting and ending points of biographies. They orient our memory and evoke metaphors and analogies of our conditions and lives—we can *pine* their loss endlessly unless we stiffen our *oaken* spines.

Others things, animate and inanimate, singularly and collectively do the same. Neuroscientist Antonio Damasio suggests that things are pertinent to our survival. Things guide and even command our homeostasis, keeping our bodies and emotions in balance and on track. They alert our sensations, spark our feelings, shape our consciousness, and embody our ideas and dreams. While serving our nutrition, health, and recreation and making and aiding our work, things make our communities and societies. They define our actions, understanding, and plans while affording the use of materials, words, and symbols.

In *The Poetics of Space* (pub. 1958 in French; trans. into English in 1964), philosopher Gaston Bachelard suggested that things call up by their singularity, importance, feelings, stories, and memories. French essayist Francis Ponge won the title "the poet of things" in his work, *The Voice of Things*

(1974, first published in French in 1942 as *Le parti pris de choses*). In this writing, what we might take as the simplest and most ordinary of subjects—a snail, a plant, a shell, a match, a cigarette, a pebble, or a piece of soap—are the objects of his reflections. His premise was *things await our words to reveal themselves*. By unlocking them to speak, the concealed and corporal givens of our everyday lives tell us our feelings and thoughts.

In *The Voice of Things*, Ponge wrote:

> Ideas are not my forte. I do not handle them with ease. They handle me instead. . . . Objects in the external world, on the other hand, delight me. They sometimes surprise me but seem in no way concerned about my approval: which they immediately acquire. I do not question them.

Here he echoed the older French philosopher Henri Bergson, who, in his doctoral dissertation (published in French in 1889 as *Les donées immediates de la conscience*), argued that what is immediate to our mind is formative of our consciousness.

Our fruition as fully conscious beings, I conclude from Ponge and Bergson, hinges on acknowledging our dependence on the immediacy of things given and before us. We come to know the body, the self, and the world through things. Things teach us the body's functions and possibilities, our work and play, our necessities and freedom. They make up our daily and seasonal worlds while affording experience and metaphors to make ourselves and myths, and know our spirits and God.

THINGS INCREASINGLY MAKE OUR MODERN LIVES

Things, as discussed in Deyan Sudjic's *The Language of Things* (2009), have a language and a design and are formed into archetypes. An aristocratic culture puts things on display in order to show standing and wealth. Today "luxury" glimmers and glitters throughout a democracy as the masses follow "fashion" and, even unknowingly, contemporary art.

In the last two centuries, an abundance of mass-produced and commercially distributed things filled and made public places as well as our private and intimate spaces. Cultural critic John Berger wrote in *Ways of Seeing* (1972), "Clothes, food, cars, cosmetics, baths, sunshine" are things that please the human body and are to be "enjoyed in themselves."

As I have stated here in various ways, the multiplication and variety of things make the modern individual and mass society. Things give work, acceleration, and diversity to our movement and the distribution and inventory of things. The body and the self are packaged lives, as things account for our labor, craft, pleasure, play, choices, masks, dreams, and our very individuality.

The very word *thing* jumps from across matter and mind. Things are words, associations, feelings, and thoughts. As an aggregate, *things* are taken by philosophers and scientists to be equivalent to nature, life, and mankind. We leave it to metaphysics and myth to kitc the paths we take to, from, and beyond things.

Throughout history, things formed a central spine of our gifts and exchanges. They elicited a sense of gratitude and fairness and called up resentment and charges of injustice. In modern times, our politics, at least the best of them, seek fairness and equity amid shifting markets, prices, and advertisements. Good and bad times commonly raise up calls for thanks and anger and shows of loyalty and revolt.

In a *Wall Street Journal* article (January 10, 2022), I read how "Studies Find Supply-Chain Turmoil Had Unprecedented Economic Impact." In another article, I considered how "a battery race" involves rending or diminishing the U.S. battery companies and their need for lithium as the key element in "The Race for Electric Vehicles." Who knows how Chinese possession of lithium gives it economical and even military superiority for the hour? I think of the economic and military competition hinged on superior sailing and fighting ships in early modern Europe and, eventually, the United States. I ponder how the spreading of electric transmission in the nineteenth century

lit up everyday life and increased the national capacity
to compete for the world's seas and seaports. States and
politics hinge on variable things and elusive satisfaction.

Around 1900, in Western Europe and North America,
rural and peasant societies and technologies, characterized
by small groups and villages, fieldwork, going on foot, and
living in darkness, began to be completely overrun by money
and goods, commerce and industry, machines and engines,
and national institutions.

A telling maxim of the poor southern Italians of the late
nineteen and early twentieth centuries was: *Chi non a/non è*
("He who hasn't, isn't"). I echoed this proverb in a line of
verse describing the condition of my impoverished Sicilian
grandparents' families on the eve of their departure for
America in the first decade of the twentieth century:

> *Without land for tillage*
> *Or a donkey to mortgage.*
> *For winter survival and spring seed*
> *Descended a mountain and crossed an ocean*
> *Left for opportunities and a life far away.*

So, lives entangled in traditional and thought to be lasting
ways entered a protean world in which things, individuals,
and hopes were continually altered. The gears of modernity
shifted to rapid change—full speed ahead. Indecipherable
dashboard lights signaled increasing speeds.

Modern life reiterated one message: We measure, count,
and assess our lives by things earned and desired and by
the money required to purchase them. Things are our great
romance.

Things are chronometers. Like all mutable and finite
matter, they clock themselves and the worlds in which they
exist. They literally tell time and change by years, seasons,
days, hours, and moments. Historians use them to mark off
millennia and centuries. While historians of nature count
and measure the thickness of tree rings that tell of seasons
and centuries of climate change and their effects, traditional

historians tell of time punctuated by wars and new weapons and marked by the rise and fall of empires and nations.

Modern historians form their chronology of changing lives out of the spread of commerce and new inventions and their dependency on machines, engines, energy, and factories. Sugar and its worldwide spread tell a story of continental changing tastes, diets, and leisure, while anthracite coal, which mainly replaced wood and fueled the furnaces of the Industrial Revolution, tells the story of regions, machines, labor, and even the dust that filled the air and covered the surfaces of water, cities, and the skins of grist mill workers and coal miners whose coughs and particle-filled spitting revealed dust penetration into the body.

TALKING THINGS

Birth names, concepts, and metaphors are things, too. They account for worlds of words that identify, explain, connect, and even consecrate the body and the self when at work or play, practicing a craft, running a machine, or organizing an industry.

Things make up the vernacular. We say: I am going to tell you a *thing or two* about *the things that count*. That is *just the thing you need*. A forgotten name is a *what's chamachig*, or to get serious is *to arrive at the heart of a thing*. And finally, there is *nothing (no-thing) like it*.

Likewise, other languages make use of *things*. The Mafia chieftain's *cosa nostra* means *our thing*. Latin attaches things "*re*" to law, reality, truth, and effects. I recall the phrase *re ipse loquitur*, ("things speak for themselves"), from days looking through my father-in-law's books. Yes, things do speak for themselves. They talk about their singular existence, the situations, places, and "*things that make the world go round*."

Things enter us into the concrete world. We derive pragmatic (useful) from the Greek word *pragmata* (meaning "a fact, a thing done"), which we translate with the word, *handy*. Even more abstractly, things are metaphoric, linking close and far, up and down, deep and high, complex and simple, and they even try to explain connections and causes between things.

By one accounting, the world is the sum of things out there. Things are not just seen, explored, touched, and taken possession of by use and habit but known, theorized, and invented. Things are not just material; they belong to mind, possibility, and spirituality; they are even the *answers* to our prayers to comprehend needs and resolve situations. Nothing captures the universality of things more than the expressions: *the nature of things, such are things,* and *things make it (life) so.* We even divide the world into things when we speak of *spiritual and material things, human and natural things,* or *intimate and public things. Things* can be a synonym for matters and elements, or they simply can be *handy* and *easy to look at.* The question *How are things going,* suggests life and *everything else* we take to be in our domain. *Things* are the synonym for life, nature, affairs, past occurrences, results, or present prospects, so we ask about *the general state of things.*

THINGS MAKE LIVES

A single thing found or given can be a magic talisman, be it a stone or a coin that can be put in a pocket, a ring, or a necklace. I affectionately wear the watch my mother bought me as her farewell. A given thing can be memorable. It forever embodies love and a pledge. Discarding or losing a thing, think of a wedding ring, resounds with meaning through space and over time. So, our lives and bodies are entangled with objects given, exchanged, and remembered. Lives can be narrated by jewelry, collections, tattoos, even scars, handmade objects, or special goods like the favorite family car.

For peasants, having or not having shoes marks the path of a lifetime. As stated by the philosopher Heidegger, a shoemaker can read his customer's work by the worn surface of their shoes as if they confess the condition of one's life. Being without shoes filled in a part of the history of my wife's relatives in the Carpathian Mountains. As children, they traveled on cold days from one foot-warming manure pile to the next foot-warming manure pile until they reached *izba babi* ("grandma's hut").

One story I read, whose title I do not recall since more than fifty years have passed, depicts how one brother took a shared pair of shoes from his brother on his farewell journey. A 1978 Italian film, *The Tree of the Wooden Clogs*, tells of a landlord who evicted a peasant family from the land to punish the peasant father who chopped down a tree to make a pair of wooden shoes for his son to walk to school in. Another story with a title I don't recall tells of a child of nineteenth-century England who was awakened very early each morning by passing workers clomping in their wooden shoes (*kloppen* in Dutch) on their way to work. Even in the countryside of Minnesota, you hear stories of children who, having only one pair of shoes, carried them to and from school to save wear and tear on them.

As recently as the post-Second World War, on the east side of prospering Detroit, shoes were valued and, along with rationed tires, were stolen, found, and traded. At my Uncle Sam's funeral, relatives claimed Sam's body was put in a half coffin by the design of a greedy and guileful undertaker who kept the shoes of the deceased. Although a single pair of shoes or two was all the poor of the countryside and city could expect up to the mid-century, thereafter, shoes crowded closet floors. Now, a pair of newly designed, engineered, and advertised tennis shoes (once simple boat shoes) has become the common footwear for leisure, play, sports, and everyday life.

Equally vivid historical novels and biographies could be told around other articles of clothing, furniture (tables, chairs, and even sofas), fireplaces, stoves, iceboxes, and refrigerators. Also, stories of wall hangings, decorations, floor coverings, tool chests, toys, and games abound. A writer with memory and imagination can spin a story around the things in a person's home, field, roads, and cities. Universally, grandmothers sew, weave, crochet, and make tapestries to win the love and memory of their grandchildren, keeping them in a lasting embrace.

Things grow and become more entangling when they enter minds as part of an image and memory of a place, time, person, and a set of actions and interactions. Humans can represent and sculpt themselves to their keepsakes. A pocket knife, key chain, watch, ring, or piece of jewelry embodies the self, memories, and affections. The tattoo, what and where it is placed on the body, and when and how it was gotten, talks of the self and signals the world. Whether simple or complex, vulgar or discrete, fresh or old, a tattoo broadcasts different programs from its station on the skin. It can speak loudly as the feathers of a bird, the outer shell of a mollusk or turtle, the hide of an animal, or a bison robe that recounts a story. Tattoos may even reveal much more—an identity, sexual disposition, type of driven motorcycle, or membership in a group. Also, tattoos can be testimonies to travel, adventures, and battles, an administered serial number from service or prison, or a formula of love, prayer, or charm.

The novelist Jack London offered this increasingly dubious comment on the possible meaning of a tattoo: "Show me a man with a tattoo, and I'll show you a man with an interesting past." Edgar Allen Poe contradicts this, saying tattoos must be read through ambiguity: "After reading all that has been written, and after thinking all that can be thought on the topics of God and the soul, the man who has a right to say that he thinks at all, will find himself face to face with the conclusion that, on these topics, the most profound thought is that which can be the least easily distinguished from the most superficial sentiment." Whereas contemporary East London and prison psychiatrist and writer Theodore Dalrymple postulated in an issue of *Psychology Today* (May 16, 2015), that a tattoo could stand for rebellion and self-chosen marginalization. He also preached that an unremoved tattoo curses the addict to continuous addiction. He authored this biting comment: "The tattoo has a profound meaning: the superficiality of modern man's existence." Tattoos that had a place in traditional cultures now belong to a time when great numbers of people, a part of the lost masses, feel compelled to discretely or overtly to take their place on the public stage by a glimpse at part of their body.

THINGS ARE US

Things received, gifted, lost, and stolen go deep into a person's emotions, relations, memories, conscience, and self. Things can be special and emotionally moving objects. They even explain motives and actions and account for lasting bonds and extreme actions and ruptures in family and friendships. For the truth of this last point, simply get a family lawyer talking about wills, and the lawyer will attest that fortunes and relations have been lost and broken while contesting the division of goods; though they lacked cash value, they told who was the heir of love. As so go things, so go our bodies, identities, feelings, and selves.

Objects touch the heart of affairs and feelings. They give rise to gratitude, fairness, equality, a sense of respect, and a range of negative feelings and thoughts. The loss of a special object can resonate an emptiness and, in minds, deeply register and account for behavior years after. Families and groups register long hurts, brood resentment, and bear grudges that last decades or for entire lives. Such was the case in my grandfather's German and Irish family, who bore grudges long after their exact causes were forgotten. A family historian falls short when failing to take notice of how division over little objects profoundly divides families. Jealousy, envy, and resentment are powerful dividers of people, and the divisions of things can mark a turning point in relations.

A person grows up and knows their self by and among things. Things constitute familiarity. They create continuity of life, places, relations, and selves. The *damnedest things* can have a compelling presence and a repeating meaning. They are like rings on fingers. They win sentiments, attachments, and identities and make shared and remembered stories.

Abundance earned, commercially given, and governmentally distributed, meant more things for all to have, be proud of, want, and envy.

Life-long friendships, romances, and marriages are woven and stitched tight out of things that incorporate us into an intimate and communal way of life. I hear this feeling echoed in the song *Little Things Mean a Lot*.

> Blow me a kiss from across the room
> Say I look nice when I'm not
> Touch my hair as you pass my chair
> Little things mean a lot. . . .

> Send me the warmth of a secret smile
> To show me you haven't forgot
> Now and forever, that always and ever
> Little things mean a lot.

Little things create habits and rituals that sew people together. A game of *bocce* and a few glasses of beer can center the local Italian club cohabited by single and widowed men. Certainly, a marriage can be centered around things used, purchased, and even regularly enjoyed and disputed. As I mourn the death of my wife, I think about what my friend and poet Jim Rogers wrote about the lingering presence of his recently passed wife, "Losing someone you love, with whom you've shared a life and a home, moves you into a world filled with ghosts—benign revenants, but ghosts all the same."

SMALL THINGS CAN BE BIG THINGS

In this age, as we seek to get our minds around the big metauniverses and hyper objects like nuclear war, global warming, relativity, and waves of energy going down black holes, our reason, imagination, and technology must consider infinitesimally small invisible pieces, bits, and particles of life and matter. They are far too small to see, touch, measure, and calculate. Germs and atoms divide and divide again. Our horizons lie along the deepening frontiers of atomic particulate. Each successive revolution in theory and technology leaves us further from the bottom and end of things.

We are condemned to say goodbye to one set of things, making them antiques and objects of memory, while being met by great sets of invented and novel things flowing from our advancing technology and theories. The world we, at least once, roughly knew becomes an unfolding universe of little and big things we barely understand.

We dine on the paradox: The more things we are entangled with, the more their growing connections, interpenetrations, and communications elude us. Limits, boundaries, movements, and connections blur, and explanations and causalities grow shaky.

One thing—surely not a distinct entity—only possibly, although not necessarily, occurs after another thing or, in the words of an old worker as quoted by a good friend, "A lot of things depend on a lot of things." I also find myself drawing on the reach of this Sicilian proverb: *Le cose longe diventanu serpenti* ("Long things, all things drawn out, become snakes").

In *Dust: A History of the Small and Invisible*, published thirty years ago, I described our collective descent, scientifically and technologically, into the growing infinity of the microcosm. I even ventured to say the small had gotten bigger than the big. Physicists plumb the death of small particles of energy and waves down black holes. Chemists seek to manipulate molecules and make new materials. Stem cell specialists seek to make mice embryos without sperm and eggs, while scientists in other fields seek to fathom neurons and identify and select DNA. Nothing is too small to search and scan and make the basis of a new theory and product. Simply listen to the daily news accounting of our seeking to understand and control COVID, another virus.

Arguably, in the last hundred fifty years of research, study, and theory, the small has actually grown bigger than the

large. The enhanced microscope sees further inward than
the telescope peers outward. From another perspective, we
are in a body and an infinite one and many. Our body's parts,
functions, and feelings connect to a myriad mind, deeper and
more complex than definition. We are an incarnate infinity of
infinities within infinities, or in the words of my recent poem:

ONE, TWO, THREE, AND MANY AND INFINITY

Who disputes the world is one, two, three
Then many,
Then infinity?
A multitude, a plentitude,
An immense stirring incertitude,
Beyond counting
A great, great many!
An infinity of infinities.

Endless things,
Up and down!
Energy and variety!
A frog plops in water,
A row of turtles follow,
Plopping one after another
As if following an eternal command,
While a nearby church bell
Rings a drowsy village awake.

Do we ever stand higher atop,
However far we abstractly hop?
Do we ever reach the bottom
Of our earthly canyon?

To get started join Archimedes
And calculate the grains of sand on a beach,
Join Leonardo
Representing all colors and shadows,
Drawing and explaining currents of wind and water.

And when through,
Sketch a straight-line end
Of gravity's curving bend
To its end.
Do your best,
You will have no rest
From this endless test.
The more you understand the connection and circuits
Of the electrified, signaling, brain,
Its distinct factory lopes and wiring synapses,
The less you comprehend the mind,
Your Socratic wisdom:
The more they know me
The less I know myself.

Little and great,
Big and small,
Singular and plural
X somehow making Y.
Yes things, objects and tools, make us
What we are.
They make our story and history,
Create the little and great,
And the white whale
Of our extraordinary tale.

CONCLUSION
ENGINES AND INDUSTRY: OUR CREATORS

We belong to the Industrial Revolution. Modern and contemporary technology goes faster than we can grasp, assimilate, and value. It connects us by body and mind to the use of coal and steam, national navies and colonies, markets and resources, factories, and the laboring class. The young Marx, a student of Hegel, taught that capitalism created and transformed labor. Its regimes emptied the proletariat, the laboring and exploited class, of its nature, inheritance, and traditional ways. With the complete emptying of the past and old self, the proletariat is potentially a free and self-defining being, everything a human can be and wants to be.

My understanding of the Industrial Revolution came from readings by a second and older American journalist, thinker, and historian, the patrician Henry Adams (1838–1918). As the heir of two American presidents and the son of the American ambassador to England during the Civil War, Adams knew much of Europe and everybody who counted as somebody in Washington.

In 1966, during my second year of graduate school at the University of Rochester, I read patrician Adams' *Education*. Written in 1905 as a sequel to his *Mont Saint Michel and Chartres* (and privately printed in 1907), Adams put forward the notion that man's history could be written as the story of his accumulating and accelerating power across the big arc of human history from fire to atom.

In a concluding chapter of the *Education*, "The Dynamo and the Virgin," he talked about how his understanding of his times was overthrown. He was more than sixty years old when he attended the Great Exposition of 1900. There he encountered a machine, the dynamo, a generator of electric energy. As he stood before the machine that "broke his

207

historical neck," he heard man's gathering energy in its hum. It sparked in him the thought that the dynamo would, in the coming century, hold the same powers that the Cross held over the Middle Ages and that the Virgin Mary held over the culture and cathedral of the high Middle Ages. As fact and as a symbol, the dynamo and the power it portended for his times transcended all previous religious symbols. History no longer belonged to God and His Providence and Mercy but to new inventions, machines, and engines of our self-making.

As Adams stated in "A Dynamic Theory of History," humanity entered a new order of being at the beginning of this revolution of scientifically and technologically quarrying the smallest units of being—atoms and particles—for new sources of energy. The sum of forces that attracted humans has been gathering things and transforming history since before recorded history. "Fire taught him secrets that no other animal could learn; running water probably taught him even more, especially in his first lessons of mechanics." With an acute sensibility beyond comparison with any other animal, humans, even before recorded history, took the world into themselves and turned it into energy and knowledge. The atom exploded all known bounds and limits. Adams queried the possibility that, in the near future, man would make a bomb of invisible matter: the atom and its kinetic energy.

Adams' vision heightened my sense of a pending apocalypse. It was only one laboratory, invention, and state away. Adams foresaw other paths to self-destruction in the imperial grasp of capitalism and the iron fist of the nation-state. He led me to conjure that mankind, with the imperial United States and Communist and totalitarian Russia in the lead, would, in competition and war, ravage nature and destroy humanity.

Neither Adams nor Lewis Mumford, a treasured undergraduate discovery, nor any other dystopian thinker like Roderick Seidenberg, author of *Post-Historic Man*, 1950, made me a historian of technology or a prophet of the future. However, collectively they convinced me that intellectual, political, and social history increasingly turned on what we made, what we ultimately don't control, and where it might lead. Rapidly advancing science and technology underpinned my view of modern and contemporary history. I believed that we were not just the inventors but the captives of new technology. It both made and imperiled life. Its machines, engines, and power, and its physics, chemistry, and inventions remade and imperiled all. Recreating, in measure, the body and the self, they changed our relation not just to space and time but also to our history and future.

SPEEDING TOWARDS AN UNKNOWN END

With the articulation of Mumford and Adams, I forged my own rough narratives of the backfire of mega-technology, the mega-city, the mega-nation-state, and our growing power over all things. In contrast to Enlightenment's progressive theories of the advance of freedom, reason, science, and humanity, I sided with conservatives in saying all changes are not advances. In fact, changes in the marketplace, science, and technological and industrial powers can blow up tradition, community, and liberty—and even deny belief in God and his calling at the end of time and beyond time.

I saw the engine room of contemporary civilization's course in the Industrial Revolution, and I concur with the opening pages of Vaclav Smil's *Energy and Civilization: A History* (2017). "Energy is the only universal currency: one of its many forms must be transformed to get anything done. . . . Humans depend . . . on many energy flows for their civilized existence. . . . The evolution of human civilization has resulted in larger populations, a growing complexity of social and productive arrangement, and a higher quality of life for growing numbers."[97]

In his Introduction several pages later, Smil concurs with Adams that mankind's advantage and advance depended on tools, which first secured food, shelter, and clothing. "The mastery of fire greatly extended our range of habitation and set us further apart from the animals. New tools led to the harnessing of the domesticated animals, the building of more

complex muscle-powered machines, and the conversion of a
tiny fraction of kinetic energies of wind and water to useful
power." Smil continues,

> Controlled combustion in fireplaces, stoves,
> and furnaces turned the chemical of plants into
> thermal energy. This heat has been used directly in
> households and in smelting metals, firing bricks, and
> processing and finishing countless products. The
> combustion of fossil fuels made all of these traditional
> direct uses of heat more widespread and efficient. A
> number of fundamental inventions made it possible
> to convert thermal energy from the burning of fossil
> fuels to mechanical energy. This was done first in
> steam and internal combustion engines, then in gas
> turbines and rockets.[98]

Then, according to Smil, the harnessing of the kinetic energy
of water in 1882 and the splitting of a uranium isotope
in 1956 turned us into "a high-energy civilization" whose
expansion now encompasses the whole planet.[99] With a
geometric increase in our engines and energy during the
last two hundred years, we have made things that make
and things that remake our bodies, lives, and the world we
live in. These things taught us how to make new things that
harvested new sources of energy that drove machines and
eventually electrified motors. Since the Industrial Revolution,
we have made ourselves, bodies and souls, inventions and
dreams, into a dynamo. With continuous inventions, we make
and remake the world that houses us and that we call home.
We go forward with our whole incarnation—the body and the
self—in great peril, at risk of self-made oblivion.

GETTING OUR HANDS ON POWER TOOLS

Over the course of five centuries, from the fifteenth
to the middle of the nineteenth century, humanity in
Western Europe moved as a great majority from scarcity
to abundance, from peasant and rural life in small and,

essentially, isolated villages to growing and changing specialized urban cities. In work and leisure, the modern industrial citizen and consumer lived amid new orders of things and choice, with participation in public and civic news and lives and the dramatically increased means of specialization, transportation, and communication. With expectations of better health and far greater longevity, the modern person assumed rights to privacy and intimacy, wealth and mobility, and even rights to certain freedoms and public education. Ever self-differentiating by choice, modern individuals took themselves to be individual persons who, by space, goods, rights, and historical inheritance, had their own singular subjectivity, personality, and happiness.

One way to sketch the path of the majority's transformation from an isolated and subordinated rural peasant to a modern protean and choice-driven individual is to follow the emergence of the court and aristocratic classes to the early upper-middle classes. First, starting in the fifteen and sixteenth centuries, we see the upper classes take up manners and styles, setting them off and above in appearance, manners, movement, and display in courts, palaces, and portraits on one's own estates, with exclusive goods, pets, and lineage. The seventeenth and eighteenth centuries followed by imitating them in increasing numbers.

Baroque court life crowned itself under gold canopies, up and down ascending and descending long curved marble stairwells, and sliding and stepping on parquet floors at exclusive court balls. Elsewhere, those of wealth produced, inherited, and accumulated themselves on exclusive property and land, among goods accumulated from new corridors of trade and control. Space became, for the rich of all sectors, a means to exhibit a superiority of power and wealth, control, and connections. Increasingly for the well-off, the good life was a full, well-served, and appointed life. The right to pursue one's happiness meant the right to have and own property and possessions. To have servants and workers to care for one's goods guaranteed one's belongings as much as ample supplies of coal and wood guaranteed the comfort of heat and light. Being dressed in special clothing and wearing good shoes and costly jewelry, along with what one ate, the coffee, tea, and beer they drank, and the tobacco they smoked, brought prestige. Satisfaction with status and class came with tableware, brass and stringed musical instruments, harpsichords and pianos, along with portraits and ritual objects like communion bells. The betrothal gifts measured one's standing and stature. Books and travel assuredly completed one's upbringing and made one educated, experienced, and cosmopolitan.

The platform of superiority expanded thanks to improved machines and mechanics. The steam engine, which moved pistons that turned gears that drove machines that lifted and fell, found a great and new source of energy in coal and provided a new source of power for pumping, milling, and turning wheels. Steam powered eighteenth-century cloth factories and powered trains and steamboats that accelerated at unimaginable speeds with great cargoes across land and sea. They dug and straightened *"our ways,"* redrawing the maps and routes of Europe and the world. Rivers and canals, crossings, tunnels, and ports caused haulers, business people, and generals to recalculate movement, money, and power. Engines and making and selling things did nothing other than remake the human experience in working, producing, possessing, dreaming of, and shopping for a future. National orders became more vulnerable as war-making machines diversified and augmented.

As I wrote in *Everyday Life, How the Ordinary Became Extraordinary*,[100] a climate of innovation captured Europe and spread to its colonies. Some eighteenth-century thinkers, both aristocrats and upper-bourgeoisie, conceived revolutionary connections with new productions, new markets, and new consumptions, which spelled a new humanity at large. Materials and technologies meant factories remade the productive lives of whole societies.

This world was spearheaded by *enlightened thinkers* who sought reasons to fashion humanity anew. It would supersede past ages. French Enlightenment thinkers began to fashion ideals for the advance of reason, science, invention, and the irreversible progress of humanity. As if somehow mankind could jump out of its skin, they subscribed to the rational improvement of all things and a new era of humanity.

Having dipped into the punch bowl of improving science, technology, and liberal trade policies, enlightened thinkers and monarchs paraded and staggered into what historian R. R. Palmer titled his magisterial work, *The Age of Democratic Revolutions*. Furthermore, the last decades of the eighteenth century saw the limitation of central and arbitrary power and an introduction of uniform laws and constitutions assuring greater group and citizens' rights. This was exemplified in the United States Constitution and Bill of Rights.

While the French Revolution suggested freedom and democracy, it quickly fell to violence and Napoleon who undertook dictatorial and imperial rule and sought continental hegemony. The first half of the nineteenth century pitched and swayed on waves of revolution and reaction and the polar influences of France and England. The Revolutions of 1848 offered a volcanic burst in freedom, rights, constitutions, and unities under new nationals and democratic and socialist governments. In 1850, the three great reactionary empires, Russia, Austria, and Turkey, turned the clock backward, and France, with a plebiscite, turned its chaotic domestic self over to a nephew of Napoleon and soon got himself dubbed Napoleon the Third.

However, beyond the skeletons of reaction, Europe and the Americas remained true to a hundred-year shift towards becoming a middle-class commercial society dominated by centralized rule, cities, and cash. Work, urbanization, money, and goods increasingly made old "nobodies" into new "somebodies." Over a generation or two or three, peasants, migrants, and workers found homes and their place and identity in their lives and public and private offerings and opportunities in emerging cities. The advancing middle class grew. Things and wealth, individual and public identities at work and play, came to life in new metropolises and urban areas.

On an unprecedented scale, earth and water resources served and were annexed to industrial, commercial, and national projects. The work of the human body and the genius of the human mind found new allies in engines and energies and in public policies in the fields of health and medicine. All would be put in the service of our bodies, lives, and dreams.

After the Civil War, the United States, followed by southern Canada, turned its ships, railroads, and energy westward, opening up great regions of the Midwest for settlements, farms, and timbering. After the war, the now-unified nation accelerated its march west, paving its way with the opening and even the gifting of public lands. The new nation explored and quarried, logged, ranched, farmed, and settled as it went. It fought, expelled, and made and broke treaties with the Native people as it went. River systems were channeled and later dammed as railroad tracks systematically crisscrossed the continent. Western towns were birthed on eastern railroad drawing boards. Not just settlers but prefabricated houses and buildings came by tracks as civilizations sprung up on the great prairie.

Everywhere in the West, people's bodies were at work, and their minds were dreaming as they joined the expansion of competitive nation-states and the metamorphic powers of machines and industries. The old world was given a new face in the nineteenth century. Construction threw up new sites with new sights, sounds, smells, emotions, and dreams. The democratic ideal turned everything over to everyone for their walking feet, renewed bodies, and invigorated minds.

Constructions defined modernity. Work meant money, food, goods, clothing, and even a chance to make one's mark. Inventions soared. More and more objects were machine-made by engines, great and small. Sanitation steadily improved. Education expanded. Public transportation grew. With bountiful cement and steel came pipes, tunnels, trestles and tracks, and even roads. With increased populations, city buildings grew larger and higher. Industry, production, commerce, and consumption were measured by miles of track and the frequency of arrivals and departures. Expanding nineteenth-century urban life shaped itself to speeding traffic, metro traffic, disciplining paved roads and sidewalks, multi-story buildings and apartments, and even the birth of department stores. Freed of hunger, the need to fetch water and wood, and the engrossing regimes of daily chores, the middle class, with money and income, had free time to dress up and select its pleasures. They could define themselves by window shopping.

Merchants, shoppers, towns, and cities concurred: life should be better, safer, healthier, more open, pleasant, and smile-filled. Roads and walkways were progressively leveled and paved as ditches and sewers were built and tucked underground. Commercial streets were widened as the storage and display of goods on them were curtailed. Near the century's end, rail and, later, bus lines crisscrossed growing urban centers. A cleaner, safer, and more accessible world was built during the last half of the nineteenth century. Municipal police were hired. Artificial lighting was added and increasingly electrified in the second half of the century. Public schools were built, and commercial property and real estate grew taller, especially with the introduction of the elevator. Recreational grounds and parks sprang up. Near the century's end, public restrooms cropped up in the most progressive cities. With water and sewage systems built, running water started to reach hospitals and homes. Bodily cleanliness and privacy became a goal, a way to avoid shame, as private homes and larger apartments offered parents a bedroom of their own. Society concurred that we should put a shine on things and a glow in our hearts.

Power became publicly accessible as coal made steam that drove turbos that spun-out electricity to light streets and homes. Cities stood taller as they set and girded themselves in steel and concrete. Wheels multiplied and sped up in machines and along roads, and tasks quickened and distances shortened. Gas, oil, diesel, and electricity drove cars, trucks, and buses while motorized armies and navies moved faster and farther.

Things, machines, engines, and new sources of energy, dramatically accelerated and expanded building and sped up and diversified activities. Lives were transformed. Bodies worked with less strain and danger. They relaxed and played more frequently. Individuals increasingly claimed rights to receive the benefits of science, medicine, and public health and converted them into needs. Things, pleasures, choices, rights, and possibilities outran traditions and beliefs while both drowned out and quieted minds, spirits, and souls.

The sources that paved our way to a better life were select inventions dating from the late eighteenth to the middle of the nineteenth century. These inventions began the transformation of our knowledge, senses, and dreams of our bodies, lives, and selves. Using Jack Challoner's *The 1001 Inventions That Changed the World* (2009), we can first choose bifocals, the safety lock, shrapnel, and the threshing machine—all of which were invented in 1784; next came the power loom and automatic flour mill in 1785; then the nail-making machine in 1790; and the guillotine in 1791. To offer a few more suggestions from years in the same period, from 1791 to 1794, the world witnessed the birth of the metric system, gas turbine, dentures, ambulance, cotton gin, and internal combustion engine; from 1800 to 1805, there was nitrous oxide anesthetic, the submarine, punch card (predecessor to computers), gas stove, locomotive, municipal water treatment, and the endoscope; macadam, truss bridge, braille, photography, friction match, screw propeller, fountain pen, and pencil sharpener represent the 1820s; the electromagnetic telegraph, grain reaper, and the Dynamo (an invention by English scientist Michael Faraday and American scientist Joseph Henry) initiated the 1830s, which went on to add to our tools, machines, engines, and industrial processes with the incandescent light bulb, mechanical computer, revolver, steam hammer, steel plow, vulcanization, and artificial fertilizer. The 1840s startled the world with the invention of the electric car, grain elevator, aneroid barometer, ether, typewriter, safety match, Morse code, and Portland cement, and ended with chewing gum and the safety pin. I end my selective list with the 1850s, which witnessed the invention of the hydraulic jack, airship, passenger elevator, rubber boots, hypodermic syringe, prism binoculars, and the Bessemer process (the first inexpensive industrial process to make steel from pig iron).

These take us only halfway to the First World War. In the decades prior to *The Great War*, we have body-changing things, tools, machines, and engines, including the portable automatic machine gun, the dissolvable pill, steel-girder skyscrapers, modern safety bicycles, motorcycles, motor cars, and, in 1903, the Wright Flyer powered airplane that took off literally and symbolically and flew us from recent modern history, where the train deposited us, into contemporary history. I jump to traffic lights and military tanks in 1914 and lipstick and the gas mask in 1915. Surely a new and revolutionary order of invention was underway prior to the First World War, truly a world war, which made use of the new order of weapons, surgical tools, procedures, and medicines to repair the fallen and mutilated on the battlefield and in the home-front hospitals.

THE MASS-MAKING OF OURSELVES

There is some truth to the contradictory notion that we are mass-made individuals. With this comes an additional paradox, or is it a contradiction, that we are driven in mass— industrially, commercially, and politically. We are made to be a single and distinct person thanks to a choice of abundant goods and rights, the recently made privacy and intimacy of our homes and bedrooms, and the divergent ways we find meaning in new work, careers, leisure, and lifestyles. There is an additional paradox that we who live and define ourselves by our thoughts and feelings have roots in our bodies, their actions, and collective work.

The Industrial Revolution, the mother of our regimenting times, has birthed us as a mass in freedom, individuality, and choice. With machines, engines, and power, the Industrial

Revolution has brought the earth's resources and things into
our service and self-making. We are bred by and born out of
accelerating collectivization, quantification, standardization,
homogenization, and centralization of the Industrial
Revolution and its heir, mass society.

The nineteenth-century movements, ideologies,
governments, bureaucracies, and specializations wrote
out the Enlightenment's progressive dreams of a rational,
benign, and self-fulfilling humanity. Omniscient science and
omnipotent technology supported multiplying commerce and
industry and centralizing and competing nations.

Power, however, lurked as colonialism and war in the last
half of the century. Power became completely unhinged in
the first half of the twentieth century. In the First World War,
nation-states fought to the exhaustion of all their resources
of bodies, things, and weapons. Totalitarian states in Italy,
Germany, and Russia sought total control of all facets of life.
Totalitarian states and, in measure, even democratic states
disregarded freedom and material well-being as secondary to
their triumph.

Arguably, because of what has occurred in during the
last two centuries, progress's secular march left humanity
without a place, tradition, community, family, and God. It
muffled spirits and the dead. It harnessed not just science
and technology but turned industry, capital, people, and
government into transformative engines of the centralizing
state. Control enslaved humanity, harnessing bodies, wills,
and dreams.

The agglomeration of mass societies, revolutionary
technology, and the centralizing power of the nation-state has
made the world more vulnerable. What has materially made
us so powerful has left the earth and us more fragile. What
offered promises also jeopardizes life. Technology placed us
on a vessel without a port or compass.

Urgency leaves us pending. Imminence dawns. And we
have left ourselves handcuffed to our machines, engines,
energies, and powers. The body and mind are fused to a
powerful state and ever-powerful society and technology.

Today, more than a century after Henry Adams wrote his *Education*, we continue to study subatomic particles, stem cells, embryos, and animal cousins. We teeter, one and all, body and soul, on the fulcrum of unknown resources and uncertain ends. We enter a world of events and consequences without the knowledge of ends and causes. We teeter and totter without knowing the ups and downs of the body and soul.

If a conclusion may be offered to this Conclusion, let me end by saying that we cannot construct an autobiography or fashion a history of our intimate, communal, and public lives without writing stories of our bodies and the histories of our bodies. The body puts us in place, time, memory, and imagination, carrying us to life and death. The equation can be broken into one body, one head, and one self to be lived and told.

The body plants us in being and nature, places and times, with and among others. It makes each of us singular and a part of others from conception and birth, through life, to death, and how we imagine and pray for the beyond. The same singular, unique, and non-duplicable one makes us a compounding and diversifying many by parts, places, experiences, language, and possibilities.

We will forever react and give meaning to the body and its changing situations. The body is the inside and outside of our experience. It is immediate, sensual, and material, yet it is how we love, think, and project ourselves. The body both differentiates and distinguishes us, and it incorporates us in a single and special other, linking us in a multitude of ways to groups, peoples, nations, traditions, times, and even civilizations.

The body, which goes with our daily contacts, exchanges, gifts, and even sacrifices, also goes with our work and affords our pleasures and sexuality. A source of our sickness and health, it can define our satisfaction, comfort, and leisure.

The body gives us our anatomy and shapes our aesthetics. The body speaks with tongue and gestures. It recognizes and classifies. It also turns things into metaphors, such as the vessels we sail, the church we attend, and the needle we thread.

The body presses upon us with the immediacy of pain and pleasure. It strikes us with terror and fills us with ecstasy. We seek it at the bottom of our microscopes and across the breadth of our metaphors. It stands at the heart of our most personal drama and testifies to the best of regimes and the worst of regimes that practice torture, slavery, and genocide.

The body goes with us wherever the mind takes us, and it takes us beyond our thought. It accompanies our consciousness and subconsciousness. It is our tool, engine, agency, and vessel across life and thought. The body roots us in life. It gives us identity and value. It is *one* and *many* that make the self *one* and *many*.

We, who live in accelerating and transformative modern times, know that the body, however much it belongs to nature and others, is as protean and mutant as our changing lives. The body's well-being and longevity belong to culture, traditions, places, and times. We moderns and contemporaries continually place the body amidst new things, on ever faster and distant travel, with increasing wants and an expanding imagination. As the body can still travel the paths of thought, wish, and prayer, we place it at the center of a plethora of goods, property, needs, choices, and ideals.

As a species, we are truly the children of Prometheus who stole fire from the gods and gave it to us. As a species, we are the Athenian craftsman Daedalus. We make and improvise all, even wings of feathers and wax which were to save our son Icarus from the Minotaur's labyrinth but Icarus flew too close to the wax-melting sun, and disappeared in the sea. Myths aside, we are—our fate is—the intricate machinea and powerful engines that multiply and diversify the powers and dreams of body and self.

The body, or at least our imagination and ever-generating wants and needs, have been both lifted and taken captive by our expanding production and abundant markets. For the sake of sciences and careers, we have joined our fates to the most specialized and the most technical laboratories. The body is atomically investigated, and our hands and tools—chiromancy and revolutionary technologies—replace organs, experiment with the splicing of animal cells, and scour the depths of the sea for DNA from the smallest sea life for our use. Our seeds are planted in pig and monkey embryos.

The collective history of the body is diversified by times and places, speeds and movements of people and things, and wealth and state. We, of the *better-off world*, know ourselves by our treatment of science, medicine, public health, and personal care. The old, for example, the three hundred residents in my senior center, tell their autobiographies as medical narratives and pharmacological adventures. They divine their future by estimating the functioning of their new devices.

The stories of our bodies may belong to science, medicine, and utopian speculations. They may be narrated by the fates and fortunes of encapsulating collectivities in peace and at war. And some of us, I surmise the majority of even we "moderns," may still believe that our bodies belong to God and the spirits of the dead. Whatever the case, we humans, as a species, will continue to think and recognize ourselves as being one *in, by,* and *with* our body, the vessel and the sea of self.

ENDNOTES

1 Richard Turner, *Inventing Leonardo* (1993), 191.

2 Clive Gamble, "Thinking inside the mask," *Containers of Change: Ancient Container Technologies from Eastern to Western Asia* (Leiden, 2023), 20–27.

3 Ibid. 24.

4 Antonio Damasio, *The Feelings of What Happens* (San Francisco, 1999), 143.

5 Jonathan Riesman, *The Unseen Body* (New York, 2021), 54–55.

6 Raymond Tallis, *The Hand, A Philosophical Inquiry to Human Being* (Edinburgh, 2003), 4.

7 Jonathan Miller, *The Body in Question* (New York, 1986), 14.

8 Emily Dickinson *The Collected Poems* (NY, 2003), 58.

9 For Gamble's elaboration of humans knowing the world through scapes, see his *Origins and Revolutions: Human Identity in Earliest Prehistory* (Cambridge, 2007).

10 Joseph A. Amato, *Surfaces: A History* (Berkeley, 2013), 210–219.

11 Joseph A. Amato, *On Foot: A History of Walking* (New York, 2004), 20.

12 Ibid., 20–21.

13 Ibid., 21.

14 Ibid., 21.

15 Ibid., 22.

16 Ibid., 21.

17 Ibid., 21–22.

18 Ibid., 22, 282.

19 Ibid., 23, 282.

20 Joseph A. Amato, *Everyday Life: How the Ordinary Became the Extraordinary* (London, 2016).

21 Ibid., 23–24.

22 Ibid., 24.

23 Ibid., 24.

24 Ibid., 24–26.

25 Ibid., 25 for text and footnote, 45 with a reference to pragmatism and the philosophy of Martin Heidegger.

26 Raymond Tallis, *The Hand: A Philosophical Inquiry into Human Being* (Edinburgh, 2003), 125.

27 Ibid., 127.

28 Diane Ackerman, *A Natural History of the Senses* (New York, 1991), 65–124.

29 Frank Wilson, *The Hand* (New York, 1998), esp. 8, 15–16, 36–37.

30 Joseph A. Amato, *Everyday Life: How the Ordinary Became the Extraordinary* (London, 2016), 26, and footnote 49.

31 Raymond Tallis, *Michelangelo's Finger: An Exploration of Everyday Transcendence* (New Haven, 2010), xx.

32 Frances Larson, *Severed: A History of Heads Lost and Found* (New York, 2014), 12.

33 Ibid., 77–136.

34 Putin and Madness," *Wall Street Journal*, March 1, 2022, A 21.

35 Joseph A. Amato, *Surfaces: A History* (Berkeley, 2013), xiv.

36 Joseph A. Amato, *Everyday Life: How the Ordinary Became Extraordinary* (London, 2016), 16. Also, note the following sections are both based on and quoted from the following pages of *Everyday Life*, 13–21, 31–37, and 85–86.

37 Tim Ingold, *Being Alive. Essays on Movement, Knowledge, and Description* (London, 2011), 239.

38 Tim Ingold, *The Perception of Environment* (London, 2000).

39 Daniel Miller, *The Comfort of Things* (Malden, MA, 2008).

40 Joseph Amato, "Where is My Brother," *Buoyancies: A Ballast Master's Log* (Crossings Press and Spoon Press, 2014), 102.

41 Joseph A. Amato, "A Buddy Afloat," *Buoyancies: A Ballast Master's Log* (Crossings Press and Spoon Press, 2014), 131–135.

42 Marcel Mauss, "Les techniques du Corps," *Journal de Psychologie*, xxxii/3–4 (March–April, 1936), 1–23.

43 Leo Stein, *The A.B.C. of Aesthetics* (New York, 1927), 44.

44 Gaston Bachelard is citied in Colin Renfrew, *Prehistory: The Making of the Human Mind* (London, 2007), 122; for Bachelard's own discussion of house as the universe, see his *Poetics of Space* (Boston, 1969), 3–73.

45 Ian Hodder, *The Domestication of Europe* (Oxford, 1990), esp. 41–43.

46 Lewis, Mumford, *The City in History* (New York, 1961), 17.

47 Renfrew, *Prehistory*, 122.

48 "Goodbye, What Were You" (Llandsyul, Wales, 1994), 13.

49 Mumford, *The City in History*, 17.

50 For two views of human evolution and development, see Ian Tattersall, *Masters of the Planet* (New York, 2012) and André Leroi-Gourhan, *The Hunter of Pre-history* (New York, 1989). For pre-historical migrants, see Clive Gamble, *Time Walkers: The Prehistory of Global Colonization* (Cambridge, 1994).

51 For building in one's *cosmic image*, see Trevor Watkins, "Building and Framing Concepts, Constructing Worlds," *Paléorient*, xxx/1 (2004), 5–23.

52 Joseph A. Amato, "A World Without Intimacy: A Portrait of a Time Before We Were Intimate Individuals and Loves," *International Social Science Review*, Vol. 61, No. 4 (Autumn, 1986), 155–168).

53 Joseph A. Amato, *On Foot: A History of Walking* (New York, 2004), esp. 71–100.

54 Maurice Cranston, *The Noble Savage, Jean-Jacques Rousseau, 1754–1762* (Chicago, 1991), III, xiii.

55 Will and Ariel Durant, *Rousseau and Revolution*, Vol. 10, *The Story of Civilization* (New York, 1967), 11.

56 His very road to Damascus, so to speak, occurred on one of his frequent six-mile walks in 1749 from Paris to Vincennes to visit his imprisoned friend, Denis Diderot, editor of the *Encyclopedie*, which was the great Enlightenment literary project. On route came the inspiration to him that won him a prize for his response to the Academy Dijon question about the relation between the nature of progress in the arts and sciences and its relation to morals. His response that a reverse relationship existed between progress and morals resulted in his early *Discourse on the Sciences and Arts*, 1750, which established him as a serious light in Paris.

57 Simon Schama, *Fate of the Empire, 1776–2000*, Vol 3 of *History of Britain* (New York: Hyperion, 2002), 12.

58 See treatment of walking and Wordsworth, Joseph A. Amato, *On Foot: A History of Walking* (New York, 2004), 104–106.

59 Ibid., 10, 18.

60 Anne D. Wallace, *Walking, Literature, and English Culture* (Oxford, 1993), 62–64.

61 Robin Jarvis, *Romantic Writing and Pedestrian Travel* (New York, 1997), 20.

62 Philip Bagwell, *Transport Revolution* (New York, 1974), esp. 35–60.

63 Treatment of and reference to Thoreau, see Joseph A. Amato, *On Foot: A History of Walking* (New York, 2004), 124, 141–149.

64 R. R. Palmer, *The Age of Democratic Revolutions: A Political History of Europe and America, 1760 to 1800* (2014).

65 Joseph A. Amato, *Everyday Life: How the Ordinary Became the Extraordinary* (London, 2016), 83–92.

66 Ibid., quoted on p. 85.

67 Ibid.

68 Ibid.

69 Ibid.

70 Ibid., 88.

71 Ibid., 88–89.

72 Ibid., 89.

73 Ibid., 90.

74 Ibid., 91.

75 Ibid., 91.

76 Ibid., 91.

77 Ibid.

78 Ibid., 92.

79 Ibid., Weber's France, Fin du siècle, p. 58, cited in Joseph A. Amato, *Everyday Life: How the Ordinary Became the Extraordinary* (London, 2016), 129.

80 Susan Bordo, *Unbearable Weight: Feminism, Western Culture, and the Body* (Berkeley, 1993), 165.

81 Ibid.

82 The definition of the five innovations were received in personal correspondence upon the author's request from William Hoffman on March 22, 2022.

From its origin in the 1970s and clinical applications in the 1980s, magnetic resonance imaging (MRI) has induced spinning protons in cells, their tissues, and organs to reveal and delineate their structures, patterns, boundaries, nooks and crannies, and organization throughout the human body, most notably in the brain, the seat of its own creation. MRI is the gold standard of imaging diagnostics. It represents a profound visual turn in medical practice that transforms the body into a picture just as Leonardo da Vinci transformed it in his anatomical drawings five centuries ago but now with atomic as well as anatomic insight. Some 40 million MRI scans are performed in the U.S. every year involving whole bodies, heads and necks, torsos, and limbs. Though it is an expensive medical technology, an MRI scan can be life-saving. In 2020, the U.S. Food and Drug Administration approved the first portable MRI system. The machine cost $50,000, which is 20 times cheaper than traditional systems, runs on 35 times less power, and weighs 10 times less than the standard MRI machine.

From its origin in the 1980s, regenerative medicine has become a critical emerging area of science that includes using stem cells and other technologies to repair or replace damaged cells, tissues, and organs to restore function. A growing number of regenerative medicine-based candidate therapies for treating cancer, diabetes, heart disease and stroke, neurological and orthopedic disorders, and rare genetic diseases are in clinical trials. In laboratory experiments, pluripotent and multipotent stem cells and progenitor cells can be directed down specific tissue development pathways to mimic the unfolding growth processes that occur in the human embryo, fetus, and infant. Stem cells can be induced to form "organoids" that resemble certain features of our bodily organs and tissues, which themselves are derived from the three germ layers: the ectoderm (outer layer), the endoderm (inner layer), and the mesoderm (middle layer). Organoids are self-assembled, three-dimensional structures that are proving to be invaluable research tools for understanding how the more than 200 specific tissues in the human body develop, function, and age.

The human immune system is arguably the most complex system in the human body, a product of many millions of years of evolution. Immunotherapies—therapies that harness the system and direct its power to kill intruders and tumors—have long been used to reduce the risk that a transplanted organ will be rejected, to dampen the effects of autoimmune diseases and allergies, and to treat cancer. Beginning in the 1990s, scientists found a way to recharge immune cells called killer T-cells to destroy cancer cells by blocking a feedback system by which cancer cells prevent killer T-cells from doing their job. Biological drugs called immune checkpoint inhibitors are now in widespread use, often to treat patients whose cancer has relapsed following conventional chemotherapy. Subsequently, investigators developed a T-cell engineering approach for treating some blood cancers, particularly childhood leukemia. T-cells are isolated from patient blood, outfitted with a tumor-targeting molecule, and reinfused to attack the tumor, a process called CAR T-cell therapy. Immune checkpoint inhibitors and CAR T-cell therapies have extended the lives of many cancer patients and even cured some. These new immunotherapies also have the potential to treat neurological, autoimmune, and infectious diseases as more is learned about how to deploy them in different organ systems.

The story of the human body is written in a four-letter alphabet dating back millions of years. Since the completion of the Human Genome Project (HGP) in 2003, the stories of our evolution, our genetic endowment, our reproduction and our vulnerability to disease have been spelled out in the DNA code present in the nucleus and mitochondria of the cell. Soon it will be possible to determine the sequence of the 3.3 billion DNA base pairs or the 6.6 billion A, T, G, C letters in our cells for as little as $100 compared to the $1 million it cost for James Watson, the co-discoverer of

DNA's double helical structure, to have his genome sequenced in 2007. The exponential growth in reading (sequencing) and writing (synthesizing) DNA was followed by genome editing, the ability to add or remove specific DNA letters in microbes and experimental animals including mammals. These revolutionary techniques, notably the CRISPR/Cas9 genome-editing system, have abundant applications in life science and healthcare. They also could alter the "unedited" course of human evolution through the manipulation of reproductive cells (eggs and sperm).

Messenger RNA (mRNA), which the body transcribes from its DNA code and uses to make protein, was first synthesized in the lab in the 1980s. It was tested as a cancer vaccine in mice in 1995. But synthetic mRNA remained largely a research backwater until it burst on the scene in spectacular fashion with the COVID-19 pandemic (2019 to present). mRNA vaccines, made and clinically tested by Pfizer and its partner BioNTech together with Moderna and its partner the National Institutes of Health, constitute an unprecedented medical innovation—safe and effective vaccines that became publicly available in less than a year from the time the SARS-CoV-2 coronavirus's DNA code was sequenced. What would normally take years was compressed into months. Millions of lives have been saved as a result. These medical miracles were created by synthesizing a key mRNA sequence for the coronavirus's spike protein and packaging its lipid (fatty) nanoparticles for delivery into the body by injection. The body translates the synthetic mRNA sequence into antigen protein that the immune system recognizes as foreign (though no foreign protein is introduced). In response, the immune system generates protective neutralizing antibodies and lasting immune cell memory. mRNA technology is now being employed to develop other vaccines and a host of therapeutic agents to treat and prevent disease.

83 Marcel Mauss, "Les Techniques du corps," is a 1934 lecture, first published in *le Journal de Psychologie*, Vol. xxxii, n 3–4, 15 March–April, 1936.

84 *Urbana* (2012), which Joseph A. Amato reviewed in *Fides et Historia* (Winter/Spring, 2014), 76-84.

85 Ian Hodder, *Entangled: An Archaeology of the Relationships between Humans and Things* (2012), 109.

86 Marcel Mauss, "Techniques of the Body," *Economy of Society*, Vol. 2: 1 (1973), 75.

87 For the distinction of tools and containers, see Clive Gamble, "Bodies, Instruments, and Containers," in *Origins and Revolutions: Human Identity in the Earliest Prehistory* (Cambridge, 2007), 87–100.

88 For an introduction to anthropology that explores objects, symbols, things, and metaphors, see the *Journal of Material Culture*, started in 1996, and a collection of recent writing on pre-history, *Deep History: The Architecture of Past and Present*, eds. Andrew Shryock and Daniel Lord Small (Berkeley: University of California Press, 2011). Also, Joseph A. Amato, *Surfaces: A History* (Berkeley, 2013), 17–108.

89 For an extended discussion of things, being, language, and metaphor, see Joseph A. Amato, *The Book of Twos: The Power of Contrasts, Polarities, and Contradictions* (Granite Falls, MN, 2015), 7–101.

90 One work of use for constructing material life and culture is Jean-Pierre Warnier, *Construire la culture matérielle: l'homme qui pensait avec ses doigts* (Paris, 1999).

91 Marcel Mauss, *The Gift Forms and Functions in Archaic Society* (in English, 1954), originally published as *L'essai sur le don* in *L'Année Sociologique* in 1925.

92 For introductory works that suggest how we, a body, mind, and self are involved in a conversation with things, see ed. Sherry Turkle, *Evocative Things: Things We Think With* (Cambridge, MA, 2007), ed. Lorraine Daston, *Things That Talk: Object Lessons from Art and Science* (New York, 2004); for a complex aesthetic of emotions and physical objects, see Peter Schwenger, *The Tears of Things* (Minneapolis, MN, 2006); for Philip Ball on the origins of science, see Philip Ball, *Curiosity: How Science Became Interested in Everything* (Chicago, IL, 2012).

93 Citation taken from Brown, "Thing Theory," 3. Brown cites the original as Leo Stein, *The A- B- C- of Aesthetics* (New York, 1927), 44.

94 Tim Ingold, *Being Alive: Essays on Movement, Knowledge, and Description* (London, 2011), 239.

95 Tim Ingold, *The Perception of the Environment: Essays on Livelihood, Dwelling and Skill* (London, 2000).

96 For the pervasive use of lines in perceiving and conceiving life, see Tim Ingold, *Lines: A Brief History* (New York, 2007).

97 Vaclav Smil, *Energy and Civilization: A History* (Boston, 2017), 1.

98 Ibid., 7.

99 Ibid., 7.

100 Joseph A. Amato, *Everyday Life: How the Ordinary Became the Extraordinary* (London, 2016), 102.

Made in the USA
Monee, IL
31 August 2023